# THE
# MOST EX-
## cellent and lamentable
## Tragedie, of Romeo
### and *Iuliet*.

*Newly corrected, augmented, and
amended :*

As it hath bene sundry times pub'iquely acted , by the
right Honourable the Lord Chamberlaine
his Seruants.

LONDON
Printed by Thomas Creede, for Cuthbert Burby, and are to
be sold at his shop neare the Exchange.
1 5 9 9.

Title page of the second edition of *The Tragedy of Romeo and Juliet*

# William Shakespeare

# The Tragedy of Romeo and Juliet

With New and Updated
Critical Essays
and a Revised Bibliography

Edited by J. A. Bryant, Jr.

THE SIGNET CLASSIC SHAKESPEARE
*General Editor: Sylvan Barnet*

A SIGNET CLASSIC

SIGNET CLASSIC
Published by New American Library, a division of
Penguin Group (USA) Inc., 375 Hudson Street,
New York, New York 10014, USA
Penguin Group (Canada), 10 Alcorn Avenue, Toronto,
Ontario M4V 3B2, Canada (a division of Pearson Penguin Canada Inc.)
Penguin Books Ltd., 80 Strand, London WC2R 0RL, England
Penguin Ireland, 25 St. Stephen's Green, Dublin 2,
Ireland (a division of Penguin Books Ltd.)
Penguin Group (Australia), 250 Camberwell Road, Camberwell, Victoria 3124,
Australia (a division of Pearson Australia Group Pty. Ltd.)
Penguin Books India Pvt. Ltd., 11 Community Centre, Panchsheel Park,
New Delhi - 110 017, India
Penguin Group (NZ), cnr Airborne and Rosedale Roads, Albany,
Auckland 1310, New Zealand (a division of Pearson New Zealand Ltd.)
Penguin Books (South Africa) (Pty.) Ltd., 24 Sturdee Avenue,
Rosebank, Johannesburg 2196, South Africa

Penguin Books Ltd., Registered Offices:
80 Strand, London WC2R 0RL, England

Published by Signet Classic, an imprint of New American Library, a division
of Penguin Group (USA) Inc. The Signet Classic edition of *The Tragedy of
Romeo and Juliet* was first published in 1964, and an updated edition was
published in 1986.

First Signet Classic Printing (Second Revised Edition), May 1998
20  19  18  17  16  15  14

Copyright © J. A. Bryant, Jr., 1964, 1986
Copyright © Sylvan Barnet, 1963, 1986, 1987, 1998
All rights reserved

 REGISTERED TRADEMARK—MARCA REGISTRADA

Library of Congress Catalog Card Number: 97-69247

Printed in the United States of America

# Contents

# Shakespeare: An Overview

## Biographical Sketch

Between the record of his baptism in Stratford on 26 April 1564 and the record of his burial in Stratford on 25 April 1616, some forty official documents name Shakespeare, and many others name his parents, his children, and his grandchildren. Further, there are at least fifty literary references to him in the works of his contemporaries. More facts are known about William Shakespeare than about any other playwright of the period except Ben Jonson. The facts should, however, be distinguished from the legends. The latter, inevitably more engaging and better known, tell us that the Stratford boy killed a calf in high style, poached deer and rabbits, and was forced to flee to London, where he held horses outside a playhouse. These traditions are only traditions; they may be true, but no evidence supports them, and it is well to stick to the facts.

Mary Arden, the dramatist's mother, was the daughter of a substantial landowner; about 1557 she married John Shakespeare, a tanner, glove-maker, and trader in wool, grain, and other farm commodities. In 1557 John Shakespeare was a member of the council (the governing body of Stratford), in 1558 a constable of the borough, in 1561 one of the two town chamberlains, in 1565 an alderman (entitling him to the appellation of "Mr."), in 1568 high bailiff—the town's highest political office, equivalent to mayor. After 1577, for an unknown reason he drops out of local politics. What *is* known is that he had to mortgage his wife's property, and that he was involved in serious litigation.

The birthday of William Shakespeare, the third child and the eldest son of this locally prominent man, is unrecorded, but the Stratford parish register records that the infant was baptized on 26 April 1564. (It is quite possible that he was born on 23 April, but this date has probably been assigned by tradition because it is the date on which, fifty-two years later, he died, and perhaps because it is the feast day of St. George, patron saint of England.) The attendance records of the Stratford grammar school of the period are not extant, but it is reasonable to assume that the son of a prominent local official attended the free school—it had been established for the purpose of educating males precisely of his class—and received substantial training in Latin. The masters of the school from Shakespeare's seventh to fifteenth years held Oxford degrees; the Elizabethan curriculum excluded mathematics and the natural sciences but taught a good deal of Latin rhetoric, logic, and literature, including plays by Plautus, Terence, and Seneca.

On 27 November 1582 a marriage license was issued for the marriage of Shakespeare and Anne Hathaway, eight years his senior. The couple had a daughter, Susanna, in May 1583. Perhaps the marriage was necessary, but perhaps the couple had earlier engaged, in the presence of witnesses, in a formal "troth plight" which would render their children legitimate even if no further ceremony were performed. In February 1585, Anne Hathaway bore Shakespeare twins, Hamnet and Judith.

That Shakespeare was born is excellent; that he married and had children is pleasant; but that we know nothing about his departure from Stratford to London or about the beginning of his theatrical career is lamentable and must be admitted. We would gladly sacrifice details about his children's baptism for details about his earliest days in the theater. Perhaps the poaching episode is true (but it is first reported almost a century after Shakespeare's death), or perhaps he left Stratford to be a schoolmaster, as another tradition holds; perhaps he was moved (like Petruchio in *The Taming of the Shrew*) by

> Such wind as scatters young men through the world,
> To seek their fortunes farther than at home
> Where small experience grows.          (1.2.49–51)

In 1592, thanks to the cantankerousness of Robert Greene, we have our first reference, a snarling one, to Shakespeare as an actor and playwright. Greene, a graduate of St. John's College, Cambridge, had become a playwright and a pamphleteer in London, and in one of his pamphlets he warns three university-educated playwrights against an actor who has presumed to turn playwright:

> There is an upstart crow, beautified with our feathers, that with his *tiger's heart wrapped in a player's hide* supposes he is as well able to bombast out a blank verse as the best of you, and being an absolute Johannes-factotum [i.e., jack-of-all-trades] is in his own conceit the only Shake-scene in a country.

The reference to the player, as well as the allusion to Aesop's crow (who strutted in borrowed plumage, as an actor struts in fine words not his own), makes it clear that by this date Shakespeare had both acted and written. That Shakespeare is meant is indicated not only by *Shake-scene* but also by the parody of a line from one of Shakespeare's plays, *3 Henry VI*: "O, tiger's heart wrapped in a woman's hide" (1.4.137). If in 1592 Shakespeare was prominent enough to be attacked by an envious dramatist, he probably had served an apprenticeship in the theater for at least a few years.

In any case, although there are no extant references to Shakespeare between the record of the baptism of his twins in 1585 and Greene's hostile comment about "Shake-scene" in 1592, it is evident that during some of these "dark years" or "lost years" Shakespeare had acted and written. There are a number of subsequent references to him as an actor. Documents indicate that in 1598 he is a "principal comedian," in 1603 a "principal tragedian," in 1608 he is one of the "men players." (We do not have, however, any solid information about which roles he may have played; later traditions say he played Adam in *As You Like It* and the ghost in *Hamlet*, but nothing supports the assertions. Probably his role as dramatist came to supersede his role as actor.) The profession of actor was not for a gentleman, and it occasionally drew the scorn of university men like Greene who resented writing speeches for persons less educated than themselves, but it was respectable enough; players, if prosperous, were in effect members of the bourgeoisie, and there is nothing to suggest that Stratford considered William Shakespeare less than a solid citizen. When, in 1596, the Shakespeares were granted a coat of arms—i.e., the right to be considered gentlemen—the grant was made to Shakespeare's father, but probably William Shakespeare had arranged the matter on his own behalf. In subsequent transactions he is occasionally styled a gentleman.

Although in 1593 and 1594 Shakespeare published two narrative poems dedicated to the Earl of Southampton, *Venus and Adonis* and *The Rape of Lucrece*, and may well have written most or all of his sonnets in the middle nineties, Shakespeare's literary activity seems to have been almost entirely devoted to the theater. (It may be significant that the two narrative poems were written in years when the plague closed the theaters for several months.) In 1594 he was a charter member of a theatrical company called the Chamberlain's Men, which in 1603 became the royal company, the King's Men, making Shakespeare the king's playwright. Until he retired to Stratford (about 1611, apparently), he was with this remarkably stable company. From 1599 the company acted primarily at the Globe theater, in which Shakespeare held a one-tenth interest. Other Elizabethan dramatists are known to have acted, but no other is known also to have been entitled to a share of the profits.

Shakespeare's first eight published plays did not have his name on them, but this is not remarkable; the most popular play of the period, Thomas Kyd's *The Spanish Tragedy*, went through many editions without naming Kyd, and Kyd's authorship is known only because a book on the profession of acting happens to quote (and attribute to Kyd) some lines on the interest of Roman emperors in the drama. What is remarkable is that after 1598 Shakespeare's name commonly appears on printed plays—some of which are not his. Presumably his name was a drawing card, and publishers used it to attract potential buyers. Another indication of his popularity comes from Francis Meres, author of *Palladis Tamia: Wit's Treasury* (1598). In this anthology of snippets accompanied by an essay on literature, many playwrights are mentioned, but Shakespeare's name occurs more often than any other, and Shakespeare is the only play-wright whose plays are listed.

From his acting, his play writing, and his share in a playhouse, Shakespeare seems to have made considerable money. He put it to work, making substantial investments in Stratford real estate. As early as 1597 he bought New Place, the second-largest house in Stratford. His family moved in soon afterward, and the house remained in the family until a granddaughter died in 1670. When Shakespeare made his will in 1616, less than a month before he died, he sought to leave his property intact to his descendants. Of small bequests to relatives and to friends (including three actors, Richard Burbage, John Heminges, and Henry Condell), that to his wife of the second-best bed has provoked the most comment. It has sometimes been taken as a sign of an unhappy marriage (other supposed signs are the appar-ently hasty marriage, his wife's seniority of eight years, and his residence in London without his family). Perhaps the second-best bed was the bed the couple had slept in, the best bed being reserved for visitors. In any case, had Shakespeare not excepted it, the bed would have gone (with the rest of his household possessions) to his daughter and her husband.

On 25 April 1616 Shakespeare was buried within the chancel of the church at Stratford. An unattractive monu-ment to his memory, placed on a wall near the grave, says that he died on 23 April. Over the grave itself are the lines, perhaps by Shakespeare, that (more than his literary fame) have kept his bones undisturbed in the crowded burial ground where old bones were often dislodged to make way for new:

> Good friend, for Jesus' sake forbear
> To dig the dust enclosed here.
> Blessed be the man that spares these stones
> And cursed be he that moves my bones.

### A Note on the Anti-Stratfordians, Especially Baconians and Oxfordians

Not until 1769—more than a hundred and fifty years after Shakespeare's death—is there any record of anyone expressing doubt about Shakespeare's authorship of the plays and poems. In 1769, however, Herbert Lawrence nominated Francis Bacon (1561–1626) in *The Life and Adventures of Common Sense*. Since then, at least two dozen other nominees have been offered, including Christopher Marlowe, Sir Walter Raleigh, Queen Elizabeth I, and Edward de Vere, 17th earl of Oxford. The impulse behind all anti-Stratfordian movements is the scarcely concealed snobbish opinion that "the man from Stratford" simply could not have written the plays because he was a country fellow without a university education and without access to high society. Anyone, the argument goes, who used so many legal terms, medical terms, nautical terms, and so forth, and who showed some familiarity with classical writing, must have attended a university, and anyone who knew so much about courtly elegance and courtly deceit must himself have moved among courtiers. The plays do indeed reveal an author whose interests were exceptionally broad, but specialists in any given field—law, medicine, arms and armor, and so on—soon find that the plays do not reveal deep knowledge in specialized matters; indeed, the playwright often gets technical details wrong.

The claim on behalf of Bacon, forgotten almost as soon as it was put forth in 1769, was independently reasserted by Joseph C. Hart in 1848. In 1856 it was reaffirmed by W. H. Smith in a book, and also by Delia Bacon in an article; in 1857 Delia Bacon published a book, arguing that Francis Bacon had directed a group of intellectuals who wrote the plays.

Francis Bacon's claim has largely faded, perhaps because it was advanced with such evident craziness by Ignatius Donnelly, who in *The Great Cryptogram* (1888) claimed to break a code in the plays that proved Bacon had written not only the plays attributed to Shakespeare but also other Renaissance works, for instance the plays of Christopher Marlowe and the essays of Montaigne.

Consider the last two lines of the Epilogue in *The Tempest*:

As you from crimes would pardoned be,
Let your indulgence set me free.

What was Shakespeare—sorry, Francis Bacon, Baron Verulam—*really* saying in these two lines? According to Baconians, the lines are an anagram reading, "Tempest of Francis Bacon, Lord Verulam; do ye ne'er divulge me, ye words." Ingenious, and it is a pity that in the quotation the letter *a* appears only twice in the cryptogram, whereas in the deciphered message it appears three times. Oh, no problem; just alter "Verulam" to "Verul'm" and it works out very nicely.

Most people understand that with sufficient ingenuity one can torture any text and find in it what one wishes. For instance: Did Shakespeare have a hand in the King James Version of the Bible? It was nearing completion in 1610, when Shakespeare was forty-six years old. If you look at the 46th Psalm and count forward for forty-six words, you will find the word *shake*. Now if you go to the end of the psalm and count backward forty-six words, you will find the word *spear*. Clear evidence, according to some, that Shakespeare slyly left his mark in the book.

Bacon's candidacy has largely been replaced in the twentieth century by the candidacy of Edward de Vere (1550–1604), 17th earl of Oxford. The basic ideas behind the Oxford theory, advanced at greatest length by Dorothy and Charlton Ogburn in *This Star of England* (1952, rev. 1955), a book of 1297 pages, and by Charlton Ogburn in *The Mysterious William Shakespeare* (1984), a book of 892 pages, are these: (1) The man from Stratford could not possibly have had the mental equipment and the experience to have written the plays—only a courtier could have written them; (2) Oxford had the requisite background (social position, education, years at Queen Elizabeth's court); (3) Oxford did not wish his authorship to be known for two basic reasons: writing for the public theater was a vulgar pursuit, and the plays show so much courtly and royal disreputable behavior that they would have compromised Oxford's position at court. Oxfordians offer countless details to support the claim. For example, Hamlet's phrase "that ever I was born to set it right" (1.5.89) barely conceals "E. Ver, I was born to set it right," an unambiguous announcement of de Vere's authorship, according to *This Star of England* (p. 654). A second example: Consider Ben

Jonson's poem entitled "To the Memory of My Beloved Master William Shakespeare," prefixed to the first collected edition of Shakespeare's plays in 1623. According to Oxfordians, when Jonson in this poem speaks of the author of the plays as the "swan of Avon," he is alluding not to William Shakespeare, who was born and died in Stratford-on-Avon and who throughout his adult life owned property there; rather, he is alluding to Oxford, who, the Ogburns say, used "William Shakespeare" as his pen name, and whose manor at Bilton was on the Avon River. Oxfordians do not offer any evidence that Oxford took a pen name, and they do not mention that Oxford had sold the manor in 1581, forty-two years before Jonson wrote his poem. Surely a reference to the Shakespeare who was born in Stratford, who had returned to Stratford, and who had died there only seven years before Jonson wrote the poem is more plausible. And exactly why Jonson, who elsewhere also spoke of Shakespeare as a playwright, and why Heminges and Condell, who had acted with Shakespeare for about twenty years, should speak of Shakespeare as the author in their dedication in the 1623 volume of collected plays is never adequately explained by Oxfordians. Either Jonson, Heminges and Condell, and numerous others were in on the conspiracy, or they were all duped—equally unlikely alternatives. Another difficulty in the Oxford theory is that Oxford died in 1604, and some of the plays are clearly indebted to works and events later than 1604. Among the Oxfordian responses are: At his death Oxford left some plays, and in later years these were touched up by hacks, who added the material that points to later dates. *The Tempest*, almost universally regarded as one of Shakespeare's greatest plays and pretty clearly dated to 1611, does indeed date from a period after the death of Oxford, but it is a crude piece of work that should not be included in the canon of works by Oxford.

The anti-Stratfordians, in addition to assuming that the author must have been a man of rank and a university man, usually assume two conspiracies: (1) a conspiracy in Elizabethan and Jacobean times, in which a surprisingly large number of persons connected with the theater knew that the actor Shakespeare did not write the plays attributed to him but for some reason or other pretended that he did; (2) a conspiracy of today's Stratfordians, the professors who teach Shakespeare in the colleges and universities, who are said to have a vested interest in preserving Shakespeare as the author of the plays they teach. In fact, (1) it is inconceivable that the secret of Shakespeare's non-authorship could have been preserved by all of the people who supposedly were in on the conspiracy, and (2) academic fame awaits any scholar today who can disprove Shakespeare's authorship.

The Stratfordian case is convincing not only because hundreds or even thousands of anti-Stratford arguments—of the sort that say "ever I was born" has the secret double meaning "E. Ver, I was born"—add up to nothing at all but also because irrefutable evidence connects the man from Stratford with the London theater and with the authorship of particular plays. The anti-Stratfordians do not seem to understand that it is not enough to dismiss the Stratford case by saying that a fellow from the provinces simply couldn't have written the plays. Nor do they understand that it is not enough to dismiss all of the evidence connecting Shakespeare with the plays by asserting that it is perjured.

## The Shakespeare Canon

We return to William Shakespeare. Thirty-seven plays as well as some nondramatic poems are generally held to constitute the Shakespeare canon, the body of authentic works. The exact dates of composition of most of the works are highly uncertain, but evidence of a starting point and/or of a final limiting point often provides a framework for informed guessing. For example, *Richard II* cannot be earlier than 1595, the publication date of some material to which it is indebted; *The Merchant of Venice* cannot be later than 1598, the year Francis Meres mentioned it. Sometimes arguments for a date hang on an alleged topical allusion, such as the lines about the unseasonable weather in *A Midsummer Night's Dream*, 2.1.81–117, but such an allusion, if indeed it is an allusion to an event in the real world, can be variously interpreted, and in any case there is always the possibility that a topical allusion was inserted years later, to bring the play up to date. (The issue of alterations in a text between the time that Shakespeare drafted it and the time that it was printed—alterations due to censorship or playhouse practice or Shakespeare's own second thoughts—will be discussed in "The Play Text as a Collaboration" later in this overview.) Dates are often attributed on the basis of style, and although conjectures about style usually rest on other conjectures (such as Shakespeare's development as a playwright, or the appropriateness of lines to character), sooner or later one must rely on one's literary sense. There is no documentary proof, for example, that *Othello* is not as early as *Romeo and Juliet*, but one feels that *Othello* is a later, more mature work, and because the first record of its performance is 1604, one is glad enough to set its composition at that date and not push it back into Shakespeare's early years. (*Romeo and Juliet* was first published in 1597, but evidence suggests that it was written a little earlier.) The following chronology, then, is indebted not only to facts but also to informed guesswork and sensitivity. The dates, necessarily imprecise for some works, indicate something like a scholarly consensus concerning the time of original composition. Some plays show evidence of later revision.

*Plays.* The first collected edition of Shakespeare, published in 1623, included thirty-six plays. These are all accepted as Shakespeare's, though for one of them, *Henry VIII*, he is thought to have had a collaborator. A thirty-seventh play, *Pericles*, published in 1609 and attributed to Shakespeare on the title page, is also widely accepted as being partly by Shakespeare even though it is not included in the 1623 volume. Still another play not in the 1623 volume, *The Two Noble Kinsmen*, was first published in 1634, with a title page attributing it to John Fletcher and Shakespeare. Probably most students of the subject now believe that Shakespeare did indeed have a hand in it. Of the remaining plays attributed at one time or another to Shakespeare, only one, *Edward III*, anonymously published in 1596, is now regarded by some scholars as a serious candidate. The prevailing opinion, however, is that this rather simpleminded play is not Shakespeare's; at most he may have revised some passages, chiefly scenes with the Countess of

Salisbury. We include *The Two Noble Kinsmen* but do not include *Edward III* in the following list.

| | |
|---|---|
| 1588–94 | *The Comedy of Errors* |
| 1588–94 | *Love's Labor's Lost* |
| 1589–91 | *2 Henry VI* |
| 1590–91 | *3 Henry VI* |
| 1589–92 | *1 Henry VI* |
| 1592–93 | *Richard III* |
| 1589–94 | *Titus Andronicus* |
| 1593–94 | *The Taming of the Shrew* |
| 1592–94 | *The Two Gentlemen of Verona* |
| 1594–96 | *Romeo and Juliet* |
| 1595 | *Richard II* |
| 1595–96 | *A Midsummer Night's Dream* |
| 1596–97 | *King John* |
| 1594–96 | *The Merchant of Venice* |
| 1596–97 | *1 Henry IV* |
| 1597 | *The Merry Wives of Windsor* |
| 1597–98 | *2 Henry IV* |
| 1598–99 | *Much Ado About Nothing* |
| 1598–99 | *Henry V* |
| 1599 | *Julius Caesar* |
| 1599–1600 | *As You Like It* |
| 1599–1600 | *Twelfth Night* |
| 1600–1601 | *Hamlet* |
| 1601–1602 | *Troilus and Cressida* |
| 1602–1604 | *All's Well That Ends Well* |
| 1603–1604 | *Othello* |
| 1604 | *Measure for Measure* |
| 1605–1606 | *King Lear* |
| 1605–1606 | *Macbeth* |
| 1606–1607 | *Antony and Cleopatra* |
| 1605–1608 | *Timon of Athens* |
| 1607–1608 | *Coriolanus* |
| 1607–1608 | *Pericles* |
| 1609–10 | *Cymbeline* |
| 1610–11 | *The Winter's Tale* |
| 1611 | *The Tempest* |

| 1612–13 | *Henry VIII* |
| 1613 | *The Two Noble Kinsmen* |

*Poems.* In 1989 Donald W. Foster published a book in which he argued that "A Funeral Elegy for Master William Peter," published in 1612, ascribed only to the initials W.S., *may* be by Shakespeare. Foster later published an article in a scholarly journal, *PMLA* 111 (1996), in which he asserted the claim more positively. The evidence begins with the initials, and includes the fact that the publisher and the printer of the elegy had published Shakespeare's *Sonnets* in 1609. But such facts add up to rather little, especially because no one has found any connection between Shakespeare and William Peter (an Oxford graduate about whom little is known, who was murdered at the age of twenty-nine). The argument is based chiefly on statistical examinations of word patterns, which are said to correlate with Shakespeare's known work. Despite such correlations, however, many readers feel that the poem does not sound like Shakespeare. True, Shakespeare has a great range of styles, but one quality that unites his work is that it is imaginative and interesting. Many readers find neither of these qualities in "A Funeral Elegy."

| 1592–93 | *Venus and Adonis* |
| 1593–94 | *The Rape of Lucrece* |
| 1593–1600 | *Sonnets* |
| 1600–1601 | *The Phoenix and the Turtle* |

## Shakespeare's English

*1. Spelling and Pronunciation.* From the philologist's point of view, Shakespeare's English is modern English. It requires footnotes, but the inexperienced reader can comprehend substantial passages with very little help, whereas for the same reader Chaucer's Middle English is a foreign language. By the beginning of the fifteenth century the chief grammatical changes in English had taken place, and the final unaccented -*e* of Middle English had been lost (though it survives even today in spelling, as in *name*); during the fif-teenth century the dialect of London, the commercial and political center, gradually displaced the provincial dialects, at least in writing; by the end of the century, printing had helped to regularize and stabilize the language, especially spelling. Elizabethan spelling may seem erratic to us (there were dozens of spellings of *Shakespeare*, and a simple word like *been* was also spelled *beene* and *bin*), but it had much in common with our spelling. Elizabethan spelling was conser-vative in that for the most part it reflected an older pronun-ciation (Middle English) rather than the sound of the language as it was then spoken, just as our spelling continues to reflect medieval pronunciation—most obviously in the now silent but formerly pronounced letters in a word such as *knight*. Elizabethan pronunciation, though not identical with ours, was much closer to ours than to that of the Middle Ages. Incidentally, though no one can be certain about what Elizabethan English sounded like, specialists tend to believe it was rather like the speech of a modern stage Irishman (*time* apparently was pronounced *toime*, *old* pronounced *awld*, *day* pronounced *die*, and *join* pronounced *jine*) and not at all like the Oxford speech that most of us think it was.

An awareness of the difference between our pronuncia-tion and Shakespeare's is crucial in three areas—in accent, or number of syllables (many metrically regular lines may look irregular to us); in rhymes (which may not look like rhymes); and in puns (which may not look like puns). Examples will be useful. Some words that were at least on occasion stressed differently from today are *aspèct*, *còmplete*, *fòrlorn*, *revènue*, and *sepùlcher*. Words that some-times had an additional syllable are *emp[e]ress*, *Hen[e]ry*, *mon[e]th*, and *villain* (three syllables, *vil-lay-in*). An addi-tional syllable is often found in possessives, like *moon*'s (pronounced *moones*) and in words ending in -*tion* or -*sion*. Words that had one less syllable than they now have are *needle* (pronounced *neel*) and *violet* (pronounced *vilet*). Among rhymes now lost are *one* with *loan*, *love* with *prove*, *beast* with *jest*, *eat* with *great*. (In reading, trust your sense of metrics and your ear, more than your eye.) An example of a pun that has become obliterated by a change in pronuncia-tion is Falstaff's reply to Prince Hal's "Come, tell us your

reason" in *1 Henry IV*: "Give you a reason on compulsion?
If reasons were as plentiful as blackberries, I would give no
man a reason upon compulsion, I" (2.4.237–40). The *ea* in
*reason* was pronounced rather like a long *a*, like the *ai* in
*raisin*, hence the comparison with blackberries.

Puns are not merely attempts to be funny; like metaphors
they often involve bringing into a meaningful relationship
areas of experience normally seen as remote. In *2 Henry IV*,
when Feeble is conscripted, he stoically says, "I care not. A
man can die but once. We owe God a death" (3.2.242–43),
punning on *debt*, which was the way *death* was pronounced.
Here an enormously significant fact of life is put into simple
commercial imagery, suggesting its commonplace quality.
Shakespeare used the same pun earlier in *1 Henry IV*, when
Prince Hal says to Falstaff, "Why, thou owest God a death,"
and Falstaff replies, " 'Tis not due yet: I would be loath
to pay him before his day. What need I be so forward with
him that calls not on me?" (5.1.126–29).

Sometimes the puns reveal a delightful playfulness;
sometimes they reveal aggressiveness, as when, replying to
Claudius's "But now, my cousin Hamlet, and my son,"
Hamlet says, "A little more than kin, and less than kind!"
(1.2.64–65). These are Hamlet's first words in the play, and
we already hear him warring verbally against Claudius.
Hamlet's "less than kind" probably means (1) Hamlet is not
of Claudius's family or nature, *kind* having the sense it still
has in our word *mankind*; (2) Hamlet is not kindly (affec-
tionately) disposed toward Claudius; (3) Claudius is not
naturally (but rather unnaturally, in a legal sense incestu-
ously) Hamlet's father. The puns evidently were not put in
as sops to the groundlings; they are an important way of
communicating a complex meaning.

2. *Vocabulary.* A conspicuous difficulty in reading Shakespeare is rooted in the fact that some of his words are no
longer in common use—for example, words concerned with
armor, astrology, clothing, coinage, hawking, horsemanship, law, medicine, sailing, and war. Shakespeare had a
large vocabulary—something near thirty thousand words—
but it was not so much a vocabulary of big words as a
vocabulary drawn from a wide range of life, and it is partly

his ability to call upon a great body of concrete language that gives his plays the sense of being in close contact with life. When the right word did not already exist, he made it up. Among words thought to be his coinages are *accommodation, all-knowing, amazement, bare-faced, countless, dexterously, dislocate, dwindle, fancy-free, frugal, indistinguishable, lackluster, laughable, overawe, premeditated, sea change, star-crossed*. Among those that have not survived are the verb *convive,* meaning to feast together, and *smilet,* a little smile.

Less overtly troublesome than the technical words but more treacherous are the words that seem readily intelligible to us but whose Elizabethan meanings differ from their modern ones. When Horatio describes the Ghost as an "erring spirit," he is saying not that the ghost has sinned or made an error but that it is wandering. Here is a short list of some of the most common words in Shakespeare's plays that often (but not always) have a meaning other than their most usual modern meaning:

| | |
|---|---|
| *'a* | he |
| *abuse* | deceive |
| *accident* | occurrence |
| *advertise* | inform |
| *an, and* | if |
| *annoy* | harm |
| *appeal* | accuse |
| *artificial* | skillful |
| *brave* | fine, splendid |
| *censure* | opinion |
| *cheer* | (1) face (2) frame of mind |
| *chorus* | a single person who comments on the events |
| *closet* | small private room |
| *competitor* | partner |
| *conceit* | idea, imagination |
| *cousin* | kinsman |
| *cunning* | skillful |
| *disaster* | evil astrological influence |
| *doom* | judgment |
| *entertain* | receive into service |

| | |
|---|---|
| *envy* | malice |
| *event* | outcome |
| *excrement* | outgrowth (of hair) |
| *fact* | evil deed |
| *fancy* | (1) love (2) imagination |
| *fell* | cruel |
| *fellow* | (1) companion (2) low person (often an insulting term if addressed to someone of approximately equal rank) |
| *fond* | foolish |
| *free* | (1) innocent (2) generous |
| *glass* | mirror |
| *hap, haply* | chance, by chance |
| *head* | army |
| *humor* | (1) mood (2) bodily fluid thought to control one's psychology |
| *imp* | child |
| *intelligence* | news |
| *kind* | natural, acting according to nature |
| *let* | hinder |
| *lewd* | base |
| *mere(ly)* | utter(ly) |
| *modern* | commonplace |
| *natural* | a fool, an idiot |
| *naughty* | (1) wicked (2) worthless |
| *next* | nearest |
| *nice* | (1) trivial (2) fussy |
| *noise* | music |
| *policy* | (1) prudence (2) stratagem |
| *presently* | immediately |
| *prevent* | anticipate |
| *proper* | handsome |
| *prove* | test |
| *quick* | alive |
| *sad* | serious |
| *saw* | proverb |
| *secure* | without care, incautious |
| *silly* | innocent |

| | |
|---|---|
| *sensible* | capable of being perceived by the senses |
| *shrewd* | sharp |
| *so* | provided that |
| *starve* | die |
| *still* | always |
| *success* | that which follows |
| *tall* | brave |
| *tell* | count |
| *tonight* | last night |
| *wanton* | playful, careless |
| *watch* | keep awake |
| *will* | lust |
| *wink* | close both eyes |
| *wit* | mind, intelligence |

All glosses, of course, are mere approximations; sometimes one of Shakespeare's words may hover between an older meaning and a modern one, and as we have seen, his words often have multiple meanings.

*3. Grammar.* A few matters of grammar may be surveyed, though it should be noted at the outset that Shakespeare sometimes made up his own grammar. As E.A. Abbott says in *A Shakespearian Grammar,* "Almost any part of speech can be used as any other part of speech": a noun as a verb ("he childed as I fathered"); a verb as a noun ("She hath made compare"); or an adverb as an adjective ("a seldom pleasure"). There are hundreds, perhaps thousands, of such instances in the plays, many of which at first glance would not seem at all irregular and would trouble only a pedant. Here are a few broad matters.

*Nouns:* The Elizabethans thought the *-s* genitive ending for nouns (as in *man's*) derived from *his*; thus the line " 'gainst the count his galleys I did some service," for "the count's galleys."

*Adjectives:* By Shakespeare's time adjectives had lost the endings that once indicated gender, number, and case. About the only difference between Shakespeare's adjectives and ours is the use of the now redundant *more* or *most* with the comparative ("some more fitter place") or superlative

("This was the most unkindest cut of all"). Like double comparatives and double superlatives, double negatives were acceptable; Mercutio "will not budge for no man's pleasure."

*Pronouns:* The greatest change was in pronouns. In Middle English *thou, thy,* and *thee* were used among familiars and in speaking to children and inferiors; *ye, your,* and *you* were used in speaking to superiors (servants to masters, nobles to the king) or to equals with whom the speaker was not familiar. Increasingly the "polite" forms were used in all direct address, regardless of rank, and the accusative *you* displaced the nominative *ye.* Shakespeare sometimes uses *ye* instead of *you,* but even in Shakespeare's day *ye* was archaic, and it occurs mostly in rhetorical appeals.

*Thou, thy,* and *thee* were not completely displaced, however, and Shakespeare occasionally makes significant use of them, sometimes to connote familiarity or intimacy and sometimes to connote contempt. In *Twelfth Night* Sir Toby advises Sir Andrew to insult Cesario by addressing him as *thou:* "If thou thou'st him some thrice, it shall not be amiss" (3.2.46–47). In *Othello* when Brabantio is addressing an unidentified voice in the dark he says, "What are you?" (1.1.91), but when the voice identifies itself as the foolish suitor Roderigo, Brabantio uses the contemptuous form, saying, "I have charged thee not to haunt about my doors" (93). He uses this form for a while, but later in the scene, when he comes to regard Roderigo as an ally, he shifts back to the polite *you,* beginning in line 163, "What said she to you?" and on to the end of the scene. For reasons not yet satisfactorily explained, Elizabethans used *thou* in addresses to God—"O God, thy arm was here," the king says in *Henry V* (4.8.108)—and to supernatural characters such as ghosts and witches. A subtle variation occurs in *Hamlet.* When Hamlet first talks with the Ghost in 1.5, he uses *thou,* but when he sees the Ghost in his mother's room, in 3.4, he uses *you,* presumably because he is now convinced that the Ghost is not a counterfeit but is his father.

Perhaps the most unusual use of pronouns, from our point of view, is the neuter singular. In place of our *its, his* was often used, as in "How far that little candle throws *his* beams." But the use of a masculine pronoun for a neuter noun came to seem unnatural, and so *it* was used for the possessive as well as the nominative: "The hedge-sparrow fed the cuckoo so long / That it had it head bit off by it young." In the late sixteenth century the possessive form *its* developed, apparently by analogy with the *-s* ending used to indicate a genitive noun, as in *book*'s, but *its* was not yet common usage in Shakespeare's day. He seems to have used *its* only ten times, mostly in his later plays. Other usages, such as "you have seen Cassio and she together" or the substitution of *who* for *whom,* cause little problem even when noticed.

*Verbs, Adverbs, and Prepositions:* Verbs cause almost no difficulty: The third person singular present form commonly ends in *s,* as in modern English (e.g., "He blesses"), but sometimes in *-eth* (Portia explains to Shylock that mercy "blesseth him that gives and him that takes"). Broadly speaking, the *-eth* ending was old-fashioned or dignified or "literary" rather than colloquial, except for the words *doth, hath,* and *saith.* The *-eth* ending (regularly used in the King James Bible, 1611) is very rare in Shakespeare's dramatic prose, though not surprisingly it occurs twice in the rather formal prose summary of the narrative poem *Lucrece.* Sometimes a plural subject, especially if it has collective force, takes a verb ending in *-s,* as in "My old bones aches." Some of our strong or irregular preterites (such as *broke*) have a different form in Shakespeare (*brake*); some verbs that now have a weak or regular preterite (such as *helped*) in Shakespeare have a strong or irregular preterite (*holp*). Some adverbs that today end in *-ly* were not inflected: "grievous sick," "wondrous strange." Finally, prepositions often are not the ones we expect: "We are such stuff as dreams are made on," "I have a king here to my flatterer."

Again, none of the differences (except meanings that have substantially changed or been lost) will cause much difficulty. But it must be confessed that for some elliptical passages there is no widespread agreement on meaning. Wise editors resist saying more than they know, and when they are uncertain they add a question mark to their gloss.

## Shakespeare's Theater

In Shakespeare's infancy, Elizabethan actors performed wherever they could—in great halls, at court, in the courtyards of inns. These venues implied not only different audiences but also different playing conditions. The innyards must have made rather unsatisfactory theaters: on some days they were unavailable because carters bringing goods to London used them as depots; when available, they had to be rented from the innkeeper. In 1567, presumably to avoid such difficulties, and also to avoid regulation by the Common Council of London, which was not well disposed toward theatricals, one John Brayne, brother-in-law of the carpenter turned actor James Burbage, built the Red Lion in an eastern suburb of London. We know nothing about its shape or its capacity; we can say only that it may have been the first building in Europe constructed for the purpose of giving plays since the end of antiquity, a thousand years earlier. Even after the building of the Red Lion theatrical activity continued in London in makeshift circumstances, in marketplaces and inns, and always uneasily. In 1574 the Common Council required that plays and playing places in London be licensed because

> sundry great disorders and inconveniences have been found to ensue to this city by the inordinate haunting of great multitudes of people, specially youth, to plays, interludes, and shows, namely occasion of frays and quarrels, evil practices of incontinency in great inns having chambers and secret places adjoining to their open stages and galleries.

The Common Council ordered that innkeepers who wished licenses to hold performance put up a bond and make contributions to the poor.

The requirement that plays and innyard theaters be licensed, along with the other drawbacks of playing at inns and presumably along with the success of the Red Lion, led James Burbage to rent a plot of land northeast of the city walls, on property outside the jurisdiction of the city. Here he built England's second playhouse, called simply the Theatre. About all that is known of its construction is that it was wood. It soon had imitators, the most famous being the Globe (1599), essentially an amphitheater built across the Thames (again outside the city's jurisdiction), constructed with timbers of the Theatre, which had been dismantled when Burbage's lease ran out.

Admission to the theater was one penny, which allowed spectators to stand at the sides and front of the stage that jutted into the yard. An additional penny bought a seat in a covered part of the theater, and a third penny bought a more comfortable seat and a better location. It is notoriously difficult to translate prices into today's money, since some things that are inexpensive today would have been expensive in the past and vice versa—a pipeful of tobacco (imported, of course) cost a lot of money, about three pennies, and an orange (also imported) cost two or three times what a chicken cost—but perhaps we can get some idea of the low cost of the penny admission when we realize that a penny could also buy a pot of ale. An unskilled laborer made about five or sixpence a day, an artisan about twelve pence a day, and the hired actors (as opposed to the sharers in the company, such as Shakespeare) made about ten pence a performance. A printed play cost five or sixpence. Of course a visit to the theater (like a visit to a baseball game today) usually cost more than the admission since the spectator probably would also buy food and drink. Still, the low entrance fee meant that the theater was available to all except the very poorest people, rather as movies and most athletic events are today. Evidence indicates that the audience ranged from apprentices who somehow managed to scrape together the minimum entrance fee and to escape from their masters for a few hours, to prosperous members of the middle class and aristocrats who paid the additional fee for admission to the galleries. The exact proportion of men to women cannot be determined, but women of all classes certainly were present. Theaters were open every afternoon but Sundays for much of the year, except in times of plague, when they were closed because of fear of infection. By the way, no evidence suggests the presence of toilet facilities. Presumably the patrons relieved themselves by making a quick trip to the fields surrounding the playhouses.

There are four important sources of information about the

structure of Elizabethan public playhouses—drawings, a contract, recent excavations, and stage directions in the plays. Of drawings, only the so-called de Witt drawing (c. 1596) of the Swan—really his friend Aernout van Buchell's copy of Johannes de Witt's drawing—is of much significance. The drawing, the only extant representation of the interior of an Elizabethan theater, shows an amphitheater of three tiers, with a stage jutting from a wall into the yard or

Johannes de Witt, a Continental visitor to London, made a drawing of the Swan theater in about the year 1596. The original drawing is lost; this is Aernout van Buchell's copy of it.

center of the building. The tiers are roofed, and part of the stage is covered by a roof that projects from the rear and is supported at its front on two posts, but the groundlings, who paid a penny to stand in front of the stage or at its sides, were exposed to the sky. (Performances in such a playhouse were held only in the daytime; artificial illumination was not used.) At the rear of the stage are two massive doors; above the stage is a gallery.

The second major source of information, the contract for the Fortune (built in 1600), specifies that although the Globe (built in 1599) is to be the model, the Fortune is to be square, eighty feet outside and fifty-five inside. The stage is to be forty-three feet broad, and is to extend into the middle of the yard, i.e., it is twenty-seven and a half feet deep.

The third source of information, the 1989 excavations of the Rose (built in 1587), indicate that the Rose was fourteen-sided, about seventy-two feet in diameter with an inner yard almost fifty feet in diameter. The stage at the Rose was about sixteen feet deep, thirty-seven feet wide at the rear, and twenty-seven feet wide downstage. The relatively small dimensions and the tapering stage, in contrast to the rectangular stage in the Swan drawing, surprised theater historians and have made them more cautious in generalizing about the Elizabethan theater. Excavations at the Globe have not yielded much information, though some historians believe that the fragmentary evidence suggests a larger theater, perhaps one hundred feet in diameter.

From the fourth chief source, stage directions in the plays, one learns that entrance to the stage was by the doors at the rear (*"Enter one citizen at one door, and another at the other"*). A curtain hanging across the doorway—or a curtain hanging between the two doorways—could provide a place where a character could conceal himself, as Polonius does, when he wishes to overhear the conversation between Hamlet and Gertrude. Similarly, withdrawing a curtain from the doorway could "discover" (reveal) a character or two. Such discovery scenes are very rare in Elizabethan drama, but a good example occurs in *The Tempest* (5.1.171), where a stage direction tells us, *"Here Prospero discovers Ferdinand and Miranda playing at chess."* There was also some sort of playing space "aloft" or "above" to represent, for instance, the top of a city's walls or a room above the street. Doubtless each theater had its own peculiarities, but perhaps we can talk about a "typical" Elizabethan theater if we realize that no theater need exactly fit the description, just as no mother is the average mother with 2.7 children.

This hypothetical theater is wooden, round, or polygonal (in *Henry V* Shakespeare calls it a "wooden *O*") capable of holding some eight hundred spectators who stood in the yard around the projecting elevated stage—these spectators were the "groundlings"—and some fifteen hundred additional spectators who sat in the three roofed galleries. The stage, protected by a "shadow" or "heavens" or roof, is entered from two doors; behind the doors is the "tiring house" (attiring house, i.e., dressing room), and above the stage is some sort of gallery that may sometimes hold spectators but can be used (for example) as the bedroom from which Romeo—according to a stage direction in one text—"goeth down." Some evidence suggests that a throne can be lowered onto the platform stage, perhaps from the "shadow"; certainly characters can descend from the stage through a trap or traps into the cellar or "hell." Sometimes this space beneath the stage accommodates a sound-effects man or musician (in *Antony and Cleopatra* "*music of the hautboys* [oboes] *is under the stage*") or an actor (in *Hamlet* the "*Ghost cries under the stage*"). Most characters simply walk on and off through the doors, but because there is no curtain in front of the platform, corpses will have to be carried off (Hamlet obligingly clears the stage of Polonius's corpse, when he says, "I'll lug the guts into the neighbor room"). Other characters may have fallen at the rear, where a curtain on a doorway could be drawn to conceal them.

Such may have been the "public theater," so called because its inexpensive admission made it available to a wide range of the populace. Another kind of theater has been called the "private theater" because its much greater admission charge (sixpence versus the penny for general admission at the public theater) limited its audience to the wealthy or the prodigal. The private theater was basically a large room, entirely roofed and therefore artificially illuminated, with a stage at one end. The theaters thus were distinct in two ways: One was essentially an amphitheater that catered to the general public; the other was a hall that catered to the wealthy. In 1576 a hall theater was established in Blackfriars, a Dominican priory in London that had been suppressed in 1538 and confiscated by the Crown and thus was not under the city's jurisdiction. All the actors in this Blackfriars theater were boys about eight to thirteen years old (in the public theaters similar boys played female parts; a boy Lady Macbeth played to a man Macbeth). Near the end of this section on Shakespeare's theater we will talk at some length about possible implications in this convention of using boys to play female roles, but for the moment we should say that it doubtless accounts for the relative lack of female roles in Elizabethan drama. Thus, in *A Midsummer Night's Dream*, out of twenty-one named roles, only four are female; in *Hamlet*, out of twenty-four, only two (Gertrude and Ophelia) are female. Many of Shakespeare's characters have fathers but no mothers—for instance, King Lear's daughters. We need not bring in Freud to explain the disparity; a dramatic company had only a few boys in it.

To return to the private theaters, in some of which all of the performers were children—the "eyrie of . . . little eyases" (nest of unfledged hawks—2.2.347–48) which Rosencrantz mentions when he and Guildenstern talk with Hamlet. The theater in Blackfriars had a precarious existence, and ceased operations in 1584. In 1596 James Burbage, who had already made theatrical history by building the Theatre, began to construct a second Blackfriars theater. He died in 1597, and for several years this second Blackfriars theater was used by a troupe of boys, but in 1608 two of Burbage's sons and five other actors (including Shakespeare) became joint operators of the theater, using it in the winter when the open-air Globe was unsuitable. Perhaps such a smaller theater, roofed, artificially illuminated, and with a tradition of a wealthy audience, exerted an influence in Shakespeare's late plays.

Performances in the private theaters may well have had intermissions during which music was played, but in the public theaters the action was probably uninterrupted, flowing from scene to scene almost without a break. Actors would enter, speak, exit, and others would immediately enter and establish (if necessary) the new locale by a few properties and by words and gestures. To indicate that the scene took place at night, a player or two would carry a torch. Here are some samples of Shakespeare establishing the scene:

> This is Illyria, lady.                    (*Twelfth Night,* 1.2.2)

> Well, this is the Forest of Arden.        (*As You Like It,* 2.4.14)

> This castle has a pleasant seat; the air
> Nimbly and sweetly recommends itself
> Unto our gentle senses.                   (*Macbeth,* 1.6.1–3)

> The west yet glimmers with some streaks of day.
> (*Macbeth,* 3.3.5)

Sometimes a speech will go far beyond evoking the minimal setting of place and time, and will, so to speak, evoke the social world in which the characters move. For instance, early in the first scene of *The Merchant of Venice* Salerio suggests an explanation for Antonio's melancholy. (In the following passage, *pageants* are decorated wagons, floats, and *cursy* is the verb "to curtsy," or "to bow.")

> Your mind is tossing on the ocean,
> There where your argosies with portly sail—
> Like signiors and rich burghers on the flood,
> Or as it were the pageants of the sea—
> Do overpeer the petty traffickers
> That cursy to them, do them reverence,
> As they fly by them with their woven wings.      (1.1.8–14)

Late in the nineteenth century, when Henry Irving produced the play with elaborate illusionistic sets, the first scene showed a ship moored in the harbor, with fruit vendors and dock laborers, in an effort to evoke the bustling and exotic life of Venice. But Shakespeare's words give us this exotic, rich world of commerce in his highly descriptive language when Salerio speaks of "argosies with portly sail" that fly with "woven wings"; equally important, through Salerio Shakespeare conveys a sense of the orderly, hierarchical

society in which the lesser ships, "the petty traffickers,"
curtsy and thereby "do . . . reverence" to their superiors, the
merchant prince's ships, which are "Like signiors and rich
burghers."

. On the other hand, it is a mistake to think that except for
verbal pictures the Elizabethan stage was bare. Although
Shakespeare's Chorus in *Henry V* calls the stage an
"unworthy scaffold" (Prologue 1.10) and urges the spectators to "eke out our performance with your mind" (Prologue
3.35), there was considerable spectacle. The last act of *Macbeth,* for instance, has five stage directions calling for *"drum
and colors,"* and another sort of appeal to the eye is indicated by the stage direction *"Enter Macduff, with Macbeth's
head."* Some scenery and properties may have been substantial; doubtless a throne was used, but the pillars sup-
porting the roof would have served for the trees on which
Orlando pins his poems in *As You Like It.*

Having talked about the public theater—"this wooden
*O*"—at some length, we should mention again that Shakespeare's plays were performed also in other locales. Alvin
Kernan, in *Shakespeare, the King's Playwright: Theater in
the Stuart Court 1603–1613* (1995) points out that "several
of [Shakespeare's] plays contain brief theatrical performances, set always in a court or some noble house. When
Shakespeare portrayed a theater, he did not, except for the
choruses in *Henry V*, imagine a public theater" (p. 195).
(Examples include episodes in *The Taming of the Shrew*, *A
Midsummer Night's Dream*, *Hamlet*, and *The Tempest*.)

### A Note on the Use of Boy Actors in Female Roles

Until fairly recently, scholars were content to mention
that the convention existed; they sometimes also mentioned
that it continued the medieval practice of using males in
female roles, and that other theaters, notably in ancient
Greece and in China and Japan, also used males in female
roles. (In classical Noh drama in Japan, males still play the
female roles.) Prudery may have been at the root of the academic failure to talk much about the use of boy actors, or
maybe there really is not much more to say than that it was
a convention of a male-centered culture (Stephen Green-

blatt's view, in *Shakespearean Negotiations* [1988]). Further, the very nature of a convention is that it is not thought about: Hamlet is a Dane and Julius Caesar is a Roman, but in Shakespeare's plays they speak English, and we in the audience never give this odd fact a thought. Similarly, a character may speak in the presence of others and we understand, again without thinking about it, that he or she is not heard by the figures on the stage (the aside); a character alone on the stage may speak (the soliloquy), and we do not take the character to be unhinged; in a realistic (box) set, the fourth wall, which allows us to see what is going on, is miraculously missing. The no-nonsense view, then, is that the boy actor was an accepted convention, accepted unthinkingly—just as today we know that Kenneth Branagh is not Hamlet, Al Pacino is not Richard II, and Denzel Washington is not the Prince of Aragon. In this view, the audience takes the performer for the role, and that is that; such is the argument we now make for race-free casting, in which African-Americans and Asians can play roles of persons who lived in medieval Denmark and ancient Rome. But gender perhaps is different, at least today. It is a matter of abundant academic study: The Elizabethan theater is now sometimes called a transvestite theater, and we hear much about cross-dressing.

Shakespeare himself in a very few passages calls attention to the use of boys in female roles. At the end of *As You Like It* the boy who played Rosalind addresses the audience, and says, "O men, . . . if I were a woman, I would kiss as many of you as had beards that pleased me." But this is in the Epilogue; the plot is over, and the actor is stepping out of the play and into the audience's everyday world. A second reference to the practice of boys playing female roles occurs in *Antony and Cleopatra*, when Cleopatra imagines that she and Antony will be the subject of crude plays, her role being performed by a boy:

> The quick comedians
> Extemporally will stage us, and present
> Our Alexandrian revels: Antony
> Shall be brought drunken forth, and I shall see
> Some squeaking Cleopatra boy my greatness.    (5.2.216–20)

In a few other passages, Shakespeare is more indirect. For instance, in *Twelfth Night* Viola, played of course by a boy, disguises herself as a young man and seeks service in the house of a lord. She enlists the help of a Captain, and (by way of explaining away her voice and her beardlessness) says,

> I'll serve this duke
> Thou shalt present me as an eunuch to him.       (1.2.55–56)

In *Hamlet*, when the players arrive in 2.2, Hamlet jokes with the boy who plays a female role. The boy has grown since Hamlet last saw him: "By'r Lady, your ladyship is nearer to heaven than when I saw you last by the altitude of a chopine" (a lady's thick-soled shoe). He goes on: "Pray God your voice . . . be not cracked" (434–38).

Exactly how sexual, how erotic, this material was and is, is now much disputed. Again, the use of boys may have been unnoticed, or rather not thought about—an unexamined convention—by most or all spectators most of the time, perhaps *all* of the time, except when Shakespeare calls the convention to the attention of the audience, as in the passages just quoted. Still, an occasional bit seems to invite erotic thoughts. The clearest example is the name that Rosalind takes in *As You Like It*, Ganymede—the beautiful youth whom Zeus abducted. Did boys dressed to play female roles carry homoerotic appeal for straight men (Lisa Jardine's view, in *Still Harping on Daughters* [1983]), or for gay men, or for some or all women in the audience? Further, when the boy actor played a woman who (for the purposes of the plot) disguised herself as a male, as Rosalind, Viola, and Portia do—so we get a boy playing a woman playing a man—what sort of appeal was generated, and for what sort of spectator?

Some scholars have argued that the convention empowered women by letting female characters display a freedom unavailable in Renaissance patriarchal society; the convention, it is said, undermined rigid gender distinctions. In this view, the convention (along with plots in which female characters for a while disguised themselves as young men) allowed Shakespeare to say what some modern gender

critics say: Gender is a constructed role rather than a bio-
logical given, something we make, rather than a fixed binary
opposition of male and female (see Juliet Dusinberre, in
*Shakespeare and the Nature of Women* [1975]). On the other
hand, some scholars have maintained that the male disguise
assumed by some female characters serves only to reaffirm
traditional social distinctions since female characters who
don male garb (notably Portia in *The Merchant of Venice*
and Rosalind in *As You Like It*) return to their female garb
and at least implicitly (these critics say) reaffirm the status
quo. (For this last view, see Clara Claiborne Park, in an
essay in *The Woman's Part*, ed. Carolyn Ruth Swift Lenz et
al. [1980].) Perhaps no one answer is right for all plays; in
*As You Like It* cross-dressing empowers Rosalind, but in
*Twelfth Night* cross-dressing comically traps Viola.

## Shakespeare's Dramatic Language: Costumes, Gestures and Silences; Prose and Poetry

Because Shakespeare was a dramatist, not merely a poet,
he worked not only with language but also with costume,
sound effects, gestures, and even silences. We have already
discussed some kinds of spectacle in the preceding section,
and now we will begin with other aspects of visual language;
a theater, after all, is literally a "place for seeing." Consider
the opening stage direction in *The Tempest*, the first play in
the first published collection of Shakespeare's plays: *"A
tempestuous noise of thunder and Lightning heard: Enter a
Ship-master, and a Boteswain."*

*Costumes:* What did that shipmaster and that boatswain
wear? Doubtless they wore something that identified them
as men of the sea. Not much is known about the costumes
that Elizabethan actors wore, but at least three points are
clear: (1) many of the costumes were splendid versions of
contemporary Elizabethan dress; (2) some attempts were
made to approximate the dress of certain occupations and of
antique or exotic characters such as Romans, Turks, and
Jews; (3) some costumes indicated that the wearer was

supernatural. Evidence for elaborate Elizabethan clothing can be found in the plays themselves and in contemporary comments about the "sumptuous" players who wore the discarded clothing of noblemen, as well as in account books that itemize such things as "a scarlet cloak with two broad gold laces, with gold buttons down the sides."

The attempts at approximation of the dress of certain occupations and nationalities also can be documented from the plays themselves, and it derives additional confirmation from a drawing of the first scene of Shakespeare's *Titus Andronicus*—the only extant Elizabethan picture of an identifiable episode in a play. (See pp. xxxviii–xxxix.) The drawing, probably done in 1594 or 1595, shows Queen Tamora pleading for mercy. She wears a somewhat medieval-looking robe and a crown; Titus wears a toga and a wreath, but two soldiers behind him wear costumes fairly close to Elizabethan dress. We do not know, however, if the drawing represents an actual stage production in the public theater, or perhaps a private production, or maybe only a reader's visualization of an episode. Further, there is some conflicting evidence: In *Julius Caesar* a reference is made to Caesar's doublet (a close-fitting jacket), which, if taken literally, suggests that even the protagonist did not wear Roman clothing; and certainly the lesser characters, who are said to wear hats, did not wear Roman garb.

It should be mentioned, too, that even ordinary clothing can be symbolic: Hamlet's "inky cloak," for example, sets him apart from the brightly dressed members of Claudius's court and symbolizes his mourning; the fresh clothes that are put on King Lear partly symbolize his return to sanity. Consider, too, the removal of disguises near the end of some plays. For instance, Rosalind in *As You Like It* and Portia and Nerissa in *The Merchant of Venice* remove their male attire, thus again becoming fully themselves.

*Gestures and Silences:* Gestures are an important part of a dramatist's language. King Lear kneels before his daughter Cordelia for a benediction (4.7.57–59), an act of humility that contrasts with his earlier speeches banishing her and that contrasts also with a comparable gesture, his ironic

kneeling before Regan (2.4.153–55). Northumberland's failure to kneel before King Richard II (3.3.71–72) speaks volumes. As for silences, consider a moment in *Coriolanus*: Before the protagonist yields to his mother's entreaties (5.3.182), there is this stage direction: *"Holds her by the hand, silent."* Another example of "speech in dumbness" occurs in *Macbeth*, when Macduff learns that his wife and children have been murdered. He is silent at first, as Malcolm's speech indicates: "What, man! Ne'er pull your hat upon your brows. Give sorrow words" (4.3.208–09). (For a discussion of such moments, see Philip C. McGuire's *Speechless Dialect: Shakespeare's Open Silences* [1985].)

Of course when we think of Shakespeare's work, we think primarily of his language, both the poetry and the prose.

*Prose:* Although two of his plays (*Richard II* and *King John*) have no prose at all, about half the others have at least one quarter of the dialogue in prose, and some have notably more: *1 Henry IV* and *2 Henry IV*, about half; *As You Like It*

and *Twelfth Night*, a little more than half; *Much Ado About Nothing*, more than three quarters; and *The Merry Wives of Windsor*, a little more than five sixths. We should remember that despite Molière's joke about M. Jourdain, who was amazed to learn that he spoke prose, most of us do not speak prose. Rather, we normally utter repetitive, shapeless, and often ungrammatical torrents; prose is something very different—a sort of literary imitation of speech at its most coherent.

Today we may think of prose as "natural" for drama; or even if we think that poetry is appropriate for high tragedy we may still think that prose is the right medium for comedy. Greek, Roman, and early English comedies, however, were written in verse. In fact, prose was not generally considered a literary medium in England until the late fifteenth century; Chaucer tells even his bàwdy stories in verse. By the end of the 1580s, however, prose had established itself on the English comic stage. In tragedy, Marlowe made some use of prose, not simply in the speeches of clownish servants but even in the speech of a tragic hero, Doctor Faustus. Still, before Shakespeare, prose normally was used in the theater only for special circumstances: (1) letters and proclamations, to set them off from the poetic dialogue; (2) mad characters, to indicate that normal thinking has become disordered; and (3) low comedy, or speeches uttered by clowns even when they are not being comic. Shakespeare made use of these conventions, but he also went far beyond them. Sometimes he begins a scene in prose and then shifts into verse as the emotion is heightened; or conversely, he may shift from verse to prose when a speaker is lowering the emotional level, as when Brutus speaks in the Forum.

Shakespeare's prose usually is not prosaic. Hamlet's prose includes not only small talk with Rosencrantz and Guildenstern but also princely reflections on "What a piece of work is a man" (2.2.312). In conversation with Ophelia, he shifts from light talk in verse to a passionate prose denunciation of women (3.1.103), though the shift to prose here is perhaps also intended to suggest the possibility of madness. (Consult Brian Vickers, *The Artistry of Shakespeare's Prose* [1968].)

*Poetry:* Drama in rhyme in England goes back to the Middle Ages, but by Shakespeare's day rhyme no longer dominated poetic drama; a finer medium, blank verse (strictly speaking, unrhymed lines of ten syllables, with the stress on every second syllable) had been adopted. But before looking at unrhymed poetry, a few things should be said about the chief uses of rhyme in Shakespeare's plays. (1) A couplet (a pair of rhyming lines) is sometimes used to convey emotional heightening at the end of a blank verse speech; (2) characters sometimes speak a couplet as they leave the stage, suggesting closure; (3) except in the latest plays, scenes fairly often conclude with a couplet, and sometimes, as in *Richard II*, 2.1.145–46, the entrance of a new character within a scene is preceded by a couplet, which wraps up the earlier portion of that scene; (4) speeches of two characters occasionally are linked by rhyme, most notably in *Romeo and Juliet*, 1.5.95–108, where the lovers speak a sonnet between them; elsewhere a taunting reply occasionally rhymes with the previous speaker's last line; (5) speeches with sententious or gnomic remarks are sometimes in rhyme, as in the duke's speech in *Othello* (1.3.199–206); (6) speeches of sardonic mockery are sometimes in rhyme—for example, Iago's speech on women in *Othello* (2.1.146–58)—and they sometimes conclude with an emphatic couplet, as in Bolingbroke's speech on comforting words in *Richard II* (1.3.301–2); (7) some characters are associated with rhyme, such as the fairies in *A Midsummer Night's Dream*; (8) in the early plays, especially *The Comedy of Errors* and *The Taming of the Shrew*, comic scenes that in later plays would be in prose are in jingling rhymes; (9) prologues, choruses, plays-within-the-play, inscriptions, vows, epilogues, and so on are often in rhyme, and the songs in the plays are rhymed.

Neither prose nor rhyme immediately comes to mind when we first think of Shakespeare's medium: It is blank verse, unrhymed iambic pentameter. (In a mechanically exact line there are five iambic feet. An iambic foot consists of two syllables, the second accented, as in *away*; five feet make a pentameter line. Thus, a strict line of iambic pentameter contains ten syllables, the even syllables being stressed more heavily than the odd syllables. Fortunately, Shakespeare usually varies the line somewhat.) The first speech in *A Midsummer Night's Dream*, spoken by Duke Theseus to his betrothed, is an example of blank verse:

> Now, fair Hippolyta, our nuptial hour
> Draws on apace. Four happy days bring in
> Another moon; but, O, methinks, how slow
> This old moon wanes! She lingers my desires,
> Like to a stepdame, or a dowager,
> Long withering out a young man's revenue.           (1.1.1–6)

As this passage shows, Shakespeare's blank verse is not mechanically unvarying. Though the predominant foot is the iamb (as in *apace* or *desires*), there are numerous variations. In the first line the stress can be placed on "fair," as the regular metrical pattern suggests, but it is likely that "Now" gets almost as much emphasis; probably in the second line "Draws" is more heavily emphasized than "on," giving us a trochee (a stressed syllable followed by an unstressed one); and in the fourth line each word in the phrase "This old moon wanes" is probably stressed fairly heavily, conveying by two spondees (two feet, each of two stresses) the oppressive tedium that Theseus feels.

In Shakespeare's early plays much of the blank verse is end-stopped (that is, it has a heavy pause at the end of each line), but he later developed the ability to write iambic pentameter verse paragraphs (rather than lines) that give the illusion of speech. His chief techniques are (1) enjambing, i.e., running the thought beyond the single line, as in the first three lines of the speech just quoted; (2) occasionally replacing an iamb with another foot; (3) varying the position of the chief pause (the caesura) within a line; (4) adding an occasional unstressed syllable at the end of a line, traditionally called a feminine ending; (5) and beginning or ending a speech with a half line.

Shakespeare's mature blank verse has much of the rhythmic flexibility of his prose; both the language, though richly figurative and sometimes dense, and the syntax seem natural. It is also often highly appropriate to a particular character. Consider, for instance, this speech from *Hamlet*, in which Claudius, King of Denmark ("the Dane"), speaks to Laertes:

> And now, Laertes, what's the news with you?
> You told us of some suit. What is't, Laertes?
> You cannot speak of reason to the Dane
> And lose your voice. What wouldst thou beg, Laertes,
> That shall not be my offer, not thy asking?    (1.2.42–46)

Notice the short sentences and the repetition of the name "Laertes," to whom the speech is addressed. Notice, too, the shift from the royal "us" in the second line to the more intimate "my" in the last line, and from "you" in the first three lines to the more intimate "thou" and "thy" in the last two lines. Claudius knows how to ingratiate himself with Laertes.

For a second example of the flexibility of Shakespeare's blank verse, consider a passage from *Macbeth*. Distressed by the doctor's inability to cure Lady Macbeth and by the imminent battle, Macbeth addresses some of his remarks to the doctor and others to the servant who is arming him. The entire speech, with its pauses, interruptions, and irresolution (in "Pull't off, I say," Macbeth orders the servant to remove the armor that the servant has been putting on him), catches Macbeth's disintegration. (In the first line, *physic* means "medicine," and in the fourth and fifth lines, *cast the water* means "analyze the urine.")

Throw physic to the dogs, I'll none of it.
Come, put mine armor on. Give me my staff.
Seyton, send out.—Doctor, the thanes fly from me.—
Come, sir, dispatch. If thou couldst, doctor, cast
The water of my land, find her disease
And purge it to a sound and pristine health,
I would applaud thee to the very echo,
That should applaud again.—Pull't off, I say.—
What rhubarb, senna, or what purgative drug,
Would scour these English hence? Hear'st thou of them?

(5.3.47–56)

Blank verse, then, can be much more than unrhymed iambic pentameter, and even within a single play Shakespeare's blank verse often consists of several styles, depending on the speaker and on the speaker's emotion at the moment.

## The Play Text as a Collaboration

Shakespeare's fellow dramatist Ben Jonson reported that the actors said of Shakespeare, "In his writing, whatsoever he penned, he never blotted out line," i.e., never crossed out material and revised his work while composing. None of Shakespeare's plays survives in manuscript (with the possible exception of a scene in *Sir Thomas More*), so we cannot fully evaluate the comment, but in a few instances the published work clearly shows that he revised his manuscript. Consider the following passage (shown here in facsimile) from the best early text of *Romeo and Juliet*, the Second Quarto (1599):

*Ro.* Would I were sleepe and peace so sweet to rest
The grey eyde morne smiles on the frowning night,
Checking the Easterne Clouds with streaks of light,
And darknesse fleckted like a drunkard reeles,
From forth daies pathway, made by *Tytans* wheeles.
Hence will I to my ghostly Friers close cell,
His helpe to craue, and my deare hap to tell.

*Exit.*

*Enter Frier alone with a basket.*         (night,
*Fri.* The grey-eyed morne smiles on the frowning
Checking the Easterne clowdes with streaks of light:
And fleckeld darknesse like a drunkard reeles,
From forth daies path, and *Titans* burning wheeles:
Now ere the sun aduance his burning eie,

Romeo rather elaborately tells us that the sun at dawn is dispelling the night (morning is smiling, the eastern clouds are checked with light, and the sun's chariot—Titan's wheels—advances), and he will seek out his spiritual father, the Friar. He exits and, oddly, the Friar enters and says pretty much the same thing about the sun. Both speakers say that "the gray-eyed morn smiles on the frowning night," but there are small differences, perhaps having more to do with the business of printing the book than with the author's composition: For Romeo's "checkring," "fleckted," and "pathway," we get the Friar's "checking," "fleckeld," and "path." (Notice, by the way, the inconsistency in Elizabethan spelling: Romeo's "clouds" become the Friar's "clowdes.")

Both versions must have been in the printer's copy, and it seems safe to assume that both were in Shakespeare's manuscript. He must have written one version—let's say he first wrote Romeo's closing lines for this scene—and then he decided, no, it's better to give this lyrical passage to the Friar, as the opening of a new scene, but neglected to delete the first version. Editors must make a choice, and they may feel that the reasonable thing to do is to print the text as Shakespeare intended it. But how can we know what he intended? Almost all modern editors delete the lines from

Romeo's speech, and retain the Friar's lines. They don't do this because they know Shakespeare's intention, however. They give the lines to the Friar because the first published version (1597) of *Romeo and Juliet* gives only the Friar's version, and this text (though in many ways inferior to the 1599 text) is thought to derive from the memory of some actors, that is, it is thought to represent a performance, not just a script. Maybe during the course of rehearsals Shakespeare—an actor as well as an author—unilaterally decided that the Friar should speak the lines; if so (remember that we don't know this to be a fact) his final intention was to give the speech to the Friar. Maybe, however, the actors talked it over and settled on the Friar, with or without Shakespeare's approval. On the other hand, despite the 1597 version, one might argue (if only weakly) on behalf of giving the lines to Romeo rather than to the Friar, thus: (1) Romeo's comment on the coming of the daylight emphasizes his separation from Juliet, and (2) the figurative language seems more appropriate to Romeo than to the Friar. Having said this, in the Signet edition we have decided in this instance to draw on the evidence provided by earlier text and to give the lines to the Friar, on the grounds that since Q1 reflects a production, in the theater (at least on one occasion) the lines were spoken by the Friar.

A playwright sold a script to a theatrical company. The script thus belonged to the company, not the author, and author and company alike must have regarded this script not as a literary work but as the basis for a play that the actors would create on the stage. We speak of Shakespeare as the author of the plays, but readers should bear in mind that the texts they read, even when derived from a single text, such as the First Folio (1623), are inevitably the collaborative work not simply of Shakespeare with his company—doubtless during rehearsals the actors would suggest alterations—but also with other forces of the age. One force was governmental censorship. In 1606 parliament passed "an Act to restrain abuses of players," prohibiting the utterance of oaths and the name of God. So where the earliest text of *Othello* gives us "By heaven" (3.3.106), the first Folio gives "Alas," presumably reflecting the compliance of stage practice with the law. Similarly, the 1623 version of *King Lear* omits the oath "Fut" (probably from "By God's foot") at 1.2.142, again presumably reflecting the line as it was spoken on the stage. Editors who seek to give the reader the play that Shakespeare initially conceived—the "authentic" play conceived by the solitary Shakespeare—probably will restore the missing oaths and references to God. Other editors, who see the play as a collaborative work, a construction made not only by Shakespeare but also by actors and compositors and even government censors, may claim that what counts is the play as it was actually performed. Such editors regard the censored text as legitimate, since it is the play that was (presumably) finally put on. A performed text, they argue, has more historical reality than a text produced by an editor who has sought to get at what Shakespeare initially wrote. In this view, the text of a play is rather like the script of a film; the script is not the film, and the play text is not the performed play. Even if we want to talk about the play that Shakespeare "intended," we will find ourselves talking about a script that he handed over to a company with the intention that it be implemented by actors. The "intended" play is the one that the actors—we might almost say "society"—would help to construct.

Further, it is now widely held that a play is also the work of readers and spectators, who do not simply receive meaning, but who create it when they respond to the play. This idea is fully in accord with contemporary post-structuralist critical thinking, notably Roland Barthes's "The Death of the Author," in *Image-Music-Text* (1977) and Michel Foucault's "What Is an Author?," in *The Foucault Reader* (1984). The gist of the idea is that an author is not an isolated genius; rather, authors are subject to the politics and other social structures of their age. A dramatist especially is a worker in a collaborative project, working most obviously with actors—parts may be written for particular actors—but working also with the audience. Consider the words of Samuel Johnson, written to be spoken by the actor David Garrick at the opening of a theater in 1747:

> The stage but echoes back the public voice;
> The drama's laws, the drama's patrons give,
> For we that live to please, must please to live.

The audience—the public taste as understood by the playwright—helps to determine what the play is. Moreover, even members of the public who are not part of the playwright's immediate audience may exert an influence through censorship. We have already glanced at governmental censorship, but there are also other kinds. Take one of Shakespeare's most beloved characters, Falstaff, who appears in three of Shakespeare's plays, the two parts of *Henry IV* and *The Merry Wives of Windsor*. He appears with this name in the earliest printed version of the first of these plays, *1 Henry IV*, but we know that Shakespeare originally called him (after an historical figure) Sir John Oldcastle. Oldcastle appears in Shakespeare's source (partly reprinted in the Signet edition of *1 Henry IV*), and a trace of the name survives in Shakespeare's play, 1.2.43–44, where Prince Hal punningly addresses Falstaff as "my old lad of the castle." But for some reason—perhaps because the family of the historical Oldcastle complained—Shakespeare had to change the name. In short, the play as we have it was (at least in this detail) subject to some sort of censorship. If we think that a text should present what we take to be the author's intention, we probably will want to replace *Falstaff* with *Oldcastle*. But if we recognize that a play is a collaboration, we may welcome the change, even if it was forced on Shakespeare. Somehow *Falstaff*, with its hint of *false-staff*, i.e., inadequate prop, seems just right for this fat knight who, to our delight, entertains the young prince with untruths. We can go as far as saying that, at least so far as a play is concerned, an insistence on the author's original intention (even if we could know it) can sometimes impoverish the text.

The tiny example of Falstaff's name illustrates the point that the text we read is inevitably only a version—something in effect produced by the collaboration of the playwright with his actors, audiences, compositors, and editors—of a fluid text that Shakespeare once wrote, just as the *Hamlet* that we see on the screen starring Kenneth Branagh is not the *Hamlet* that Shakespeare saw in an open-air playhouse starring Richard Burbage. *Hamlet* itself, as we shall note in a moment, also exists in several versions. It is not surprising that there is now much talk about the *instability* of Shakespeare's texts.

Because he was not only a playwright but was also an actor and a shareholder in a theatrical company, Shakespeare probably was much involved with the translation of the play from a manuscript to a stage production. He may or may not have done some rewriting during rehearsals, and he may or may not have been happy with cuts that were made. Some plays, notably *Hamlet* and *King Lear*, are so long that it is most unlikely that the texts we read were acted in their entirety. Further, for both of these plays we have more than one early text that demands consideration. In *Hamlet*, the Second Quarto (1604) includes some two hundred lines not found in the Folio (1623). Among the passages missing from the Folio are two of Hamlet's reflective speeches, the "dram of evil" speech (1.4.13–38) and "How all occasions do inform against me" (4.4.32–66). Since the Folio has more numerous and often fuller stage directions, it certainly looks as though in the Folio we get a theatrical version of the play, a text whose cuts were probably made—this is only a hunch, of course—not because Shakespeare was changing his conception of Hamlet but because the playhouse demanded a modified play. (The problem is complicated, since the Folio not only cuts some of the Quarto but adds some material. Various explanations have been offered.)

Or take an example from *King Lear*. In the First and Second Quarto (1608, 1619), the final speech of the play is given to Albany, Lear's surviving son-in-law, but in the First Folio version (1623), the speech is given to Edgar. The Quarto version is in accord with tradition—usually the highest-ranking character in a tragedy speaks the final words. Why does the Folio give the speech to Edgar? One possible answer is this: The Folio version omits some of Albany's speeches in earlier scenes, so perhaps it was decided (by Shakespeare? by the players?) not to give the final lines to so pale a character. In fact, the discrepancies are so many between the two texts, that some scholars argue we do not simply have texts showing different theatrical productions. Rather, these scholars say, Shakespeare substantially revised the play, and we really have two versions of *King Lear* (and of *Othello* also, say some)—two different plays—not simply two texts, each of which is in some ways imperfect.

In this view, the 1608 version of *Lear* may derive from Shakespeare's manuscript, and the 1623 version may derive from his later revision. The Quartos have almost three hundred lines not in the Folio, and the Folio has about a hundred lines not in the Quartos. It used to be held that all the texts were imperfect in various ways and from various causes— some passages in the Quartos were thought to have been set from a manuscript that was not entirely legible, other passages were thought to have been set by a compositor who was new to setting plays, and still other passages were thought to have been provided by an actor who misremembered some of the lines. This traditional view held that an editor must draw on the Quartos and the Folio in order to get Shakespeare's "real" play. The new argument holds (although not without considerable strain) that we have two authentic plays, Shakespeare's early version (in the Quarto) and Shakespeare's—or his theatrical company's—revised version (in the Folio). Not only theatrical demands but also Shakespeare's own artistic sense, it is argued, called for extensive revisions. Even the titles vary: Q1 is called *True Chronicle Historie of the life and death of King Lear and his three Daughters*, whereas the Folio text is called *The Tragedie of King Lear*. To combine the two texts in order to produce what the editor thinks is the play that Shakespeare intended to write is, according to this view, to produce a text that is false to the history of the play. If the new view is correct, and we do have texts of two distinct versions of *Lear* rather than two imperfect versions of one play, it supports in a textual way the poststructuralist view that we cannot possibly have an unmediated vision of (in this case) a play by Shakespeare; we can only recognize a plurality of visions.

## Editing Texts

Though eighteen of his plays were published during his lifetime, Shakespeare seems never to have supervised their publication. There is nothing unusual here; when a playwright sold a play to a theatrical company he surrendered his ownership to it. Normally a company would not publish the play, because to publish it meant to allow competitors to acquire the piece. Some plays did get published: Apparently hard-up actors sometimes pieced together a play for a publisher; sometimes a company in need of money sold a play; and sometimes a company allowed publication of a play that no longer drew audiences. That Shakespeare did not concern himself with publication is not remarkable; of his contemporaries, only Ben Jonson carefully supervised the publication of his own plays.

In 1623, seven years after Shakespeare's death, John Heminges and Henry Condell (two senior members of Shakespeare's company, who had worked with him for about twenty years) collected his plays—published and unpublished—into a large volume, of a kind called a folio. (A folio is a volume consisting of large sheets that have been folded once, each sheet thus making two leaves, or four pages. The size of the page of course depends on the size of the sheet—a folio can range in height from twelve to sixteen inches, and in width from eight to eleven; the pages in the 1623 edition of Shakespeare, commonly called the First Folio, are approximately thirteen inches tall and eight inches wide.) The eighteen plays published during Shakespeare's lifetime had been issued one play per volume in small formats called quartos. (Each sheet in a quarto has been folded twice, making four leaves, or eight pages, each page being about nine inches tall and seven inches wide, roughly the size of a large paperback.)

Heminges and Condell suggest in an address "To the great variety of readers" that the republished plays are presented in better form than in the quartos:

> Before you were abused with diverse stolen and surreptitious copies, maimed and deformed by the frauds and stealths of injurious impostors that exposed them; even those, are now offered to your view cured and perfect of their limbs, and all the rest absolute in their numbers, as he [i.e., Shakespeare] conceived them.

There is a good deal of truth to this statement, but some of the quarto versions are better than others; some are in fact preferable to the Folio text.

Whoever was assigned to prepare the texts for publication

in the first Folio seems to have taken the job seriously and yet not to have performed it with uniform care. The sources of the texts seem to have been, in general, good unpublished copies or the best published copies. The first play in the collection, *The Tempest*, is divided into acts and scenes, has unusually full stage directions and descriptions of spectacle, and concludes with a list of the characters, but the editor was not able (or willing) to present all of the succeeding texts so fully dressed. Later texts occasionally show signs of carelessness: in one scene of *Much Ado About Nothing* the names of actors, instead of characters, appear as speech prefixes, as they had in the Quarto, which the Folio reprints; proofreading throughout the Folio is spotty and apparently was done without reference to the printer's copy; the pagination of *Hamlet* jumps from 156 to 257. Further, the proofreading was done while the presses continued to print, so that each play in each volume contains a mix of corrected and uncorrected pages.

Modern editors of Shakespeare must first select their copy; no problem if the play exists only in the Folio, but a considerable problem if the relationship between a Quarto and the Folio—or an early Quarto and a later one—is unclear. In the case of *Romeo and Juliet*, the First Quarto (Q1), published in 1597, is vastly inferior to the Second (Q2), published in 1599. The basis of Q1 apparently is a version put together from memory by some actors. Not surprisingly, it garbles many passages and is much shorter than Q2. On the other hand, occasionally Q1 makes better sense than Q2. For instance, near the end of the play, when the parents have assembled and learned of the deaths of Romeo and Juliet, in Q2 the Prince says (5.3.208–9),

> Come, *Montague;* for thou art early vp
> To see thy sonne and heire, now earling downe.

The last three words of this speech surely do not make sense, and many editors turn to Q1, which instead of "now earling downe" has "more early downe." Some modern editors take only "early" from Q1, and print "now early down"; others take "more early," and print "more early down." Further, Q1 (though, again, quite clearly a garbled and abbreviated text) includes some stage directions that are not found in Q2, and today many editors who base their text on Q2 are glad to add these stage directions, because the directions help to give us a sense of what the play looked like on Shakespeare's stage. Thus, in 4.3.58, after Juliet drinks the potion, Q1 gives us this stage direction, not in Q2: *"She falls upon her bed within the curtains."*

In short, an editor's decisions do not end with the choice of a single copy text. First of all, editors must reckon with Elizabethan spelling. If they are not producing a facsimile, they probably modernize the spelling, but ought they to preserve the old forms of words that apparently were pronounced quite unlike their modern forms—*lanthorn, alablaster*? If they preserve these forms are they really preserving Shakespeare's forms or perhaps those of a compositor in the printing house? What is one to do when one finds *lanthorn* and *lantern* in adjacent lines? (The editors of this series in general, but not invariably, assume that words should be spelled in their modern form, unless, for instance, a rhyme is involved.) Elizabethan punctuation, too, presents problems. For example, in the First Folio, the only text for the play, Macbeth rejects his wife's idea that he can wash the blood from his hand (2.2.60–62):

> No: this my Hand will rather
> The multitudinous Seas incarnardine,
> Making the Greene one, Red.

Obviously an editor will remove the superfluous capitals, and will probably alter the spelling to "incarnadine," but what about the comma before "Red"? If we retain the comma, Macbeth is calling the sea "the green one." If we drop the comma, Macbeth is saying that his bloody hand will make the sea ("the Green") *uniformly* red.

An editor will sometimes have to change more than spelling and punctuation. Macbeth says to his wife (1.7.46–47):

> I dare do all that may become a man,
> Who dares no more, is none.

For two centuries editors have agreed that the second line is unsatisfactory, and have emended "no" to "do": "Who dares do more is none." But when in the same play (4.2.21–22) Ross says that fearful persons

> Floate vpon a wilde and violent Sea
> Each way, and moue,

need we emend the passage? On the assumption that the compositor misread the manuscript, some editors emend "each way, and move" to "and move each way"; others emend "move" to "none" (i.e., "Each way and none"). Other editors, however, let the passage stand as in the original. The editors of the Signet Classic Shakespeare have restrained themselves from making abundant emendations. In their minds they hear Samuel Johnson on the dangers of emendation: "I have adopted the Roman sentiment, that it is more honorable to save a citizen than to kill an enemy." Some departures (in addition to spelling, punctuation, and lineation) from the copy text have of course been made, but the original readings are listed in a note following the play, so that readers can evaluate the changes for themselves.

Following tradition, the editors of the Signet Classic Shakespeare have prefaced each play with a list of characters, and throughout the play have regularized the names of the speakers. Thus, in our text of *Romeo and Juliet*, all speeches by Juliet's mother are prefixed "Lady Capulet," although the 1599 Quarto of the play, which provides our copy text, uses at various points seven speech tags for this one character: *Capu. Wi.* (i.e., Capulet's wife), *Ca. Wi., Wi., Wife, Old La.* (i.e., Old Lady), *La.,* and *Mo.* (i.e., Mother). Similarly, in *All's Well That Ends Well*, the character whom we regularly call "Countess" is in the Folio (the copy text) variously identified as *Mother, Countess, Old Countess, Lady,* and *Old Lady.* Admittedly there is some loss in regularizing, since the various prefixes may give us a hint of the way Shakespeare (or a scribe who copied Shakespeare's manuscript) was thinking of the character in a particular scene—for instance, as a mother, or as an old lady. But too much can be made of these differing prefixes, since the social relationships implied are *not* always relevant to the given scene.

We have also added line numbers and in many cases act and scene divisions as well as indications of locale at the beginning of scenes. The Folio divided most of the plays into acts and some into scenes. Early eighteenth-century editors increased the divisions. These divisions, which provide a convenient way of referring to passages in the plays, have been retained, but when not in the text chosen as the basis for the Signet Classic text they are enclosed within square brackets, [ ], to indicate that they are editorial additions. Similarly, though no play of Shakespeare's was equipped with indications of the locale at the heads of scene divisions, locales have here been added in square brackets for the convenience of readers, who lack the information that costumes, properties, gestures, and scenery afford to spectators. Spectators can tell at a glance they are in the throne room, but without an editorial indication the reader may be puzzled for a while. It should be mentioned, incidentally, that there are a few authentic stage directions—perhaps Shakespeare's, perhaps a prompter's—that suggest locales, such as *"Enter Brutus in his orchard,"* and *"They go up into the Senate house."* It is hoped that the bracketed additions in the Signet text will provide readers with the sort of help provided by these two authentic directions, but it is equally hoped that the reader will remember that the stage was not loaded with scenery.

## Shakespeare on the Stage

Each volume in the Signet Classic Shakespeare includes a brief stage (and sometimes film) history of the play. When we read about earlier productions, we are likely to find them eccentric, obviously wrongheaded—for instance, Nahum Tate's version of *King Lear*, with a happy ending, which held the stage for about a century and a half, from the late seventeenth century until the end of the first quarter of the nineteenth. We see engravings of David Garrick, the greatest actor of the eighteenth century, in eighteenth-century garb as King Lear, and we smile, thinking how absurd the production must have been. If we are more thoughtful, we say, with the English novelist L. P. Hartley, "The past is a foreign country: they do things differently there." But if the eighteenth-century staging is a foreign country, what of the plays of the late sixteenth and seventeenth centuries? A foreign language, a foreign theater, a foreign audience.

Probably all viewers of Shakespeare's plays, beginning with Shakespeare himself, at times have been unhappy with the plays on the stage. Consider three comments about production that we find in the plays themselves, which suggest Shakespeare's concerns. The Chorus in *Henry V* complains that the heroic story cannot possibly be adequately staged:

> But pardon, gentles all,
> The flat unraisèd spirits that hath dared
> On this unworthy scaffold to bring forth
> So great an object. Can this cockpit hold
> The vasty fields of France? Or may we cram
> Within this wooden *O* the very casques
> That did affright the air at Agincourt?
>
> . . . . . . . . . . . .
>
> Piece out our imperfections with your thoughts.
>
> (Prologue 1.8–14,23)

Second, here are a few sentences (which may or may not represent Shakespeare's own views) from Hamlet's longish lecture to the players:

> Speak the speech, I pray you, as I pronounced it to you, trippingly on the tongue. But if you mouth it, as many of our players do, I had as lief the town crier spoke my lines. . . . O, it offends me to the soul to hear a robustious periwig-pated fellow tear a passion to tatters, to very rags, to split the ears of the groundlings. . . . And let those that play your clowns speak no more than is set down for them, for there be of them that will themselves laugh, to set on some quantity of barren spectators to laugh too, though in the meantime some necessary question of the play be then to be considered. That's villainous and shows a most pitiful ambition in the fool that uses it. (3.2.1–47)

Finally, we can quote again from the passage cited earlier in this introduction, concerning the boy actors who played the female roles. Cleopatra imagines with horror a theatrical version of her activities with Antony:

> The quick comedians
> Extemporally will stage us, and present
> Our Alexandrian revels: Antony
> Shall be brought drunken forth, and I shall see
> Some squeaking Cleopatra boy my greatness
> I' th' posture of a whore.               (5.2.216–21)

It is impossible to know how much weight to put on such passages—perhaps Shakespeare was just being modest about his theater's abilities—but it is easy enough to think that he was unhappy with some aspects of Elizabethan production. Probably no production can fully satisfy a playwright, and for that matter, few productions can fully satisfy *us;* we regret this or that cut, this or that way of costuming the play, this or that bit of business.

One's first thought may be this: Why don't they just do "authentic" Shakespeare, "straight" Shakespeare, the play as Shakespeare wrote it? But as we read the plays—words written to be performed—it sometimes becomes clear that we do not know *how* to perform them. For instance, in *Antony and Cleopatra* Antony, the Roman general who has succumbed to Cleopatra and to Egyptian ways, says, "The nobleness of life / Is to do thus" (1.1.36–37). But what is "thus"? Does Antony at this point embrace Cleopatra? Does he embrace and kiss her? (There are, by the way, very few scenes of kissing on Shakespeare's stage, possibly because boys played the female roles.) Or does he make a sweeping gesture, indicating the Egyptian way of life?

This is not an isolated example; the plays are filled with lines that call for gestures, but we are not sure what the gestures should be. *Interpretation* is inevitable. Consider a passage in *Hamlet.* In 3.1, Polonius persuades his daughter, Ophelia, to talk to Hamlet while Polonius and Claudius eavesdrop. The two men conceal themselves, and Hamlet encounters Ophelia. At 3.1.131 Hamlet suddenly says to her, "Where's your father?" Why does Hamlet, apparently out of nowhere—they have not been talking about Polonius—ask this question? Is this an example of the "antic disposition" (fantastic behavior) that Hamlet earlier (1.5.172) had told Horatio and others—including us—he would display? That is, is the question about the whereabouts of her father a seemingly irrational one, like his earlier question (3.1.103) to Ophelia, "Ha, ha! Are you honest?" Or, on the other hand, has Hamlet (as in many productions) suddenly glimpsed Polonius's foot protruding from beneath a drapery at the rear? That is, does Hamlet ask the question because he has suddenly seen something suspicious and now is testing Ophelia? (By the way, in productions that do give Hamlet a physical cue, it is almost always Polonius rather than Claudius who provides the clue. This itself is an act of interpretation on the part of the director.) Or (a third possibility) does Hamlet get a clue from Ophelia, who inadvertently betrays the spies by nervously glancing at their place of hiding? This is the interpretation used in the BBC television version, where Ophelia glances in fear toward the hiding place just after Hamlet says "Why wouldst thou be a breeder of sinners?" (121–22). Hamlet, realizing that he is being observed, glances here and there *before* he asks "Where's your father?" The question thus is a climax to what he has been doing while speaking the preceding lines. Or (a fourth interpretation) does Hamlet suddenly, without the aid of any clue whatsoever, intuitively (insightfully, mysteriously, wonderfully) sense that someone is spying? Directors must decide, of course—and so must readers.

Recall, too, the preceding discussion of the texts of the plays, which argued that the texts—though they seem to be before us in permanent black on white—are unstable. The Signet text of *Hamlet*, which draws on the Second Quarto (1604) and the First Folio (1623) is considerably longer than any version staged in Shakespeare's time. Our version, even if spoken very briskly and played without any intermission, would take close to four hours, far beyond "the two hours' traffic of our stage" mentioned in the Prologue to *Romeo and Juliet*. (There are a few contemporary references to the duration of a play, but none mentions more than three hours.) Of Shakespeare's plays, only *The Comedy of Errors*, *Macbeth*, and *The Tempest* can be done in less than three hours without cutting. And even if we take a play that exists only in a short text, *Macbeth*, we cannot claim that we are experiencing the very play that Shakespeare conceived, partly because some of the Witches' songs almost surely are non-Shakespearean additions, and partly because we are not willing to watch the play performed without an intermission and with boys in the female roles.

Further, as the earlier discussion of costumes mentioned, the plays apparently were given chiefly in contemporary, that is, in Elizabethan dress. If today we give them in the costumes that Shakespeare probably saw, the plays seem not contemporary but curiously dated. Yet if we use our own dress, we find lines of dialogue that are at odds with what we see; we may feel that the language, so clearly not our own, is inappropriate coming out of people in today's dress. A common solution, incidentally, has been to set the plays in the nineteenth century, on the grounds that this attractively distances the plays (gives them a degree of foreignness, allowing for interesting costumes) and yet doesn't put them into a museum world of Elizabethan England.

Inevitably our productions are adaptations, *our* adaptations, and inevitably they will look dated, not in a century but in twenty years, or perhaps even in a decade. Still, we cannot escape from our own conceptions. As the director Peter Brook has said, in *The Empty Space* (1968):

> It is not only the hair-styles, costumes and make-ups that look dated. All the different elements of staging—the shorthands of behavior that stand for emotions; gestures, gesticulations and tones of voice—are all fluctuating on an invisible stock exchange all the time. . . . A living theatre that thinks it can stand aloof from anything as trivial as fashion will wilt. (p. 16)

As Brook indicates, it is through today's hairstyles, costumes, makeup, gestures, gesticulations, tones of voice—this includes our *conception* of earlier hairstyles, costumes, and so forth if we stage the play in a period other than our own—that we inevitably stage the plays.

It is a truism that every age invents its own Shakespeare, just as, for instance, every age has invented its own classical world. Our view of ancient Greece, a slave-holding society in which even free Athenian women were severely circum-scribed, does not much resemble the Victorians' view of ancient Greece as a glorious democracy, just as, perhaps, our view of Victorianism itself does not much resemble theirs. We cannot claim that the Shakespeare on our stage is the true Shakespeare, but in our stage productions we find a Shakespeare that speaks to us, a Shakespeare that our ancestors doubtless did not know but one that seems to us to be the true Shakespeare—at least for a while.

Our age is remarkable for the wide variety of kinds of staging that it uses for Shakespeare, but one development deserves special mention. This is the now common practice of race-blind or color-blind or nontraditional casting, which allows persons who are not white to play in Shakespeare. Previously blacks performing in Shakespeare were limited to a mere three roles, Othello, Aaron (in *Titus Andronicus*), and the Prince of Morocco (in *The Merchant of Venice*), and there were no roles at all for Asians. Indeed, African-Americans rarely could play even one of these three roles, since they were not welcome in white companies. Ira Aldridge (c.1806–1867), a black actor of undoubted talent, was forced to make his living by performing Shakespeare in England and in Europe, where he could play not only Othello but also—in whiteface—other tragic roles such as King Lear. Paul Robeson (1898–1976) made theatrical history when he played Othello in London in 1930, and there was some talk about bringing the production to the United States, but there was more talk about whether American audiences would tolerate the sight of a black man—a real black man, not a white man in blackface—kissing and then killing a white woman. The idea was tried out in summer stock in 1942, the reviews were enthusiastic, and in the following year Robeson opened on Broadway in a production that ran an astounding 296 performances. An occasional all-black company sometimes performed Shakespeare's plays, but otherwise blacks (and other minority members) were in effect shut out from performing Shakespeare. Only since about 1970 has it been common for nonwhites to play major roles along with whites. Thus, in a 1996–97 production of *Antony and Cleopatra*, a white Cleopatra, Vanessa Red-grave, played opposite a black Antony, David Harewood.

Multiracial casting is now especially common at the New York Shakespeare Festival, founded in 1954 by Joseph Papp, and in England, where even siblings such as Claudio and Isabella in *Measure for Measure* or Lear's three daughters may be of different races. Probably most viewers today soon stop worrying about the lack of realism, and move beyond the color of the performers' skin to the quality of the performance.

Nontraditional casting is not only a matter of color or race; it includes sex. In the past, occasionally a distinguished woman of the theater has taken on a male role—Sarah Bernhardt (1844–1923) as Hamlet is perhaps the most famous example—but such performances were widely regarded as eccentric. Although today there have been some performances involving cross-dressing (a drag *As You Like It* staged by the National Theatre in England in 1966 and in the United States in 1974 has achieved considerable fame in the annals of stage history), what is more interesting is the casting of women in roles that traditionally are male but that need not be. Thus, a 1993–94 English production of *Henry V* used a woman—*not* cross-dressed—in the role of the governor of Harfleur. According to Peter Holland, who reviewed the production in *Shakespeare Survey* 48 (1995), "having a female Governor of Harfleur feminized the city and provided a direct response to the horrendous threat of rape and murder that Henry had offered, his language and her body in direct connection and opposition" (p. 210). Ten years from now the device may not play so effectively, but today it speaks to us. Shakespeare, born in the Elizabethan Age, has been dead nearly four hundred years, yet he is, as Ben Jonson said, "not of an age but for all time." We must understand, however, that he is "for all time" precisely because each age finds in his abundance something for itself and something of itself.

And here we come back to two issues discussed earlier in this introduction—the instability of the text and, curiously, the Bacon/Oxford heresy concerning the authorship of the plays. *Of course* Shakespeare wrote the plays, and we should daily fall on our knees to thank him for them—and yet there is something to the idea that he is not their only author. Every editor, every director and actor, and every reader to some degree shapes them, too, for when we edit, direct, act, or read, we inevitably become Shakespeare's collaborator and re-create the plays. The plays, one might say, are so cunningly contrived that they guide our responses, tell us how we ought to feel, and make a mark on us, but (for better or for worse) we also make a mark on them.

—SYLVAN BARNET
*Tufts University*

# Introduction

*Romeo and Juliet,* even in the mutilated versions that Restoration and eighteenth-century audiences knew, has always been one of Shakespeare's most popular plays. Since 1845, when Charlotte and Susan Cushman finally brought a version approaching Shakespeare's original back to the stage, it has been a coveted vehicle among actors and actresses alike, on both sides of the Atlantic; and some of the theater's greatest names have been associated with it. In recent years audiences have also been enjoying it in film versions and on television. Among professional scholars the play has sparked less enthusiasm. In this quarter one hears praise for the ingenuity of the language, for the brilliance of the characterizations, and for the portrayal of young love; but such praise is frequently qualified by the uneasy admission that *Romeo and Juliet* resists measurement by the rules conventionally applied to Shakespeare's later tragedies. Scholarly critics continue to express misgivings about the emphasis on pathos, the absence of ethical purpose, and what appears to be a capricious shifting of tone, particularly between the first two acts and the last three.

Such misgivings among modern readers are understandable, but one may question whether the Elizabethans would have felt or even understood them. Apparently most of Shakespeare's contemporaries still considered an ending in death the principal requirement for tragedy; and since *Romeo and Juliet* offered six deaths, five of them on stage and two of them the deaths of protagonists, audiences in those days probably thought it more tragic than many plays so labeled. Elizabethan audiences would have found equally strange the objection that the play lacks ethical purpose. They knew by training what to think of impetuous young lovers who deceived their parents and sought advice from friars. Arthur Brooke, whose *Tragicall Historye of Romeus and Juliet* (1562) was most likely Shakespeare's only source, had spelled it all out as follows:

> To this ende (good Reader) is this tragicall matter written, to describe unto thee a coople of unfortunate lovers, thralling themselves to unhonest desire, neglecting the authoritie and advise of parents and frendes, conferring their principall counsels with dronken gossyppes, and superstitious friers (the naturally fitte instrumentes of unchastitie) attemptyng all adventures of peryll, for thattaynyng of their wished lust, usying auriculer confession (the kay of whoredome, and treason) for furtheraunce of theyre purpose, abusyng the honorable name of lawefull mariage, the cloke the shame of stolne contractes, finallye, by all means of unhonest lyfe, hastyng to most unhappy deathe.

In addition, Elizabethans also knew that suicide was the devil's business and usually meant damnation; in their view, therefore, *Romeo and Juliet* must have had automatically an abundance of ethical import. Shakespeare probably should be given some kind of credit for not challenging these deep-seated convictions of his contemporary auditors and readers; for, ironically, the modern feeling that his play is ethically deficient stems partly from the modern ability to see that Shakespeare has really approved the love of Romeo and Juliet, condoned their deceptions, and laid the blame for their deaths, even though by suicide, upon their elders.

A better explanation for the modern reader's uneasiness about ranking *Romeo and Juliet* with the so-called major tragedies lies in the widespread assumption that Shakespeare meant the play to be deterministic. Shakespeare seems to invite such a view when he promises in the Prologue to show the "misadventured piteous overthrows" of "a pair of star-crossed lovers" and thereafter lets the principals make references to fate and the stars and has them express various kinds of premonition. Romeo, for example, says in Act 1 that his "mind misgives / Some consequence yet hanging in the stars" (1.4.106–7); Friar Lawrence tries to reassure himself with uneasy prayers but soon observes that "violent delights have violent ends" (2.6.9); and Juliet, on taking leave of her husband, cries, "O Fortune, Fortune! All men call thee fickle" (3.5.60). These and other references make it easy to argue that the characters are, as they themselves sometimes imply, little better than puppets, pitiful perhaps but ethically uninteresting and scarcely due the fearful respect that one gives to the heroes of Shakespeare's later tragedies. Actually, the text as a whole gives little justification for such a view. It is true that Romeo says, as he is about to enter the Capulet's great hall,

> . . . my mind misgives
> Some consequence yet hanging in the stars
> Shall bitterly begin his fearful date
> With this night's revels and expire the term
> Of a despisèd life, closed in my breast,
> By some vile forfeit of untimely death.

> (1.4.106–11)

But he immediately adds, ". . . he that hath the steerage of my course / Direct my sail!" The first part of this quotation is typical of what we find—and find not so often as some imagine—in *Romeo and Juliet*: premonitions, prayers, misgivings, references to Fortune, all uttered much as we ourselves utter such things, without necessarily implying real belief in astral influence. Sometimes the character's premonition is confirmed by later events; sometimes not, as is true of the auspicious part of Romeo's dream on the night before his suicide. The second part of the quotation is typical, too; for almost as often as these characters speak of fate they speak of a superior Providence, mysteriously directing but never absolutely determining human destiny. Moreover, accident-prone as Romeo and Juliet may occasionally seem, they are really no more than Hamlet, who also has his share of premonitions; and their actions are no more clearly determined by supernatural influence than those of Macbeth. Like its successors, *Romeo and Juliet* takes place in a universe where there is a special providence in the fall of a sparrow and where what will be, assuredly will be. All that is asked of the inhabitants of this Shakespearean world of tragedy is that they achieve readiness or ripeness for what is to come, and in this tragedy as in the others they are allowed and expected to do that much for themselves. The things to consider are whether or not the protagonists have succeeded in meeting this requirement and, if it appears they have failed, whether one had any right to suppose they would do otherwise.

A final source of uneasiness for contemporary readers of *Romeo and Juliet* is the impression, got mainly from the first two acts, that Verona is really a part of the world of comedy. Many things contribute to this impression. An amusing street fight and a masked ball in the first act, a lovers' meeting in the orchard in the second, a doting young man carrying courtly conventions to laughable excess, parents who would be custom-bound to interfere if they only knew of the affair going on under their noses, an affected troublemaker bent on vindicating honor to the letter in duels conducted with precious precision, a bawdy nurse and an even bawdier friend—such things as these in an Elizabethan play ordinarily lead to the triumph of young love and a marriage or two, with forgiveness and feasting all around. In this play, however, the familiar dream of courtly comedy shatters when Mercutio is slain, and from that point on the lightness quickly dissolves. Romeo is banished, the "comfortable" Friar falls back on desperate remedies, old Capulet grows testy and intolerant, Lady Capulet calls for blood, the amusing Nurse suggests bigamy as a practical course, and Juliet, who has scarcely known life, prepares to be familiar with death. Even the weather adapts itself to the shift in tone: it suddenly gets hot in Act 3, and in Act 4 it rains; the sky is still overcast as the play comes to an end.

The contrast that Shakespeare gets here between the tone of the first two acts and that of the remaining three is probably intentional and, in any case, more apparent than real. Unless a reader is genuinely sophisticated, his response to literature is always at least partly a matter of habit; he laughs and shudders on signal. Thus there will always be those who find the first two acts of *Romeo and Juliet* mainly laughable, just as there will always be some who consider *Othello* the tragedy of a handkerchief, a farce with unfortunate consequences. Shakespeare must not be held responsible for responses of this kind. The first two acts of *Romeo and Juliet* will appear to be consistently comic only if we read them in the limited light of other, very different things—second-rate farces, dramatic and nondramatic, hack work generally, certain comic strips, even—in which the same conventions have been used. The corrective is to pay attention, for Shakespeare allows us to carry any initial impression of comedy we may have got only so far as the climax of the street brawl in Scene 1. At that point, while the servants are still battling, Tybalt still fighting with Benvolio, Capulet yelling for a long sword, and his wife telling him to call for a crutch instead, he brings us up sharply with the Prince's words:

> What, ho! You men, you beasts,
> That quench the fire of your pernicious rage
> With purple fountains issuing from your veins!
>
> (1.1.86–88)

Comedy can thrive indefinitely on beasts that pass for men, but it cannot long tolerate a reminder of original sin such as lurks in "pernicious rage" or a reminder of royal humanity's self-destructiveness like "purple fountains"; and it is with these in our ears that we pass on to the rest of the Prince's dignified rebuke and thence to the speeches of Benvolio and the Montagues which express their human concern for a youthful friend and son, the absent Romeo. When Romeo himself appears, later in the same scene, juggling words in a fashionable euphuistic manner and complaining of the contradictions of love, we are more cautious with our laughter. Laugh as we may, Romeo clearly lives in a world where folly can have serious and irrevocable consequences; and we are no longer confident that the conventions of comedy will save him from those consequences or spare us the pain of seeing him destroyed.

The remaining scenes in Acts 1 and 2 contain much that confirms our uneasiness. For example, Capulet, who has been very funny calling for his long sword, says tenderly of his daughter in Scene 2:

> . . . too soon marred are those so early made.
> Earth hath swallowed all my hopes but she;
> She is the hopeful lady of my earth.

(1.2.13–15)

These three lines are enough to establish him as a dramatic figure who will probably invite our sympathy as readily as he has provoked our ridicule. They also prepare us for Juliet, who never has much of the comic about her and least of all when she disturbs us with a prophetic "My grave is like to be my wedding bed" (1.5.137). Mercutio's bawdiness is perhaps the best argument for taking these two acts as comic, but an attentive listener will receive it all with the long Queen Mab speech still in mind, see that Mercutio's bawdiness and fancy are simply complementary aspects of a single creative and remarkably perceptive imagination, and be prepared to recognize that Verona's one hope of restoration without tragedy has vanished when he dies.

In any case, a feeling that the play represents relatively mature work has disposed most scholars to seek a late date for it. The latest that can reasonably be given is 1596, since the first edition appeared early in 1597 and described the play as having been performed by "Lord Hunsdon's servants," a title that Shakespeare's company held only from July 1596 until the following March. The preferred date seems to be 1595, which is also the preferred date for *Richard II* and *A Midsummer Night's Dream*. The reason usually given for putting these plays in the same year is that the same intense lyricism characterizes all three, but it has also been suggested that *A Midsummer Night's Dream,* in its special concern with the difficulties of young love, reveals itself to be a product of the same mood or preoccupation that caused Shakespeare to write *Romeo and Juliet.* Some interesting parallels have been noted. For example, in the first scene of *A Midsummer Night's Dream* Lysander says:

> Brief as the lightning in the collied night,
> That, in a spleen, unfolds both heaven and earth,
> And ere a man hath power to say "Behold!"
> The jaws of darkness do devour it up:
> So quick bright things come to confusion.

> (1.1.145–49)

To this Hermia replies, "If then true lovers have been ever crossed, / It stands as an edict in destiny." This exchange has been related plausibly both to Juliet's "too rash, too unadvised, too sudden; / Too like the lightning, which doth cease to be / Ere one can say it lightens" (2.2.118–20) and to the "star-crossed lovers" of the Prologue. But beyond the realm of the plausible in this matter we cannot go. Those who regard the play as immature usually prefer an earlier date, insisting that the Nurse's " 'Tis since the earthquake now eleven years" (1.3.23), by which she remembers the time of Juliet's weaning, refers to a famous earthquake which struck England in 1580 and that Shakespeare meant to date his play 1591 by having the Nurse mention something that everyone in the audience could date precisely. Against this view one might argue that there were two other earthquakes in England during the 1580s and at least one on the Continent; Shakespeare could easily have referred to one of these or just as easily to no earthquake at all. Moreover, while it is certainly reasonable to suppose that in mentioning an earthquake he would have thought of some earthquake he knew, it is hardly reasonable to think he would have bothered to fix as contemporary the date of a play that apparently had nothing to gain by being considered topical. Everything taken into account, the play seems to come after plays like *The Two Gentlemen of Verona* and *Love's Labor's Lost* and before *The Merchant of Venice* and the Henry IV plays. The most likely date, therefore, is still 1595.

Whatever the date, the style of *Romeo and Juliet* places it at a point which marks the poet's achievement of self-awareness and confidence in his mastery over the medium. The play is rich in set pieces and memorable scenes, so much so in fact that insensitive producers have sometimes turned it into a collection of dramatic recitals. Yet Shakespeare's virtuosity, intrinsically interesting as it is whenever we choose to isolate some specimen of it, never fails to function as a part of the general action of the play; and that is as true in this work, where he seems to be rejoicing openly in his creative power, as it is in the later tragedies, where the power is felt rather than seen. Nothing in *Romeo and Juliet* really stands alone, not even a startling passage like the Queen Mab speech, which almost immediately proves to be an indispensable part of Mercutio's complex personality, just as Mercutio with all his complexity ultimately proves indispensable to the meaning of the play. The creativity displayed in this passage is Shakespeare's, to be sure, but his greatest achievement is in making it credibly Mercutio's. Equally remarkable is the much-admired lyrical quality of the next scene, in which Romeo meets Juliet for the first time; but this scene is remarkable for another reason. Here we have two young people who presumably have had no opportunity to develop any special gift for language. Juliet's talk up to this point has commanded no particular attention; and Romeo's, best displayed perhaps in his first exchange with Benvolio (1.1), has been characterized by extravagant paradoxes and an occasional fortuitous couplet. Suddenly, with Juliet in sight, he begins to make something like poetry:

> O, she doth teach the torches to burn bright!
> It seems she hangs upon the cheek of night

> As a rich jewel in an Ethiop's ear—
> Beauty too rich for use, for earth too dear!

(1.5.46–49)

Capulet and Tybalt briefly obscure the young man from view, but as these move aside, we see that he has not only taken Juliet by the hand but has begun spinning sonnets with her; and even before the Nurse interrupts, we have sensed the rightness of this unexpected attachment and its potential for permanence. We are thus prepared for the orchard, or balcony, scene of Act 2 and for the lovely *aubade* that the two perform at the parting in Act 3—both among the memorable scenes in Shakespeare because without any formal patterning they achieve a unity all their own and still serve the larger function of suggesting the integrity that love can confer briefly upon two young people who, apart from each other, will remain children to the end.

In characterization Shakespeare had always been able to make language work for him, but with *Romeo and Juliet* he mastered it so completely that the play almost became a gallery of individuals. The language of the extremes in the social scale must have been easiest to catch, with the banter of servingmen at one end and the formal periods of Prince Escalus at the other; but in between the extremes we get the Nurse's peasant speech, most noticeably of peasant origin when she tries to imitate her betters, beautifully contrasted with the self-assured and warmly healthy country-gentry talk of old Capulet; Mercutio's mature command of language at all levels and Tybalt's narrow range of sharp insolence; Friar Lawrence's moralizing, formal and sententious but never tedious, and the tiny voice of the complaisant Apothecary. Some of these characters change attitude as external circumstances require, but in general their personalities simply unfold in the language that establishes them. This is also true of Benvolio, Paris, and Lady Capulet. Romeo and Juliet, however, undergo development, and he undergoes more than she. From her first appearance the younger Juliet is more mature than her lover. Romeo is fertile in figures and can occasionally invent fresh things like "Night's candles are burnt out, and jocund day / Stands tiptoe on the misty mountaintops" (3.5.9–10); but it is always Juliet who leads the talk in their two great scenes together, and it is also she who knows what language cannot do:

> Conceit, more rich in matter than in words,
> Brags of his substance, not of ornament.
> They are but beggars that can count their worth;
> But my true love is grown to such excess
> I cannot sum up sum of half my wealth.
>
> (2.6.30–34)

Her best lines are those in which she draws upon language to invent for her the images of death which she must confront before Romeo can be permanently hers (4.3.14–58); yet when she wakes to find Romeo lifeless, she can muster no language capable of helping her in such an extremity and quickly joins her lover in death. By contrast, Romeo's best speech is perhaps the one he delivers in the tomb; with it he gives dignity, meaning, and finality to the one act he plans and executes, however unwisely, without the help of friends, Friar, or Juliet. His language here, like the deed, is his own, as the courtly conventions and fashionable euphuism of many of his earlier scenes were not. His paradoxes, his puns, even his lamentations in the Friar's cell, are borrowed things, as his mature friends know; yet Romeo's "misshapen chaos of well-seeming forms" is catalyzed into inchoate poetry whenever Juliet comes upon the scene, and in the end he achieves in her presence a man's power to act if not a man's gift of discretion.

If *Romeo and Juliet* fails to achieve the highest rank of tragedy, the reason for that failure must be sought in the protagonists themselves and not in some extraterrestrial power or agency. The reason Romeo and Juliet do not stand out clearly as protagonists in a great tragedy is simply that Shakespeare created them to be protagonists in a different kind of play, one which has many of the circumstances that we find in the other tragedies but which lacks at the center a figure capable of achieving the terrible but satisfying perception of man's involvement in the mystery of creation. "Failure" is an inappropriate word for such an achievement. The notable thing about Romeo and Juliet is not that they fail to reach a Hamlet's degree of awareness but that as very young people they behave better and mature more rapidly in that direction than we have any right to expect them to. They learn that Verona is flawed, but they do not dream that the whole world is flawed in the same way. They discover that some actions are good and some bad, but never achieve the Friar's catholic view that only will can make an action bad and only grace can redeem it. They confront imperfection courageously; they fail to see in it an image of themselves. Death overtakes them in their innocence and their unknowing; and we remember them not as we remember tragic heroes, in pity and fear, but in admiration for their loveliness, as we remember dead children.

All things considered, the Verona which serves as their testing ground is not a bad place. The Prologue refers darkly to "the continuance of their parents' rage, / Which but their children's end, naught could remove"; but as H. B. Charlton has observed, the old people in the play seem to have little interest in continuing a quarrel. Apart from the ancient rift, one might describe the city as a reservoir of high spirits and good will, full of attractive people like the witty Mercutio, Benvolio and Paris, the wise and tolerant Friar, and the young ladies who brighten the evenings in Capulet's great hall. Yet the Prologue is right. The rift created by the old people's almost forgotten rage is still there, wide enough for irresponsible young servingmen to see and make a game of and wide enough, too, for irresponsible young noblemen, like Tybalt, to aggravate into a civic crisis. One might say of it, as Mercutio says of his death wound, " 'Tis not so deep as a well, nor so wide as a church door; but 'tis enough, 'twill serve." In the end it has served as a conduit for some of the best blood in the city, including Mercutio's own, and for the tears of all the rest.

Apart from the two protagonists, the people of Verona, or rather those that Shakespeare has presented to us, may be arranged in two groups. The first of these, by far the larger, includes all the supernumeraries, such minor characters as Peter and the Apothecary, and a few relatively important figures like Tybalt, the Capulets, the Nurse, Paris, and Benvolio. These are the static or "flat" characters, who are "by nature" what they are; and their functions are to present the limited range of values they embody and to make the plot go. Tybalt, for example, is by nature choleric and determined to pick quarrels; Benvolio, by nature the opposite, is equally determined to avoid them. There are no surprises in either, even when Tybalt precipitates the climactic crisis of the play, just as there are no surprises in Paris and should be none in the Nurse. The latter is interesting to us precisely because Shakespeare's detailed unfolding of her reveals a consistent personality, yet she too is static. From the beginning, she is garrulous, corruptible, and insensitive; and as long as nothing requires her to be otherwise, she can also be amusing. At her crisis, when Juliet asks her to be wise, the Nurse can only suggest bigamy, a course quite in keeping with the values she herself is made of. Here the Nurse is no longer funny, but she has not changed. It is Juliet who has done that. The other characters in this group do not change either. They may be said to represent the abiding conditions of human intercourse in any representative community; and a lesser playwright, assembling a similar collection, would probably have included the same kind of servants and dignitaries, a Nurse or someone like her, Tybalts and Benvolios, all performing essentially the same functions as Shakespeare's and exhibiting many of the same qualities. The unique excellence of the static characters in *Romeo and Juliet* comes from Shakespeare's having particularized them so deftly that, like the protagonists in the play, we hopefully take them at first for people of larger dimensions. Their vitality tempts us to expect them to be more than they are and to give more than they have any capacity for giving. Thus when Tybalt fails to respond to Romeo's generous appeal and Lady Capulet proves blind to her daughter's need for sympathy, we feel the disappointment as sharply as if we were discovering for ourselves the limitations of common humanity.

The second group consists of three characters who give a doubly strong impression of life because they include among their qualities some degree of perception or understanding. Prince Escalus, slight as he is, is one of these, and Friar Lawrence another. Normally we should expect a magistrate to belong to the group of static or flat characters, but Shakespeare has given his magistrate a conscience and a growing presentiment of what must happen to everyone in Verona if the wound in the civil body cannot be healed. Others want to keep the peace, too, but mainly because they have a perfunctory sense of duty or perhaps because they dislike fighting. Escalus knows from the beginning that keeping the peace here is a matter of life or death, and in the end he readily takes his share of responsibility for the bloody sacrifice he has failed to avert:

> Capulet, Montague,
> See what a scourge is laid upon your hate,
> That heaven finds means to kill your joys with love.
> And I, for winking at your discords too,
> Have lost a brace of kinsmen. All are punished.
>
> (5.3.291–95)

The Friar is included in this "all"; and the Friar, moreover, has preceded the Prince in accepting blame:

> . . . if aught in this
> Miscarried by my fault, let my old life
> Be sacrificed some hour before his time
> Unto the rigor of severest law.
>
> (266–69)

Like the Prince, the Friar has had from the start a clear perception of the danger latent in the old quarrel, and like the Prince he has taken steps appropriate to his position to mend the differences and restore order. Yet whereas the Prince by nature has moved openly and erred in not moving vigorously enough, Friar Lawrence by nature works in secret and his secrecy does him in. Actually his much-criticized plan for ending the quarrel is sound enough in principle. Any faithful son of the Church, accustomed to cementing alliances with the sacrament of matrimony, would naturally have considered the young people's sudden affection for each other an opportunity sent by Heaven. Friar Lawrence's error lies all in the execution of the thing, in letting a Heaven-made marriage remain an affair of secret messages, rope ladders, and unorthodox sleeping potions, a clandestine remedy doomed to miscarriage long before the thwarted message determines the shape of the inevitable catastrophe. What was desperately needed in this case was a combination of virtues, the forthrightness of the Prince and the vigor and ingenuity of the Friar; and these virtues were combined only in Mercutio, who fell victim to the deficiencies of both in that he confronted a needlessly active Tybalt at a disadvantage caused in part by bumbling Romeo's adherence to the Friar's secret plot.

Mercutio, who is the third member of this more perceptive group, stands next to Romeo and Juliet in importance in the play. In fact, some critics who consider him more interesting than the two protagonists have suggested that Shakespeare finished him off in Act 3 out of necessity. This is almost as absurd as the view that Shakespeare wrote Falstaff out of *Henry V* because the fat man had become unmanageable. Others have found Mercutio's wit embarrassing and tried to relieve Shakespeare of the responsibility for some parts of it, but this is absurd too. An edited Mercutio becomes either sentimental or obscene; he also becomes meaningless, and without him the play as a whole reverts to the condition of melodrama that it had in Shakespeare's source. Consider for a moment the climax of the play, which is almost solely Shakespeare's invention. In Brooke the matter is relatively simple: Tybalt provokes Romeo, and Romeo slays him. Shakespeare has it that Tybalt deliberately sought to murder Romeo and Romeo so badly underestimated his challenger that he declined to defend himself; whereupon Mercutio, in defense of both Romeo's honor and his person, picked up the challenge and would have killed Tybalt but for Romeo's intervention. Tybalt then killed Mercutio, and Romeo killed Tybalt in revenge. But, one should ask, what if Romeo had not intervened? Tybalt would have been slain, surely, and Mercutio would have survived to receive the Prince's rebuke; at most, however, he would have been punished only slightly, for Mercutio was of the Prince's line and not of the feuding families. The feud thus would have died with Tybalt, and in time Capulet and Montague might have been reconciled openly, as Friar Lawrence hoped. In short, Mercutio was on the point of bringing to pass what neither civil authority nor well-intentioned but misplaced ingenuity had been able to accomplish, and Romeo with a single sentimental action ("I thought all for the best," he says) destroyed his only hope of averting tragedy long enough to achieve the maturity he needed in order to avoid it altogether.

Many critics have commented on the breathless pace of this play, and no wonder. Shakespeare has made it the story of a race against time. What Romeo needs most of all is a teacher, and the only one capable of giving him instruction worth having and giving it quickly is Mercutio. All the rest are unavailable, or ineffectual, like Benvolio, or unapt for dealing practically with human relations. Mercutio, however, for all his superficial show of irresponsibility, is made in the image of his creator; he is a poet, who gives equal value to flesh and spirit, sees them as inseparable aspects of total being, and accepts each as the necessary mode of the other. His first line in the play, discharged at a young fool who is playing the ascetic for love, is revealing: "Nay, gentle Romeo, we must have you dance" (1.4.13). And when gentle Romeo persists in daydreaming, he says, "Be rough with love," declares that love is a mire and that dreamers are often liars. The long fairy speech which follows dignifies idle dreams by marrying them to earth; its intent is to compel Romeo to acknowledge his senses and to bring him to an honest and healthy confession of what he is really looking for, but Romeo is too wrapped up in self-deception to listen. In

Act 2 Mercutio tries harder, speaks more plainly, but prompts from his pupil only the fatuous "He jests at scars that never felt a wound." Later still, in the battle of wits (2.4), Mercutio imagines briefly that he has succeeded: "Why, is not this better now than groaning for love? Now art though sociable, now art thou Romeo; now art thou what thou art, by art as well as by nature" (92–95). There are no wiser words in the whole play, and none more ironic; for Romeo even here has not found his identity and is never really to find it except for those fleeting moments when Juliet is there to lead him by the hand.

Time runs out for both principals in this play, but it is Juliet who makes the race exciting. Her five-day maturation is a miracle which only a Shakespeare could have made credible; yet at the end she is still a fourteen-year-old girl, and she succumbs to an adolescent's despair. Mercutio might have helped had he been available, but Mercutio is dead. All the others have deserted her—parents, Nurse, the Friar, who takes fright at the crucial moment, and Romeo, who lies dead at her feet. She simply has not lived long enough in her wisdom to stand entirely alone. This is really the source of pathos in *Romeo and Juliet*. One hears much about the portrayal of young love here, about the immortality of the lovers and the eternality of their love; but such talk runs toward vapid sentimentality and does an injustice to Shakespeare. No one has more poignantly described the beauty of young love than he, and no one has portrayed more honestly than he the destructiveness of any love which ignores the mortality of those who make it. Romeo struggled toward full understanding but fell far short of achievement, leaving a trail of victims behind him. Juliet came much closer than we had any right to expect, but she too failed. Both have a legitimate claim to our respect, she more than he; and the youth of both relieves them of our ultimate censure, which falls not on the stars but on all those whose thoughtlessness denied them the time they so desperately needed.

—J. A. BRYANT, JR.
*The University of Kentucky*

# The Prologue.

### Corus.

Two housholds both alike in dignitie,
  (In faire Verona where we lay our Scene)
From auncient grudge, breake to new mutinie,
Where ciuill bloud makes ciuill hands vncleane:
From forth the fatall loynes of these two foes,
A paire of starre-crost louers, take their life:
Whose misaduentur'd pittious ouerthrowes,
Doth with their death burie their Parents strife.
The fearfull passage of their death-markt loue,
And the continuance of their Parents rage:
Which but their childrens end nought could remoue:
Is now the two houres trafficque of our Stage.
The which if you with patient eares attend,
What heare shall misse, our toyle shall striue to mend.

*A 2*

From the 1599 edition

# THE MOST EX-
## cellent and lamentable
Tragedie, of *Romeo* and *Iuliet*.

*Enter* Sampson *and* Gregorie *, with Swords and Bucklers, of the house of* Capulet.

*Samp. Gregorie,* on my word weele not carrie Coles.

*Greg.* No, for then we should be Collyers.

*Samp.* I meane, and we be in choller, weele draw.

*Greg.* I while you liue, draw your necke out of choller.

*Samp.* I strike quickly being moued.

*Greg.* But thou art not quickly moued to strike.

*Samp.* A dog of the house of *Mountague* moues me.

*Grego.* To moue is to stirre, and to be valiant, is to stand:
Therefore if thou art moued thou runst away.

*Samp.* A dog of that house shall moue me to stand:
I will take the wall of any man or maide of *Mounta-*
*gues.*

*Grego.* That shewes thee a weake slaue, for the weakest goes
to the wall.

*Samp.* Tis true, & therfore women being the weaker vessels
are euer thrust to the wall: therfore I wil push *Mountagues* men
from the wall, and thrust his maides to the wall.

*Greg.* The quarell is betweene our maisters , and vs their
men.

*Samp.* Tis all one, I will shew my selfe a tyrant, when I haue
fought with the men, I will be ciuil with the maides, I will cut
off their heads.

A 3 *Grego.* The

# The Tragedy of Romeo and Juliet

## [Dramatis Personae

Chorus
Escalus, Prince of Verona
Paris, a young count, kinsman to the Prince
Montague
Capulet
An old man, of the Capulet family
Romeo, son to Montague
Mercutio, kinsman to the Prince and friend to Romeo
Benvolio, nephew to Montague and friend to Romeo
Tybalt, nephew to Lady Capulet
Friar Lawrence } Franciscans
Friar John
Balthasar, servant to Romeo
Sampson } servants to Capulet
Gregory
Peter, servant to Juliet's nurse
Abram, servant to Montague
An Apothecary
Three Musicians
An Officer
Lady Montague, wife to Montague
Lady Capulet, wife to Capulet
Juliet, daughter to Capulet
Nurse to Juliet
Citizens of Verona, Gentlemen and Gentlewomen of both
    houses, Maskers, Torchbearers, Pages, Guards, Watch-
    men, Servants, and Attendants
                *Scene:* Verona; Mantua]

# The Tragedy of Romeo and Juliet

## THE PROLOGUE

### [*Enter Chorus.*]

*Chorus.* Two households, both alike in dignity,°¹
   In fair Verona, where we lay our scene,
From ancient grudge break to new mutiny,°
   Where civil blood makes civil hands unclean.
From forth the fatal loins of these two foes          5
   A pair of star-crossed° lovers take their life;
Whose misadventured piteous overthrows
   Doth with their death bury their parents' strife.
The fearful passage of their death-marked love,
   And the continuance of their parents' rage,       *10*
Which, but their children's end, naught could
     remove,
   Is now the two hours' traffic of our stage;°
The which if you with patient ears attend,
What here shall miss, our toil shall strive to mend.
                            [*Exit.*]

---

¹ The degree sign (°) indicates a footnote, which is keyed to the text by line number. Text references are printed in **boldface** type; the annotation follows in roman type.
Prologue 1 **dignity** rank   3 **mutiny** violence   6 **star-crossed** fated to disaster   12 **two hours' traffic of our stage** i.e., the business of our play

# [ACT 1

### Scene 1. *Verona. A public place.*]

*Enter Sampson and Gregory, with swords and bucklers,° of the house of Capulet.*

*Sampson.* Gregory, on my word, we'll not carry coals.°

*Gregory.* No, for then we should be colliers.°

*Sampson.* I mean, and° we be in choler, we'll draw.°

*Gregory.* Ay, while you live, draw your neck out of
5    collar.

*Sampson.* I strike quickly, being moved.

*Gregory.* But thou art not quickly moved to strike.

*Sampson.* A dog of the house of Montague moves me.

*Gregory.* To move is to stir, and to be valiant is to
10    stand. Therefore, if thou art moved, thou run'st
    away.

*Sampson.* A dog of that house shall move me to
    stand. I will take the wall° of any man or maid of
    Montague's.

---

1.1.s.d. **bucklers** small shields   1 **carry coals** endure insults   2 **colliers** coal venders (this leads to puns on "choler" = anger, and "collar" = hangman's noose)   3 **and** if   3 **draw** draw swords   13 **take the wall** take the preferred place on the walk

*Gregory.* That shows thee a weak slave; for the weak-    *15*
est goes to the wall.°

*Sampson.* 'Tis true; and therefore women, being the
weaker vessels, are ever thrust to the wall.° Therefore I will push Montague's men from the wall and
thrust his maids to the wall.    *20*

*Gregory.* The quarrel is between our masters and us
their men.

*Sampson.* 'Tis all one. I will show myself a tyrant.
When I have fought with the men, I will be civil
with the maids—I will cut off their heads.    *25*

*Gregory.* The heads of the maids?

*Sampson.* Ay, the heads of the maids or their maiden-
heads. Take it in what sense thou wilt.

*Gregory.* They must take it in sense that feel it.

*Sampson.* Me they shall feel while I am able to stand;    *30*
and 'tis known I am a pretty piece of flesh.

*Gregory.* 'Tis well thou art not fish; if thou hadst,
thou hadst been Poor John.° Draw thy tool!° Here
comes two of the house of Montagues.

*Enter two other Servingmen [Abram and Balthasar].*

*Sampson.* My naked weapon is out. Quarrel! I will    *35*
back thee.

*Gregory.* How? Turn thy back and run?

*Sampson.* Fear me not.

*Gregory.* No, marry.° I fear thee!


15–16 **weakest goes to the wall** i.e., is pushed to the rear    18 **thrust to
the wall** assaulted against the wall    33 **Poor John** hake salted and
dried (poor man's fare)    33 **tool** weapon (with bawdy innuendo)
39 **marry** (an interjection, from "By the Virgin Mary")

40 *Sampson.* Let us take the law of our sides;° let them
     begin.

*Gregory.* I will frown as I pass by, and let them take
     it as they list.

*Sampson.* Nay, as they dare. I will bite my thumb° at
45    them, which is disgrace to them if they bear it.

*Abram.* Do you bite your thumb at us, sir?

*Sampson.* I do bite my thumb, sir.

*Abram.* Do you bite your thumb at us, sir?

*Sampson.* [*Aside to Gregory*] Is the law of our side
50    if I say ay?

*Gregory.* [*Aside to Sampson*] No.

*Sampson.* No, sir, I do not bite my thumb at you, sir;
     but I bite my thumb, sir.

*Gregory.* Do you quarrel, sir?

55 *Abram.* Quarrel, sir? No, sir.

*Sampson.* But if you do, sir, I am for you. I serve as
     good a man as you.

*Abram.* No better.

*Sampson.* Well, sir.

                    *Enter Benvolio.*

60 *Gregory.* Say "better." Here comes one of my master's
     kinsmen.

*Sampson.* Yes, better, sir.

*Abram.* You lie.

*Sampson.* Draw, if you be men. Gregory, remember
65    thy swashing° blow.                    *They fight.*

---

40 **take the law of our sides** keep ourselves in the right    44 **bite my
thumb** i.e., make a gesture of contempt    65 **swashing** slashing

*Benvolio.* Part, fools!
 Put up your swords. You know not what you do.

    *Enter Tybalt.*

*Tybalt.* What, art thou drawn among these heartless
 hinds?°
 Turn thee, Benvolio; look upon thy death.

*Benvolio.* I do but keep the peace. Put up thy sword,  70
 Or manage it to part these men with me.

*Tybalt.* What, drawn, and talk of peace? I hate the
 word
 As I hate hell, all Montagues, and thee.
 Have at thee, coward!    [*They fight.*]

  *Enter [an Officer, and] three or four Citizens*
    *with clubs or partisans.*

*Officer.* Clubs, bills, and partisans!° Strike! Beat them  75
 down! Down with the Capulets! Down with the
 Montagues!

  *Enter old Capulet in his gown, and his Wife.*

*Capulet.* What noise is this? Give me my long sword,
 ho!

*Lady Capulet.* A crutch, a crutch! Why call you for
 a sword?

*Capulet.* My sword, I say! Old Montague is come  80
 And flourishes his blade in spite° of me.

  *Enter old Montague and his Wife.*

*Montague.* Thou villain Capulet!—Hold me not; let
 me go.

*Lady Montague.* Thou shalt not stir one foot to seek
 a foe.

---

68 **heartless hinds** cowardly rustics 75 **bills, and partisans** varieties
of halberd, a combination spear and battle-ax 81 **spite** defiance

*Enter Prince Escalus, with his Train.*

*Prince.* Rebellious subjects, enemies to peace,
85     Profaners of this neighbor-stainèd steel—
       Will they not hear? What, ho! You men, you beasts,
       That quench the fire of your pernicious rage
       With purple fountains issuing from your veins!
       On pain of torture, from those bloody hands
90     Throw your mistempered° weapons to the ground
       And hear the sentence of your movèd prince.
       Three civil brawls, bred of an airy word
       By thee, old Capulet, and Montague,
       Have thrice disturbed the quiet of our streets
95     And made Verona's ancient citizens
       Cast by their grave beseeming° ornaments
       To wield old partisans, in hands as old,
       Cank'red with peace, to part your cank'red° hate.
       If ever you disturb our streets again,
100    Your lives shall pay the forfeit of the peace.
       For this time all the rest depart away.
       You, Capulet, shall go along with me;
       And, Montague, come you this afternoon,
       To know our farther pleasure in this case,
105    To old Freetown, our common judgment place.
       Once more, on pain of death, all men depart.
                              *Exeunt [all but Montague, his Wife,*
                                        *and Benvolio].*

*Montague.* Who set this ancient quarrel new abroach?°
       Speak, nephew, were you by when it began?

*Benvolio.* Here were the servants of your adversary
110    And yours, close fighting ere I did approach.
       I drew to part them. In the instant came
       The fiery Tybalt, with his sword prepared;
       Which, as he breathed defiance to my ears,
       He swung about his head and cut the winds,

---

90 **mistempered** (1) ill-made (2) used with ill will    96 **grave beseeming**
dignified and appropriate    98 **cank'red ... cank'red** rusted ... malignant    107 **new abroach** newly open

Who, nothing hurt withal,° hissed him in scorn.    *115*
While we were interchanging thrusts and blows,
Came more and more, and fought on part and
    part,°
Till the Prince came, who parted either part.

*Lady Montague.* O, where is Romeo? Saw you him
    today?
Right glad I am he was not at this fray.    *120*

*Benvolio.* Madam, an hour before the worshiped sun
Peered forth the golden window of the East,
A troubled mind drave me to walk abroad;
Where, underneath the grove of sycamore
That westward rooteth from this city side,    *125*
So early walking did I see your son.
Towards him I made, but he was ware° of me
And stole into the covert of the wood.
I, measuring his affections by my own,
Which then most sought where most might not be
    found,°    *130*
Being one too many by my weary self,
Pursued my humor not pursuing his,°
And gladly shunned who gladly fled from me.

*Montague.* Many a morning hath he there been seen,
With tears augmenting the fresh morning's dew,    *135*
Adding to clouds more clouds with his deep sighs;
But all so soon as the all-cheering sun
Should in the farthest East begin to draw
The shady curtains from Aurora's° bed,
Away from light steals home my heavy° son    *140*
And private in his chamber pens himself,
Shuts up his windows, locks fair daylight out,
And makes himself an artificial night.

---

115 **withal** thereby    117 **on part and part** some on one side, some on
another    127 **ware** aware    130 **most sought ... found** i.e., wanted
most to be alone    132 **Pursued ... his** i.e., followed my own inclination by not inquiring into his mood    139 **Aurora** goddess of the dawn
140 **heavy** melancholy, moody

Black and portentous must this humor° prove
145   Unless good counsel may the cause remove.

*Benvolio.* My noble uncle, do you know the cause?

*Montague.* I neither know it nor can learn of him.

*Benvolio.* Have you importuned him by any means?

*Montague.* Both by myself and many other friends;
150   But he, his own affections' counselor,
Is to himself—I will not say how true—
But to himself so secret and so close,
So far from sounding° and discovery,
As is the bud bit with an envious° worm
155   Ere he can spread his sweet leaves to the air
Or dedicate his beauty to the sun.
Could we but learn from whence his sorrows grow,
We would as willingly give cure as know.

*Enter Romeo.*

*Benvolio.* See, where he comes. So please you step
aside;
160   I'll know his grievance, or be much denied.

*Montague.* I would thou wert so happy° by thy stay
To hear true shrift.° Come, madam, let's away.
*Exeunt [Montague and Wife].*

*Benvolio.* Good morrow,° cousin.

*Romeo.*                           Is the day so young?

*Benvolio.* But new struck nine.

*Romeo.*                  Ay me! Sad hours seem long.
165   Was that my father that went hence so fast?

*Benvolio.* It was. What sadness lengthens Romeo's
hours?

---

144 **humor** mood   153 **So far from sounding** so far from measuring the depth of his mood   154 **envious** malign   161 **happy** lucky   162 **true shrift** i.e., Romeo's confession of the truth   163 **morrow** morning

*Romeo.* Not having that which having makes them
  short.

*Benvolio.* In love?

*Romeo.* Out—

*Benvolio.* Of love?                                              *170*

*Romeo.* Out of her favor where I am in love.

*Benvolio.* Alas that love, so gentle in his view,°
  Should be so tyrannous and rough in proof!

*Romeo.* Alas that love, whose view is muffled still,°
  Should without eyes see pathways to his will!          *175*
  Where shall we dine? O me! What fray was here?
  Yet tell me not, for I have heard it all.
  Here's much to do with hate, but more with love.°
  Why then, O brawling love, O loving hate,
  O anything, of nothing first created!°                   *180*
  O heavy lightness, serious vanity,
  Misshapen chaos of well-seeming forms,
  Feather of lead, bright smoke, cold fire, sick health,
  Still-waking sleep, that is not what it is!
  This love feel I, that feel no love in this.            *185*
  Dost thou not laugh?

*Benvolio.*              No, coz,° I rather weep.

*Romeo.* Good heart, at what?

*Benvolio.*              At thy good heart's oppression.

*Romeo.* Why, such is love's transgression.
  Griefs of mine own lie heavy in my breast,
  Which thou wilt propagate, to have it prest°       *190*
  With more of thine. This love that thou hast shown

---

172 **gentle in his view** mild in appearance   174 **muffled still** always
blindfolded   178 **more with love** i.e., the combatants enjoyed their fighting   180 **O anything, of nothing first created** (Romeo here relates his
own succession of witty paradoxes to the dogma that God created
everything out of nothing)   186 **coz** cousin (relative)   190 **Which . . .
prest** i.e., which griefs you will increase by burdening my breast

Doth add more grief to too much of mine own.
Love is a smoke made with the fume of sighs;
Being purged, a fire sparkling in lovers' eyes;
195　Being vexed, a sea nourished with loving tears.
What is it else? A madness most discreet,°
A choking gall, and a preserving sweet.
Farewell, my coz.

*Benvolio.*　　　　　　Soft!° I will go along.
And if° you leave me so, you do me wrong.

200　*Romeo.* Tut! I have lost myself; I am not here;
This is not Romeo, he's some other where.

*Benvolio.* Tell me in sadness,° who is that you love?

*Romeo.* What, shall I groan and tell thee?

*Benvolio.*　　　　　　Groan? Why, no;
But sadly° tell me who.

205　*Romeo.* Bid a sick man in sadness° make his will.
Ah, word ill urged to one that is so ill!
In sadness, cousin, I do love a woman.

*Benvolio.* I aimed so near when I supposed you loved.

*Romeo.* A right good markman. And she's fair I love.

210　*Benvolio.* A right fair mark,° fair coz, is soonest hit.

*Romeo.* Well, in that hit you miss. She'll not be hit
With Cupid's arrow. She hath Dian's wit,°
And, in strong proof° of chastity well armed,
From Love's weak childish bow she lives un-
　　charmed.
215　She will not stay° the siege of loving terms,
Nor bide° th' encounter of assailing eyes,

196 **discreet** discriminating　198 **Soft** hold on　199 **And if** if　202 **in sadness** in all seriousness　204 **sadly** seriously　205 **in sadness** (1) in seriousness (2) in unhappiness at the prospect of death　210 **fair mark** target easily seen　212 **Dian's wit** the cunning of Diana, huntress and goddess of chastity　213 **proof** tested power　215 **stay** submit to　216 **bide** abide (put up with)

Nor ope her lap to saint-seducing gold.
O, she is rich in beauty; only poor
That, when she dies, with beauty dies her store.°

*Benvolio.* Then she hath sworn that she will still° live
    chaste?                                                    *220*

*Romeo.* She hath, and in that sparing make huge
    waste;
For beauty, starved with her severity,
Cuts beauty off from all posterity.
She is too fair, too wise, wisely too fair,
To merit bliss° by making me despair.                        *225*
She hath forsworn to love, and in that vow
Do I live dead that live to tell it now.

*Benvolio.* Be ruled by me; forget to think of her.

*Romeo.* O, teach me how I should forget to think!

*Benvolio.* By giving liberty unto thine eyes.               *230*
Examine other beauties.

*Romeo.*                          'Tis the way
To call hers, exquisite, in question° more.
These happy masks that kiss fair ladies' brows,
Being black puts us in mind they hide the fair.
He that is strucken blind cannot forget                     *235*
The precious treasure of his eyesight lost.
Show me a mistress that is passing fair:
What doth her beauty serve but as a note°
Where I may read who passed that passing fair?
Farewell. Thou canst not teach me to forget.                *240*

*Benvolio.* I'll pay that doctrine, or else die in debt.°
                                     *Exeunt.*

---

219 **with beauty dies her store** i.e., she will leave no progeny to perpetuate her beauty   220 **still** always   225 **merit bliss** win heavenly
bliss   232 **To call hers ... in question** to keep bringing her beauty to
mind   238 **note** written reminder   241 **I'll ... debt** I will teach you or
else die trying

[Scene 2. *A street.*]

*Enter Capulet, County Paris, and the Clown,*
[*his Servant*].

*Capulet.* But Montague is bound° as well as I,
    In penalty alike; and 'tis not hard, I think,
    For men so old as we to keep the peace.

*Paris.* Of honorable reckoning° are you both,
5    And pity 'tis you lived at odds so long.
    But now, my lord, what say you to my suit?

*Capulet.* But saying o'er what I have said before:
    My child is yet a stranger in the world,
    She hath not seen the change of fourteen years;
10    Let two more summers wither in their pride
    Ere we may think her ripe to be a bride.

*Paris.* Younger than she are happy mothers made.

*Capulet.* And too soon marred are those so early
    made.
    Earth hath swallowèd all my hopes° but she;
15    She is the hopeful lady of my earth.
    But woo her, gentle Paris, get her heart;
    My will to her consent is but a part.
    And she agreed,° within her scope of choice°
    Lies my consent and fair according° voice.
20    This night I hold an old accustomed° feast,
    Whereto I have invited many a guest,
    Such as I love; and you among the store,
    One more, most welcome, makes my number more.

1.2.1 **bound** under bond   4 **reckoning** reputation   14 **hopes** children
18 **And she agreed** if she agrees   18 **within her scope of choice**
among those she favors   19 **according** agreeing   20 **accustomed** established by custom

At my poor house look to behold this night
Earth-treading stars° that make dark heaven light.    25
Such comfort as do lusty young men feel
When well-appareled April on the heel
Of limping Winter treads, even such delight
Among fresh fennel° buds shall you this night
Inherit° at my house. Hear all, all see,                        30
And like her most whose merit most shall be;
Which, on more view of many, mine, being one,
May stand in number,° though in reck'ning none.°
Come, go with me. [*To Servant, giving him a paper*]
   Go, sirrah,° trudge about
Through fair Verona; find those persons out         35
Whose names are written there, and to them say
My house and welcome on their pleasure stay.°
                                        *Exit* [*with Paris*].

*Servant.* Find them out whose names are written here?
   It is written that the shoemaker should meddle with
   his yard and the tailor with his last, the fisher with    40
   his pencil and the painter with his nets;° but I am
   sent to find those persons whose names are here
   writ, and can never find° what names the writing
   person hath here writ. I must to the learned. In
   good time!°                                                            45

               *Enter Benvolio and Romeo.*

*Benvolio.* Tut, man, one fire burns out another's
                  burning;
   One pain is less'ned by another's anguish;°
   Turn giddy, and be holp by backward turning;°

One desperate grief cures with another's languish.
50  Take thou some new infection to thy eye,
And the rank poison of the old will die.

*Romeo.* Your plantain leaf is excellent for that.

*Benvolio.* For what, I pray thee?

*Romeo.*                 For your broken° shin.

*Benvolio.* Why, Romeo, art thou mad?

55  *Romeo.* Not mad, but bound more than a madman is;
Shut up in prison, kept without my food,
Whipped and tormented and—God-den,° good fel-
low.

*Servant.* God gi' go-den. I pray, sir, can you read?

*Romeo.* Ay, mine own fortune in my misery.

60  *Servant.* Perhaps you have learned it without book.
But, I pray, can you read anything you see?

*Romeo.* Ay, if I know the letters and the language.°

*Servant.* Ye say honestly. Rest you merry.°

*Romeo.* Stay, fellow; I can read.  *He reads the letter.*
65  "Signior Martino and his wife and daughters;
County Anselm and his beauteous sisters;
The lady widow of Vitruvio;
Signior Placentio and his lovely nieces;
Mercutio and his brother Valentine;
70  Mine uncle Capulet, his wife and daughters;
My fair niece Rosaline; Livia;
Signior Valentio and his cousin Tybalt;
Lucio and the lively Helena."
A fair assembly. Whither should they come?

75  *Servant.* Up.

---

53 **broken** scratched   57 **God-den** good evening (good afternoon)
62 **if I know the letters and the language** i.e., if I already know what
the writing says   63 **Rest you merry** may God keep you merry

*Romeo.* Whither? To supper?

*Servant.* To our house.

*Romeo.* Whose house?

*Servant.* My master's.

*Romeo.* Indeed I should have asked you that before.      80

*Servant.* Now I'll tell you without asking. My master
is the great rich Capulet; and if you be not of the
house of Montagues, I pray come and crush a cup°
of wine. Rest you merry.                    [*Exit.*]

*Benvolio.* At this same ancient° feast of Capulet's      85
Sups the fair Rosaline whom thou so loves;
With all the admirèd beauties of Verona.
Go thither, and with unattainted° eye
Compare her face with some that I shall show,
And I will make thee think thy swan a crow.          90

*Romeo.* When the devout religion of mine eye
    Maintains such falsehood, then turn tears to fires;
And these, who, often drowned, could never die,
    Transparent° heretics, be burnt for liars!
One fairer than my love? The all-seeing sun          95
Ne'er saw her match since first the world begun.

*Benvolio.* Tut! you saw her fair, none else being by,
Herself poised° with herself in either eye;
But in that crystal scales° let there be weighed
Your lady's love against some other maid              100
That I will show you shining at this feast,
And she shall scant° show well that now seems best.

*Romeo.* I'll go along, no such sight to be shown,
But to rejoice in splendor of mine own.° [*Exeunt.*]

---

83 **crush a cup** have a drink   85 **ancient** established by custom
88 **unattainted** impartial   94 **Transparent** obvious   98 **poised** balanced
99 **crystal scales** i.e., Romeo's pair of eyes   102 **scant** scarcely
104 **splendor of mine own** my own lady's splendor

[Scene 3. *A room in Capulet's house.*]

*Enter Capulet's Wife, and Nurse.*

*Lady Capulet.* Nurse, where's my daughter? Call her
forth to me.

*Nurse.* Now, by my maidenhead at twelve year old,
I bade her come. What,° lamb! What, ladybird!
God forbid, where's this girl? What, Juliet!

*Enter Juliet.*

*Juliet.* How now? Who calls?

*Nurse.* Your mother.

5 *Juliet.* Madam, I am here.
What is your will?

*Lady Capulet.* This is the matter—Nurse, give leave
awhile;
We must talk in secret. Nurse, come back again.
I have rememb'red me; thou 's° hear our counsel.
10 Thou knowest my daughter's of a pretty age.

*Nurse.* Faith, I can tell her age unto an hour.

*Lady Capulet.* She's not fourteen.

*Nurse.* I'll lay fourteen of my teeth—
And yet, to my teen° be it spoken, I have but
four—
She's not fourteen. How long is it now
To Lammastide?°

15 *Lady Capulet.* A fortnight and odd days.

1.3.3 **What** (an impatient call)   9 **thou 's** thou shalt   13 **teen** sorrow
15 **Lammastide** August 1

*Nurse.* Even or odd, of all days in the year,
  Come Lammas Eve at night shall she be fourteen.
  Susan and she (God rest all Christian souls!)
  Were of an age.° Well, Susan is with God;
  She was too good for me. But, as I said,                   20
  On Lammas Eve at night shall she be fourteen;
  That shall she, marry; I remember it well.
  'Tis since the earthquake° now eleven years;
  And she was weaned (I never shall forget it),
  Of all the days of the year, upon that day;               25
  For I had then laid wormwood to my dug,
  Sitting in the sun under the dovehouse wall.
  My lord and you were then at Mantua.
  Nay, I do bear a brain.° But, as I said,
  When it did taste the wormwood on the nipple              30
  Of my dug and felt it bitter, pretty fool,
  To see it tetchy° and fall out with the dug!
  Shake, quoth the dovehouse!° 'Twas no need, I
    trow,°
  To bid me trudge.
  And since that time it is eleven years,                    35
  For then she could stand high-lone;° nay, by th'
    rood,°
  She could have run and waddled all about;
  For even the day before, she broke her brow;
  And then my husband (God be with his soul!
  'A° was a merry man) took up the child.                    40
  "Yea," quoth he, "dost thou fall upon thy face?
  Thou wilt fall backward when thou hast more wit;
  Wilt thou not, Jule?" and, by my holidam,°
  The pretty wretch left crying and said, "Ay."
  To see now how a jest shall come about!                    45
  I warrant, and I should live a thousand years,

---

19 **of an age** the same age    23 **earthquake** (see Introduction)    29 **I do
bear a brain** i.e., my mind is still good    32 **tetchy** irritable    33 **Shake,
quoth the dovehouse** i.e., the dovehouse (which the Nurse personifies)
began to tremble    33 **trow** believe    36 **high-lone** alone    36 **rood** cross
40 **'A** he    43 **holidam** holy thing, relic

   I never should forget it. "Wilt thou not, Jule?"
      quoth he,
   And, pretty fool, it stinted° and said, "Ay."

*Lady Capulet.* Enough of this. I pray thee hold thy
      peace.

50 *Nurse.* Yes, madam. Yet I cannot choose but laugh
   To think it should leave crying and say, "Ay."
   And yet, I warrant, it had upon it° brow
   A bump as big as a young cock'rel's stone;
   A perilous knock; and it cried bitterly.
55 "Yea," quoth my husband, "fall'st upon thy face?
   Thou wilt fall backward when thou comest to age,
   Wilt thou not, Jule?" It stinted and said, "Ay."

*Juliet.* And stint thou too, I pray thee, nurse, say I.

*Nurse.* Peace, I have done. God mark thee to His
      grace!
60 Thou wast the prettiest babe that e'er I nursed.
   And I might live to see thee married once,
   I have my wish.

*Lady Capulet.* Marry,° that "marry" is the very theme
   I came to talk of. Tell me, daughter Juliet,
65 How stands your dispositions to be married?

*Juliet.* It is an honor that I dream not of.

*Nurse.* An honor? Were not I thine only nurse,
   I would say thou hadst sucked wisdom from thy
      teat.

*Lady Capulet.* Well, think of marriage now. Younger
      than you,
70 Here in Verona, ladies of esteem,
   Are made already mothers. By my count,
   I was your mother much upon these years°
   That you are now a maid. Thus then in brief:
   The valiant Paris seeks you for his love.

---

48 **stinted** stopped   52 **it** its   63 **Marry** indeed   72 **much upon these
years** the same length of time

*Nurse.* A man, young lady! Lady, such a man      75
  As all the world— Why, he's a man of wax.°

*Lady Capulet.* Verona's summer hath not such a
  flower.

*Nurse.* Nay, he's a flower, in faith—a very flower.

*Lady Capulet.* What say you? Can you love the gentle-
  man?
  This night you shall behold him at our feast.      80
  Read o'er the volume of young Paris' face,
  And find delight writ there with beauty's pen;
  Examine every married lineament,°
  And see how one another lends content;°
  And what obscured in this fair volume lies      85
  Find written in the margent° of his eyes.
  This precious book of love, this unbound° lover,
  To beautify him only lacks a cover.°
  The fish lives in the sea, and 'tis much pride
  For fair without the fair within to hide.°      90
  That book in many's eyes doth share the glory,
  That in gold clasps locks in the golden story;
  So shall you share all that he doth possess,
  By having him making yourself no less.

*Nurse.* No less? Nay, bigger! Women grow by men.      95

*Lady Capulet.* Speak briefly, can you like of° Paris'
  love?

*Juliet.* I'll look to like, if looking liking move;
  But no more deep will I endart mine eye
  Than your consent gives strength to make it fly.

                *Enter Servingman.*

*Servingman.* Madam, the guests are come, supper      100

---

76 **man of wax** man of perfect figure   83 **married lineament** harmo-
nious feature   84 **one another lends content** all enhance one another
86 **margent** marginal commentary   87 **unbound** (1) without cover (2)
uncaught   88 **only lacks a cover** i.e., only a wife is lacking   89–90 **The
fish . . . to hide** i.e., the fair sea is made even fairer by hiding fair fish
within it   96 **like of** be favorable to

served up, you called, my young lady asked for,
the nurse cursed° in the pantry, and everything in
extremity. I must hence to wait.° I beseech you
follow straight.°                              [*Exit.*]

*Lady Capulet.* We follow thee. Juliet, the County
105      stays.°

*Nurse.* Go, girl, seek happy nights to happy days.
                                             *Exeunt.*


[Scene 4. *A street.*]


*Enter Romeo, Mercutio, Benvolio, with five
or six other Maskers; Torchbearers.*

*Romeo.* What, shall this speech be spoke for our
      excuse?°
Or shall we on without apology?

*Benvolio.* The date is out of such prolixity.°
We'll have no Cupid hoodwinked° with a scarf,
5      Bearing a Tartar's painted bow of lath,
Scaring the ladies like a crowkeeper;°
Nor no without-book prologue,° faintly spoke
After the prompter, for our entrance;
But, let them measure° us by what they will,
10      We'll measure them a measure° and be gone.

*Romeo.* Give me a torch. I am not for this ambling.
Being but heavy, I will bear the light.


102 **the nurse cursed** i.e., because she is not helping    103 **to wait** to
serve    104 **straight** straightway    105 **the County stays** the Count is
waiting    1.4.1 **shall ... excuse** i.e., shall we introduce ourselves with
the customary prepared speech    3 **date ... prolixity** i.e., such wordi-
ness is out of fashion    4 **hoodwinked** blindfolded    6 **crowkeeper** boy
set to scare crows away    7 **without-book prologue** memorized speech
9 **measure** judge    10 **measure them a measure** dance one dance with
them

*Mercutio.* Nay, gentle Romeo, we must have you
   dance.

*Romeo.* Not I, believe me. You have dancing shoes
   With nimble soles; I have a soul of lead    15
   So stakes me to the ground I cannot move.

*Mercutio.* You are a lover. Borrow Cupid's wings
   And soar with them above a common bound.°

*Romeo.* I am too sore enpiercèd with his shaft
   To soar with his light feathers; and so bound    20
   I cannot bound a pitch° above dull woe.
   Under love's heavy burden do I sink.

*Mercutio.* And, to sink in it, should you burden love—
   Too great oppression for a tender thing.

*Romeo.* Is love a tender thing? It is too rough,    25
   Too rude, too boist'rous, and it pricks like thorn.

*Mercutio.* If love be rough with you, be rough with
   love;
   Prick love for pricking,° and you beat love down.
   Give me a case to put my visage in.
   A visor for a visor! What care I    30
   What curious eye doth quote deformities?°
   Here are the beetle brows° shall blush° for me.

*Benvolio.* Come, knock and enter; and no sooner in
   But every man betake him to his legs.°

*Romeo.* A torch for me! Let wantons light of heart    35
   Tickle the senseless rushes° with their heels;
   For I am proverbed with a grandsire phrase,°
   I'll be a candleholder° and look on;

---

18 **bound** (1) leap (2) limit    21 **pitch** height (as in a falcon's soaring)
28 **Prick love for pricking** i.e., give love the spur in return    29–31
**Give ... deformities** i.e., give me a bag for my mask. A mask for a
mask. What do I care who notices my ugliness?    32 **beetle brows**
bushy eyebrows (?)    32 **blush** be red, i.e., be grotesque    34 **betake**
**him to his legs** begin dancing    36 **rushes** (used for floor covering)
37 **grandsire phrase** old saying    38 **candleholder** attendant

The game was ne'er so fair, and I am done.°

*Mercutio.* Tut! Dun's the mouse, the constable's own
40       word!°
If thou art Dun,° we'll draw thee from the mire
Of this sir-reverence° love, wherein thou stickest
Up to the ears. Come, we burn daylight,° ho!

*Romeo.* Nay, that's not so.

*Mercutio.*             I mean, sir, in delay
45   We waste our lights° in vain, like lights by day.
Take our good meaning, for our judgment sits
Five times in that° ere once in our five wits.

*Romeo.* And we mean well in going to this masque,
But 'tis no wit° to go.

*Mercutio.*          Why, may one ask?

*Romeo.* I dreamt a dream tonight.°

50  *Mercutio.*           And so did I.

*Romeo.* Well, what was yours?

*Mercutio.*         That dreamers often lie.

*Romeo.* In bed asleep, while they do dream things true.

*Mercutio.* O, then I see Queen Mab° hath been with
      you.
She is the fairies' midwife, and she comes
55  In shape no bigger than an agate stone

---

39 **The game … done** i.e., I'll give up dancing, now that I have
enjoyed it as much as I ever shall   40 **Dun's … word** (Mercutio puns
on Romeo's last clause, saying in effect "You are not done [i.e., "dun":
"dark," by extension, "silent"] but the mouse is, and it's time to be
quiet)   41 **Dun** (a common name for a horse, used in an old game,
"Dun is in the mire," in which the players try to haul a heavy log)
42 **sir-reverence** save your reverence (an apologetic expression, used to
introduce indelicate expressions; here used humorously with the word
"love")   43 **burn daylight** delay   45 **lights** (1) torches (2) mental fac-
ulties   47 **that** i.e., our good meaning   49 **'tis no wit** it shows no discretion   50 **tonight** last night   53 **Queen Mab** Fairy Queen (Celtic)

On the forefinger of an alderman,
Drawn with a team of little atomies°
Over men's noses as they lie asleep;
Her wagon spokes made of long spinners'° legs,
The cover, of the wings of grasshoppers;                    60
Her traces, of the smallest spider web;
Her collars, of the moonshine's wat'ry beams;
Her whip, of cricket's bone; the lash, of film;°
Her wagoner, a small gray-coated gnat,
Not half so big as a round little worm                      65
Pricked from the lazy finger of a maid;°
Her chariot is an empty hazelnut,
Made by the joiner squirrel or old grub,°
Time out o' mind the fairies' coachmakers.
And in this state° she gallops night by night             70
Through lovers' brains, and then they dream of
      love;
On courtiers' knees, that dream on curtsies straight;
O'er lawyers' fingers, who straight dream on fees;
O'er ladies' lips, who straight on kisses dream,
Which oft the angry Mab with blisters plagues,            75
Because their breath with sweetmeats tainted are.
Sometime she gallops o'er a courtier's nose,
And then dreams he of smelling out a suit;°
And sometime comes she with a tithe pig's° tail
Tickling a parson's nose as 'a lies asleep,               80
Then he dreams of another benefice.°
Sometime she driveth o'er a soldier's neck,
And then dreams he of cutting foreign throats,
Of breaches, ambuscadoes, Spanish blades,
Of healths° five fathom deep; and then anon               85
Drums in his ear, at which he starts and wakes,
And being thus frighted, swears a prayer or two

---

57 **atomies** tiny creatures   59 **spinners** spiders   63 **film** fine filament
of some kind   65–66 **worm . . . maid** (lazy maids were said to have
worms breeding in their fingers)   68 **joiner squirrel or old grub** (both
woodworkers and adept at hollowing out nuts)   70 **state** stately array
78 **suit** i.e., a petitioner, who may be induced to pay for the courtier's
influence   79 **tithe pig** tenth pig (considered part of the parson's tithe)
81 **benefice** income, "living"   85 **healths** toasts

And sleeps again. This is that very Mab
That plats the manes of horses in the night
90 And bakes the elflocks° in foul sluttish hairs,
Which once untangled much misfortune bodes.
This is the hag,° when maids lie on their backs,
That presses them and learns them first to bear,
Making them women of good carriage.°
This is she—

95 *Romeo.*          Peace, peace, Mercutio, peace!
Thou talk'st of nothing.

*Mercutio.*                    True, I talk of dreams;
Which are the children of an idle brain,
Begot of nothing but vain fantasy;°
Which is as thin of substance as the air,
100 And more inconstant than the wind, who woos
Even now the frozen bosom of the North
And, being angered, puffs away from thence,
Turning his side to the dew-dropping South.

*Benvolio.* This wind you talk of blows us from ourselves.
105 Supper is done, and we shall come too late.

*Romeo.* I fear, too early; for my mind misgives
Some consequence° yet hanging in the stars
Shall bitterly begin his fearful date°
With this night's revels and expire the term
110 Of a despisèd life, closed in my breast,
By some vile forfeit of untimely death.°
But he that hath the steerage of my course
Direct my sail! On, lusty gentlemen!

*Benvolio.* Strike, drum.
                    *They march about the stage, and*
                    *[retire to one side].*

90 **elflocks** hair tangled by elves   92 **hag** nightmare or incubus   94 **carriage** (1) posture (2) capacity for carrying children   98 **fantasy** fancy
107 **consequence** future event   108 **date** duration (of the consequence
or event)   109–11 **expire ... death** (the event is personified here as
one who deliberately lends in expectation that the borrower will have to
forfeit at great loss)

[Scene 5. *A hall in Capulet's house.*]

*Servingmen come forth with napkins.*°

**First Servingman.** Where's Potpan, that he helps not
to take away? He shift a trencher!° He scrape a
trencher!

**Second Servingman.** When good manners shall lie all
in one or two men's hands, and they unwashed too,     5
'tis a foul thing.

**First Servingman.** Away with the join-stools,° remove
the court cupboard,° look to the plate. Good thou,
save me a piece of marchpane,° and, as thou loves
me, let the porter let in Susan Grindstone and Nell.     10
Anthony, and Potpan!

**Second Servingman.** Ay, boy, ready.

**First Servingman.** You are looked for and called for,
asked for and sought for, in the great chamber.

**Third Servingman.** We cannot be here and there too.     15
Cheerly, boys! Be brisk awhile, and the longer liver
take all.                                          *Exeunt.*

*Enter [Capulet, his Wife, Juliet, Tybalt, Nurse, and]*
*all the Guests and Gentlewomen to the Maskers.*

**Capulet.** Welcome, gentlemen! Ladies that have their
toes

---

1.5.s.d. (although for reference purposes this edition employs the conventional post-Elizabethan divisions into scenes, the reader is reminded
that they are merely editorial; in the quarto this stage direction is part of
the preceding one)   2 **trencher** wooden plate   7 **join-stools** stools fitted
together by a joiner   8 **court cupboard** sideboard, displaying plate
9 **marchpane** marzipan, a confection made of sugar and almonds

Unplagued with corns will walk a bout° with you.
20 Ah, my mistresses, which of you all
Will now deny° to dance? She that makes dainty,°
She I'll swear hath corns. Am I come near ye now?
Welcome, gentlemen! I have seen the day
That I have worn a visor and could tell
25 A whispering tale in a fair lady's ear,
Such as would please. 'Tis gone, 'tis gone, 'tis gone.
You are welcome, gentlemen! Come, musicians, play.
                    *Music plays, and they dance.*
A hall,° a hall! Give room! And foot it, girls.
More light, you knaves, and turn the tables up,
30 And quench the fire; the room is grown too hot.
Ah, sirrah, this unlooked-for sport° comes well.
Nay, sit; nay, sit, good cousin Capulet;
For you and I are past our dancing days.
How long is't now since last yourself and I
Were in a mask?

35 *Second Capulet.*    By'r Lady, thirty years.

*Capulet.* What, man? 'Tis not so much, 'tis not so
    much;
'Tis since the nuptial of Lucentio,
Come Pentecost as quickly as it will,
Some five-and-twenty years, and then we masked.

*Second Capulet.* 'Tis more, 'tis more. His son is elder,
40    sir;
His son is thirty.

*Capulet.*          Will you tell me that?
. His son was but a ward° two years ago.

*Romeo.* [*To a Servingman*] What lady's that which
    doth enrich the hand
Of yonder knight?

45 *Servingman.* I know not, sir.

---

19 **walk a bout** dance a turn   21 **deny** refuse   21 **makes dainty** seems
to hesitate   28 **A hall** clear the floor   31 **unlooked-for sport** (they had
not expected maskers)   42 **ward** minor

*Romeo.* O, she doth teach the torches to burn bright!
  It seems she hangs upon the cheek of night
  As a rich jewel in an Ethiop's ear—
  Beauty too rich for use, for earth too dear!
  So shows a snowy dove trooping with crows          50
  As yonder lady o'er her fellows shows.
  The measure done, I'll watch her place of stand
  And, touching hers, make blessèd my rude° hand.
  Did my heart love till now? Forswear it, sight!
  For I ne'er saw true beauty till this night.          55

*Tybalt.* This, by his voice, should be a Montague.
  Fetch me my rapier, boy. What! Dares the slave
  Come hither, covered with an antic face,°
  To fleer° and scorn at our solemnity?
  Now, by the stock and honor of my kin,          60
  To strike him dead I hold it not a sin.

*Capulet.* Why, how now, kinsman? Wherefore storm
      you so?

*Tybalt.* Uncle, this is a Montague, our foe,
  A villain, that is hither come in spite°
  To scorn at our solemnity this night.          65

*Capulet.* Young Romeo is it?

*Tybalt.*                          'Tis he, that villain Romeo.

*Capulet.* Content thee, gentle coz, let him alone.
  'A bears him like a portly° gentleman,
  And, to say truth, Verona brags of him
  To be a virtuous and well-governed youth.          70
  I would not for the wealth of all this town
  Here in my house do him disparagement.
  Therefore be patient; take no note of him.
  It is my will, the which if thou respect,
  Show a fair presence and put off these frowns,          75
  An ill-beseeming semblance for a feast.

*Tybalt.* It fits when such a villain is a guest.

53 **rude** rough   58 **antic face** fantastic mask   59 **fleer** jeer   64 **in spite**
insultingly   68 **portly** of good deportment

I'll not endure him.

*Capulet.*                    He shall be endured.
    What, goodman° boy! I say he shall. Go to!°
80    Am I the master here, or you? Go to!
    You'll not endure him, God shall mend my soul!°
    You'll make a mutiny° among my guests!
    You will set cock-a-hoop.° You'll be the man!

*Tybalt.* Why, uncle, 'tis a shame.

*Capulet.*                    Go to, go to!
85    You are a saucy boy. Is't so, indeed?
    This trick may chance to scathe° you. I know what.
    You must contrary me! Marry, 'tis time—
    Well said, my hearts!—You are a princox°—go!
    Be quiet, or— More light, more light!—For shame!
90    I'll make you quiet. What!—Cheerly, my hearts!

*Tybalt.* Patience perforce° with willful choler° meeting
    Makes my flesh tremble in their different greeting.
    I will withdraw; but this intrusion shall,
    Now seeming sweet, convert to bitt'rest gall. *Exit.*

95 *Romeo.* If° I profane with my unworthiest hand
    This holy shrine,° the gentle sin is this:°
    My lips, two blushing pilgrims, ready stand
    To smooth that rough touch with a tender kiss.

*Juliet.* Good pilgrim, you do wrong your hand too
    much,
100    Which mannerly devotion shows in this;
    For saints have hands that pilgrims' hands do touch,
    And palm to palm is holy palmers'° kiss.

---

79 **goodman** (a term applied to someone below the rank of gentleman)
79 **Go to** (impatient exclamation)   81 **God shall mend my soul**
(roughly equivalent to our "Indeed")   82 **mutiny** disturbance   83 **set
cock-a-hoop** be cock of the walk   86 **scathe** hurt, harm   88 **princox**
impertinent youngster   91 **Patience perforce** enforced self-control
91 **choler** anger   95 **If** (here begins an English, or Shakespearean,
sonnet)   96 **shrine** i.e., Juliet's hand   96 **the gentle sin is this** this is
the sin of well-bred people   102 **palmer** religious pilgrim (the term
originally signified one who carried a palm branch; here it is used as a
pun meaning one who holds another's hand)

*Romeo.* Have not saints lips, and holy palmers too?

*Juliet.* Ay, pilgrim, lips that they must use in prayer.

*Romeo.* O, then, dear saint, let lips do what hands do! 105
 They pray; grant thou, lest faith turn to despair.

*Juliet.* Saints do not move,° though grant for prayers'
 sake.

*Romeo.* Then move not while my prayer's effect I take.
 Thus from my lips, by thine my sin is purged.
            [*Kisses her.*]

*Juliet.* Then have my lips the sin that they have took. 110

*Romeo.* Sin from my lips? O trespass sweetly urged!
 Give me my sin again.    [*Kisses her.*]

*Juliet.*      You kiss by th' book.°

*Nurse.* Madam, your mother craves a word with you.

*Romeo.* What is her mother?

*Nurse.*      Marry, bachelor,
 Her mother is the lady of the house, 115
 And a good lady, and a wise and virtuous.
 I nursed her daughter that you talked withal.°
 I tell you, he that can lay hold of her
 Shall have the chinks.°

*Romeo.*     Is she a Capulet?
 O dear account! My life is my foe's debt.° 120

*Benvolio.* Away, be gone; the sport is at the best.

*Romeo.* Ay, so I fear; the more is my unrest.

*Capulet.* Nay, gentlemen, prepare not to be gone;
 We have a trifling foolish banquet towards.°
 Is it e'en so?° Why then, I thank you all. 125

107 **do not move** (1) do not initiate action (2) stand still 112 **kiss by
th' book** i.e., you take my words literally to get more kisses 117 **withal**
with 119 **the chinks** plenty of money 120 **My life is my foe's debt**
my foe now owns my life 124 **towards** in preparation 125 **Is it e'en
so?** (the maskers insist on leaving)

I thank you, honest gentlemen. Good night.
More torches here! Come on then; let's to bed.
Ah, sirrah, by my fay,° it waxes late;
I'll to my rest.    [*Exeunt all but Juliet and Nurse.*]

130  *Juliet.* Come hither, nurse. What is yond gentleman?

*Nurse.* The son and heir of old Tiberio.

*Juliet.* What's he that now is going out of door?

*Nurse.* Marry, that, I think, be young Petruchio.

*Juliet.* What's he that follows here, that would not
dance?

135  *Nurse.* I know not.

*Juliet.* Go ask his name.—If he is marrièd,
My grave is like to be my wedding bed.

*Nurse.* His name is Romeo, and a Montague,
The only son of your great enemy.

140  *Juliet.* My only love, sprung from my only hate!
Too early seen unknown, and known too late!
Prodigious° birth of love it is to me
That I must love a loathèd enemy.

*Nurse.* What's this? What's this?

*Juliet.*                          A rhyme I learnt even now
145  Of one I danced withal.   *One calls within,* "Juliet."

*Nurse.*                          Anon,° anon!
Come, let's away; the strangers all are gone.
                                        *Exeunt.*

128 **fay** faith   142 **Prodigious** (1) monstrous (2) of evil portent
145 **Anon** at once

# [ACT 2

*Enter]* Chorus.

*Chorus.* Now old desire doth in his deathbed lie,
    And young affection gapes° to be his heir;
That fair° for which love groaned for and would
    die,
    With tender Juliet matched, is now not fair.
Now Romeo is beloved and loves again,          5
    Alike bewitchèd° by the charm of looks;
But to his foe supposed he must complain,°
    And she steal love's sweet bait from fearful
    hooks.
Being held a foe, he may not have access
    To breathe such vows as lovers use to° swear,     *10*
And she as much in love, her means much less
    To meet her new belovèd anywhere;
But passion lends them power, time means, to meet,
Temp'ring extremities with extreme sweet.° [*Exit.*]

---

2. Prologue    2 **young affection gapes** the new love is eager    3 **That
fair** i.e., Rosaline    6 **Alike bewitchèd** i.e., both are bewitched
7 **complain** address his lover's suit    10 **use to** customarily    14 **Temp'-
ring ... sweet** softening difficulties with extraordinary delights

[Scene 1.   *Near Capulet's orchard.*]

*Enter Romeo alone.*

*Romeo.* Can I go forward when my heart is here?
    Turn back, dull earth, and find thy center out.°

*Enter Benvolio with Mercutio. [Romeo retires.]*

*Benvolio.* Romeo! My cousin Romeo! Romeo!

*Mercutio.*                               He is wise
    And, on my life, hath stol'n him home to bed.

5  *Benvolio.* He ran this way and leapt this orchard wall.
    Call, good Mercutio.

*Mercutio.*            Nay, I'll conjure too.
    Romeo! Humors! Madman! Passion! Lover!
    Appear thou in the likeness of a sigh;
    Speak but one rhyme, and I am satisfied!
    Cry but "Ay me!" pronounce but "love" and
10    "dove";
    Speak to my gossip° Venus one fair word,
    One nickname for her purblind° son and heir,
    Young Abraham Cupid,° he that shot so true
    When King Cophetua loved the beggar maid!°
15  He heareth not, he stirreth not, he moveth not;
    The ape is dead,° and I must conjure him.
    I conjure thee by Rosaline's bright eyes,
    By her high forehead and her scarlet lip,

2.1.1–2 **Can ... out** (Romeo refuses to pass Capulet's house, commanding his body, or *earth,* to stop and join its proper soul, or *center*— i.e., Juliet)   11 **gossip** crony   12 **purblind** quite blind   13 **Abraham Cupid** (the phrase may mean "ancient youth" or, since "abram man" was slang for "trickster," "rascally Cupid")   14 **King Cophetua ... maid** (reference to an old familiar ballad)   16 **The ape is dead** i.e., Romeo plays dead, like a performing ape

By her fine foot, straight leg, and quivering thigh,
And the demesnes° that there adjacent lie,                    20
That in thy likeness thou appear to us!

*Benvolio.* And if° he hear thee, thou wilt anger him.

*Mercutio.* This cannot anger him. 'Twould anger him
To raise a spirit in his mistress' circle°
Of some strange nature, letting it there stand              25
Till she had laid it and conjured it down.
That were some spite;° my invocation
Is fair and honest:° in his mistress' name,
I conjure only but to raise up him.

*Benvolio.* Come, he hath hid himself among these trees   30
To be consorted° with the humorous° night.
Blind is his love and best befits the dark.

*Mercutio.* If love be blind, love cannot hit the mark.
Now will he sit under a medlar tree
And wish his mistress were that kind of fruit              35
As maids call medlars° when they laugh alone.
O, Romeo, that she were, O that she were
An open *et cetera,* thou a pop'rin° pear!
Romeo, good night. I'll to my truckle bed;°
This field bed is too cold for me to sleep.               40
Come, shall we go?

*Benvolio.*                     Go then, for 'tis in vain
To seek him here that means not to be found.
                                        *Exit [with others].*

---

20 **demesnes** domains    22 **And if** if    24 **circle** (conjurers worked
within a magic circle, but there is also a bawdy innuendo, as in *stand,
laid, down, raise*)    27 **spite** vexation    28 **fair and honest** respectable
31 **consorted** associated    31 **humorous** (1) damp (2) moody    36 **med-
lars** applelike fruit, eaten when decayed (like **pop'rin,** in line 38, the
word was often used to refer to sexual organs)    39 **I'll to my truckle
bed** I'll go to my trundle bed, or baby bed (i.e., I'm innocent in affairs
of this kind)

[Scene 2. *Capulet's orchard.*]

*Romeo.* [*Coming forward*] He jests at scars that never
    felt a wound.

[*Enter Juliet at a window.*]

    But soft! What light through yonder window breaks?
    It is the East, and Juliet is the sun!
    Arise, fair sun, and kill the envious moon,
5    Who is already sick and pale with grief
    That thou her maid° art far more fair than she.
    Be not her maid, since she is envious.
    Her vestal livery° is but sick and green,°
    And none but fools do wear it. Cast it off.
10    It is my lady! O, it is my love!
    O, that she knew she were!
    She speaks, yet she says nothing. What of that?
    Her eye discourses; I will answer it.
    I am too bold; 'tis not to me she speaks.
15    Two of the fairest stars in all the heaven,
    Having some business, do entreat her eyes
    To twinkle in their spheres° till they return.
    What if her eyes were there, they in her head?
    The brightness of her cheek would shame those stars
20    As daylight doth a lamp; her eyes in heaven
    Would through the airy region stream so bright
    That birds would sing and think it were not night.
    See how she leans her cheek upon her hand!
    O, that I were a glove upon that hand,
    That I might touch that cheek!

*Juliet.*                   Ay me!

2.2.6 **her maid** (the moon is here thought of as Diana, goddess and
patroness of virgins)   8 **vestal livery** i.e., virginity   8 **sick and green**
sickly, bearing the characteristics of greensickness, the virgin's malady
17 **spheres** orbits

*Romeo.*                              She speaks.     25
  O, speak again, bright angel, for thou art
  As glorious to this night, being o'er my head,
  As is a wingèd messenger of heaven
  Unto the white-upturnèd wond'ring eyes
  Of mortals that fall back to gaze on him     30
  When he bestrides the lazy puffing clouds
  And sails upon the bosom of the air.

*Juliet.* O Romeo, Romeo! Wherefore art thou Romeo?
  Deny thy father and refuse thy name;
  Or, if thou wilt not, be but sworn my love,     35
  And I'll no longer be a Capulet.

*Romeo.* [*Aside*] Shall I hear more, or shall I speak
     at this?

*Juliet.* 'Tis but thy name that is my enemy.
  Thou art thyself, though not° a Montague.
  What's Montague? It is nor hand, nor foot,     40
  Nor arm, nor face. O, be some other name
  Belonging to a man.
  What's in a name? That which we call a rose
  By any other word would smell as sweet.
  So Romeo would, were he not Romeo called,     45
  Retain that dear perfection which he owes°
  Without that title. Romeo, doff thy name;
  And for thy name, which is no part of thee,
  Take all myself.

*Romeo.*           I take thee at thy word.
  Call me but love, and I'll be new baptized;     50
  Henceforth I never will be Romeo.

*Juliet.* What man art thou, that, thus bescreened in
     night,
  So stumblest on my counsel?

*Romeo.*                         By a name
  I know not how to tell thee who I am.
  My name, dear saint, is hateful to myself     55

39 **though not** even if you were not   46 **owes** owns

Because it is an enemy to thee.
Had I it written, I would tear the word.

*Juliet.* My ears have yet not drunk a hundred words
Of thy tongue's uttering, yet I know the sound.
60      Art thou not Romeo, and a Montague?

*Romeo.* Neither, fair maid, if either thee dislike.°

*Juliet.* How camest thou hither, tell me, and where-
        fore?
The orchard walls are high and hard to climb,
And the place death, considering who thou art,
65      If any of my kinsmen find thee here.

*Romeo.* With love's light wings did I o'erperch° these
        walls;
For stony limits cannot hold love out,
And what love can do, that dares love attempt.
Therefore thy kinsmen are no stop to me.

70  *Juliet.* If they do see thee, they will murder thee.

*Romeo.* Alack, there lies more peril in thine eye
Than twenty of their swords! Look thou but sweet,
And I am proof° against their enmity.

*Juliet.* I would not for the world they saw thee here.

75  *Romeo.* I have night's cloak to hide me from their eyes;
And but° thou love me, let them find me here.
My life were better ended by their hate
Than death proroguèd,° wanting of thy love.

*Juliet.* By whose direction found'st thou out this place?

80  *Romeo.* By love, that first did prompt me to inquire.
He lent me counsel, and I lent him eyes.
I am no pilot; yet, wert thou as far
As that vast shore washed with the farthest sea,
I should adventure° for such merchandise.

85  *Juliet.* Thou knowest the mask of night is on my face;

61 **dislike** displeases  66 **o'erperch** fly over  73 **proof** protected
76 **but** if only  78 **proroguèd** deferred  84 **adventure** risk the
journey

Else would a maiden blush bepaint my cheek
For that which thou hast heard me speak tonight.
Fain would I dwell on form—fain, fain deny
What I have spoke; but farewell compliment!°
Dost thou love me? I know thou wilt say "Ay"; 90
And I will take thy word. Yet, if thou swear'st,
Thou mayst prove false. At lovers' perjuries,
They say Jove laughs. O gentle Romeo,
If thou dost love, pronounce it faithfully.
Or if thou thinkest I am too quickly won, 95
I'll frown and be perverse and say thee nay,
So thou wilt woo; but else, not for the world.
In truth, fair Montague, I am too fond,°
And therefore thou mayst think my havior° light;
But trust me, gentleman, I'll prove more true 100
Than those that have more cunning to be strange.°
I should have been more strange, I must confess,
But that thou overheard'st, ere I was ware,
My truelove passion. Therefore pardon me,
And not impute this yielding to light love, 105
Which the dark night hath so discoverèd.°

*Romeo.* Lady, by yonder blessèd moon I vow,
That tips with silver all these fruit-tree tops—

*Juliet.* O, swear not by the moon, th' inconstant moon,
That monthly changes in her circle orb, 110
Lest that thy love prove likewise variable.

*Romeo.* What shall I swear by?

*Juliet.*                        Do not swear at all;
Or if thou wilt, swear by thy gracious self,
Which is the god of my idolatry,
And I'll believe thee.

*Romeo.*                 If my heart's dear love— 115

*Juliet.* Well, do not swear. Although I joy in thee,
I have no joy of this contract tonight.

89 **compliment** formal courtesy 98 **fond** (1) affectionate (2) fool-
ishly tender 99 **havior** behavior 101 **strange** aloof 106 **discoverèd**
revealed

It is too rash, too unadvised, too sudden;
Too like the lightning, which doth cease to be
120  Ere one can say it lightens. Sweet, good night!
This bud of love, by summer's ripening breath,
May prove a beauteous flow'r when next we meet.
Good night, good night! As sweet repose and rest
Come to thy heart as that within my breast!

125  *Romeo.* O, wilt thou leave me so unsatisfied?

*Juliet.* What satisfaction canst thou have tonight?

*Romeo.* Th' exchange of thy love's faithful vow for
mine.

*Juliet.* I gave thee mine before thou didst request it;
And yet I would it were to give again.

*Romeo.* Wouldst thou withdraw it? For what purpose,
130  love?

*Juliet.* But to be frank° and give it thee again.
And yet I wish but for the thing I have.
My bounty° is as boundless as the sea,
My love as deep; the more I give to thee,
135  The more I have, for both are infinite.
I hear some noise within. Dear love, adieu!
                              [*Nurse calls within.*]
Anon, good nurse! Sweet Montague, be true.
Stay but a little, I will come again.          [*Exit.*]

*Romeo.* O blessèd, blessèd night! I am afeard,
140  Being in night, all this is but a dream,
Too flattering-sweet to be substantial.

                    [*Enter Juliet again.*]

*Juliet.* Three words, dear Romeo, and good night
indeed.
If that thy bent° of love be honorable,
Thy purpose marriage, send me word tomorrow,
145  By one that I'll procure to come to thee,
Where and what time thou wilt perform the rite;

131 **frank** generous   133 **bounty** capacity for giving   143 **bent** aim

And all my fortunes at thy foot I'll lay
And follow thee my lord throughout the world.

[*Nurse. Within*] Madam!

*Juliet.* I come anon.—But if thou meanest not well, *150*
I do beseech thee—

[*Nurse. Within*] Madam!

*Juliet.*     By and by° I come.—
To cease thy strife° and leave me to my grief.
Tomorrow will I send.

*Romeo.*     So thrive my soul—

*Juliet.* A thousand times good night!  [*Exit.*]

*Romeo.* A thousand times the worse, to want thy light! *155*
Love goes toward love as schoolboys from their
 books;
But love from love, toward school with heavy looks.

     *Enter Juliet again.*

*Juliet.* Hist! Romeo, hist! O for a falc'ner's voice
To lure this tassel gentle° back again!
Bondage is hoarse° and may not speak aloud, *160*
Else would I tear the cave where Echo lies
And make her airy tongue more hoarse than mine
With repetition of "My Romeo!"

*Romeo.* It is my soul that calls upon my name.
How silver-sweet sound lovers' tongues by night, *165*
Like softest music to attending° ears!

*Juliet.* Romeo!

*Romeo.*  My sweet?

*Juliet.*     What o'clock tomorrow
Shall I send to thee?

---

151 **By and by** at once 152 **strife** efforts 159 **tassel gentle** tercel gentle, male falcon 160 **Bondage is hoarse** i.e., being surrounded by "protectors," I cannot cry loudly 166 **attending** attentive

*Romeo.*                    By the hour of nine.

*Juliet.* I will not fail. 'Tis twenty year till then.
170  I have forgot why I did call thee back.

*Romeo.* Let me stand here till thou remember it.

*Juliet.* I shall forget, to have thee still stand there,
     Rememb'ring how I love thy company.

*Romeo.* And I'll still stay, to have thee still forget,
175  Forgetting any other home but this.

*Juliet.* 'Tis almost morning. I would have thee gone—
     And yet no farther than a wanton's° bird,
     That lets it hop a little from his hand,
     Like a poor prisoner in his twisted gyves,°
180  And with a silken thread plucks it back again,
     So loving-jealous of his liberty.

*Romeo.* I would I were thy bird.

*Juliet.*                         Sweet, so would I.
     Yet I should kill thee with much cherishing.
     Good night, good night! Parting is such sweet
         sorrow
185  That I shall say good night till it be morrow.°
                                        [*Exit.*]

*Romeo.* Sleep dwell upon thine eyes, peace in thy
         breast!
     Would I were sleep and peace, so sweet to rest!°
     Hence will I to my ghostly friar's° close cell,
     His help to crave and my dear hap° to tell.    *Exit.*

---

177 **wanton's** capricious child's   179 **gyves** fetters   185 **morrow** morning   187 **rest** (the four lines that follow in the quarto are here deleted because they are virtually identical with the first four lines of the next scene. See Textual Note. Apparently Shakespeare wrote them and then decided to use them at the start of the next scene, but forgot to delete their first occurrence)   188 **ghostly friar** spiritual father (i.e., confessor)   189 **dear hap** good fortune

### [Scene 3.   *Friar Lawrence's cell.*]

*Enter Friar [Lawrence] alone, with a basket.*

*Friar.* The gray-eyed morn smiles on the frowning
        night,
  Check'ring the eastern clouds with streaks of light;
  And fleckèd° darkness like a drunkard reels
  From forth day's path and Titan's burning wheels.°
  Now, ere the sun advance his burning eye          5
  The day to cheer and night's dank dew to dry,
  I must upfill this osier cage° of ours
  With baleful° weeds and precious-juicèd flowers.
  The earth that's nature's mother is her tomb.
  What is her burying grave, that is her womb;       10
  And from her womb children of divers kind
  We sucking on her natural bosom find,
  Many for many virtues excellent,
  None but for some, and yet all different.
  O, mickle° is the powerful grace that lies         15
  In plants, herbs, stones, and their true qualities;
  For naught so vile that on the earth doth live
  But to the earth some special good doth give;
  Nor aught so good but, strained° from that fair use,
  Revolts from true birth,° stumbling on abuse.      20
  Virtue itself turns vice, being misapplied,
  And vice sometime by action dignified.°

        *Enter Romeo.°*

2.3.3 **fleckèd** spotted   4 **Titan's burning wheels** wheels of the sun's
chariot   7 **osier cage** willow basket   8 **baleful** (1) evil. (2) poisonous
15 **mickle** much   19 **strained** diverted   20 **Revolts from true birth** falls
away from its real purpose   22 **dignified** made worthy   22 s.d. **Enter
Romeo** (the entry of Romeo at this point, unseen by the Friar, emphasizes the appropriateness of the remaining eight lines of the Friar's
speech, not only to the flower but to Romeo)

Within the infant rind° of this weak flower
Poison hath residence and medicine° power;
For this, being smelt, with that part cheers each
25      part;°
Being tasted, stays all senses with the heart.
Two such opposèd kings encamp them still°
In man as well as herbs—grace and rude will;
And where the worser is predominant,
30      Full soon the canker° death eats up that plant.

*Romeo.* Good morrow, father.

*Friar.*                          *Benedicite!°*
What early tongue so sweet saluteth me?
Young son, it argues a distemperèd head°
So soon to bid good morrow to thy bed.
35      Care keeps his watch in every old man's eye,
And where care lodges, sleep will never lie;
But where unbruisèd youth with unstuffed° brain
Doth couch his limbs, there golden sleep doth reign.
Therefore thy earliness doth me assure
40      Thou art uproused with some distemp'rature;
Or if not so, then here I hit it right—
Our Romeo hath not been in bed tonight.

*Romeo.* That last is true. The sweeter rest was mine.

*Friar.* God pardon sin! Wast thou with Rosaline?

45   *Romeo.* With Rosaline, my ghostly father? No.
I have forgot that name and that name's woe.

*Friar.* That's my good son! But where hast thou been
      then?

*Romeo.* I'll tell thee ere thou ask it me again.
I have been feasting with mine enemy,
50      Where on a sudden one hath wounded me
That's by me wounded. Both our remedies

23 **infant rind** tender bark, skin   24 **medicine** medicinal   25 **For . . .
part** i.e., being smelled, this flower stimulates every part of the body
27 **still** always   30 **canker** cankerworm, larva that feeds on leaves
31 **Benedicite** bless you   33 **distemperèd head** troubled mind   37 **un-
stuffed** untroubled

Within thy help and holy physic° lies.
I bear no hatred, blessèd man, for, lo,
My intercession° likewise steads° my foe.

*Friar.* Be plain, good son, and homely in thy drift.°      55
Riddling confession finds but riddling shrift.°

*Romeo.* Then plainly know my heart's dear love is set
On the fair daughter of rich Capulet;
As mine on hers, so hers is set on mine,
And all combined,° save what thou must combine      60
By holy marriage. When and where and how
We met, we wooed, and made exchange of vow,
I'll tell thee as we pass; but this I pray,
That thou consent to marry us today.

*Friar.* Holy Saint Francis! What a change is here!      65
Is Rosaline, that thou didst love so dear,
So soon forsaken? Young men's love then lies
Not truly in their hearts, but in their eyes.
Jesu Maria! What a deal of brine
Hath washed thy sallow cheeks for Rosaline!      70
How much salt water thrown away in waste
To season° love, that of it doth not taste!
The sun not yet thy sighs from heaven clears,
Thy old groans ring yet in mine ancient ears.
Lo, here upon thy cheek the stain doth sit      75
Of an old tear that is not washed off yet.
If e'er thou wast thyself, and these woes thine,
Thou and these woes were all for Rosaline.
And art thou changed? Pronounce this sentence
     then:
Women may fall° when there's no strength° in men.      80

*Romeo.* Thou chidst me oft for loving Rosaline.

*Friar.* For doting, not for loving, pupil mine.

---

52 **physic** medicine  54 **intercession** entreaty  54 **steads** helps
55 **homely in thy drift** plain in your talk  56 **shrift** absolution
60 **combined** (1) brought into unity (2) settled  72 **season** (1) preserve
(2) flavor  80 **may fall** i.e., may be expected to be fickle  80 **strength**
constancy

*Romeo.* And badst me bury love.

*Friar.*                  Not in a grave
   To lay one in, another out to have.

85  *Romeo.* I pray thee chide me not. Her I love now
   Doth grace° for grace and love for love allow.
   The other did not so.

*Friar.*             O, she knew well
   Thy love did read by rote, that could not spell.°
   But come, young waverer, come go with me.
90    In one respect° I'll thy assistant be;
   For this alliance may so happy prove
   To turn your households' rancor to pure love.

*Romeo.* O, let us hence! I stand on° sudden haste.

*Friar.* Wisely and slow. They stumble that run fast.
                              *Exeunt.*


[Scene 4. *A street.*]


*Enter Benvolio and Mercutio.*


*Mercutio.* Where the devil should this Romeo be?
   Came he not home tonight?

*Benvolio.* Not to his father's. I spoke with his man.

*Mercutio.* Why, that same pale hardhearted wench,
   that Rosaline,
5    Torments him so that he will sure run mad.

*Benvolio.* Tybalt, the kinsman to old Capulet,
   Hath sent a letter to his father's house.

*Mercutio.* A challenge, on my life.

---

86 **grace** favor    88 **did read ... spell** i.e., said words without understanding them    90 **In one respect** with respect to one particular
93 **stand on** insist on

*Benvolio.* Romeo will answer it.

*Mercutio.* Any man that can write may answer a letter.    *10*

*Benvolio.* Nay, he will answer the letter's master, how he dares, being dared.

*Mercutio.* Alas, poor Romeo, he is already dead: stabbed with a white wench's black eye; run through the ear with a love song; the very pin° of his heart   *15* cleft with the blind bow-boy's butt-shaft;° and is he a man to encounter Tybalt?

*Benvolio.* Why, what is Tybalt?

*Mercutio.* More than Prince of Cats.° O, he's the courageous captain of compliments.° He fights as   *20* you sing pricksong°—keeps time, distance, and proportion; he rests his minim rests,° one, two, and the third in your bosom! The very butcher of a silk button,° a duelist, a duelist! A gentleman of the very first house,° of the first and second cause.°   *25* Ah, the immortal *passado!*° The *punto reverso!*° The hay!°

*Benvolio.* The what?

*Mercutio.* The pox of such antic, lisping, affecting fantasticoes°—these new tuners of accent! "By   *30* Jesu, a very good blade! A very tall° man! A very good whore!" Why, is not this a lamentable thing, grandsir, that we should be thus afflicted with these

---

2.4.15 **pin** center (of a target)   16 **blind bow-boy's butt-shaft** Cupid's blunt arrow   19 **Prince of Cats** (Tybalt's name, or some variant of it, was given to the cat in medieval stories of Reynard the Fox)   20 **compliments** formal courtesies   21 **sing pricksong** (1) sing from a text (2) sing with attention to accuracy   22 **he rests his minim rests** i.e., he scrupulously observes every formality (literally, he observes even the shortest rests in the notation)   24 **button** (on his opponent's shirt) 25 **first house** first rank   25 **first and second cause** (dueling terms, meaning formal grounds for taking offense and giving a challenge) 26 **passado** lunge   26 **punto reverso** backhanded stroke   27 **hay** home thrust (Italian *hai*)   30 **fantasticoes** fops   31 **tall** brave

strange flies, these fashionmongers, these pardon-
35  me's,° who stand so much on the new form° that
they cannot sit at ease on the old bench? O, their
bones,° their bones!

*Enter Romeo.*

*Benvolio.* Here comes Romeo! Here comes Romeo!

*Mercutio.* Without his roe,° like a dried herring. O
40  flesh, flesh, how art thou fishified! Now is he for
the numbers° that Petrarch flowed in. Laura,° to
his lady, was a kitchen wench (marry, she had a
better love to berhyme her), Dido° a dowdy,°
Cleopatra a gypsy,° Helen and Hero° hildings° and
45  harlots, Thisbe° a gray eye° or so, but not to the
purpose. Signior Romeo, *bon jour!* There's a French
salutation to your French slop.° You gave us the
counterfeit fairly last night.

*Romeo.* Good morrow to you both. What counterfeit
50  did I give you?

*Mercutio.* The slip,° sir, the slip. Can you not con-
ceive?

*Romeo.* Pardon, good Mercutio. My business was
great, and in such a case as mine a man may strain
55  courtesy.

*Mercutio.* That's as much as to say, such a case° as
yours constrains a man to bow in the hams.

---

34–35 **pardon-me's** i.e., persons who affect foreign phrases (cf. Italian
*perdona mi*)   35 **form** (1) fashion (2) bench   37 **bones** (pun on French
*bon*)   39 **Without his roe** i.e., (1) emaciated like a fish that has
spawned or (2) stripped of "Ro," leaving only "me-o" (a sigh)   41 **numbers** verses   41 **Laura** (Petrarch's beloved)   43 **Dido** (Queen of Car-
thage, enamored of Aeneas)   43 **dowdy** a drab woman   44 **gypsy** a
deceitful woman (gypsies were commonly believed to be Egyptians)
44 **Helen and Hero** (beloved respectively of Paris and Leander)
44 **hildings** good-for-nothings   45 **Thisbe** (beloved of Pyramus in a
story analogous to that of Romeo and Juliet)   45 **gray eye** i.e., gleam
in the eye   47 **slop** loose breeches   51 **slip** (1) escape (2) counterfeit
coin   56 **case** (1) situation (2) physical condition

*Romeo.* Meaning, to curtsy.

*Mercutio.* Thou hast most kindly hit° it.

*Romeo.* A most courteous exposition. 60

*Mercutio.* Nay, I am the very pink° of courtesy.

*Romeo.* Pink for flower.

*Mercutio.* Right.

*Romeo.* Why, then is my pump° well-flowered.°

*Mercutio.* Sure wit, follow me this jest now till thou 65
hast worn out thy pump, that, when the single sole
of it is worn, the jest may remain, after the wearing,
solely singular.°

*Romeo.* O single-soled jest, solely singular for the
singleness! 70

*Mercutio.* Come between us, good Benvolio! My wits
faints.

*Romeo.* Swits° and spurs, swits and spurs; or I'll cry
a match.°

*Mercutio.* Nay, if our wits run the wild-goose chase,° 75
I am done; for thou hast more of the wild goose in
one of thy wits than, I am sure, I have in my whole
five. Was I with you there for the goose?°

*Romeo.* Thou wast never with me for anything when
thou wast not there for the goose.° 80

*Mercutio.* I will bite thee by the ear for that jest.

59 **most kindly hit** most politely interpreted   61 **pink** perfection (but
Romeo proceeds to exploit two other meanings: [1] flower [2] punches
in an ornamental design)   64 **pump** shoe   64 **well-flowered** orna-
mented with pinking (with pun on "floored")   68 **solely singular** (1)
single-soled (i.e., weak) (2) uniquely remarkable (literally, "uniquely
unique")   73 **Swits** switches   73–74 **cry a match** claim a victory
75 **wild-goose chase** cross-country game of "follow the leader" on
horseback   78 **goose** end of the chase (i.e., end of the punning match)
80 **goose** prostitute

*Romeo.* Nay, good goose, bite not!°

*Mercutio.* Thy wit is a very bitter sweeting;° it is a most sharp sauce.

85 *Romeo.* And is it not, then, well served in to a sweet goose?°

*Mercutio.* O, here's a wit of cheveril,° that stretches from an inch narrow to an ell broad!°

*Romeo.* I stretch it out for that word "broad," which
90 added to the goose, proves thee far and wide a broad° goose.

*Mercutio.* Why, is not this better now than groaning for love? Now art thou sociable, now art thou Romeo; now art thou what thou art, by art as well
95 as by nature. For this driveling love is like a great natural° that runs lolling° up and down to hide his bauble° in a hole.

*Benvolio.* Stop there, stop there!

*Mercutio.* Thou desirest me to stop in my tale against
100 the hair.°

*Benvolio.* Thou wouldst else have made thy tale large.°

*Mercutio.* O, thou art deceived! I would have made it short; for I was come to the whole depth of my
105 tale, and meant indeed to occupy the argument° no longer.

*Romeo.* Here's goodly gear!°

---

82 **good goose, bite not** (proverbial for "Spare me!") 83 **bitter sweeting** tart kind of apple 85–86 **sweet goose** tender goose (here probably referring to Mercutio; but the expression "Sour sauce for sweet meat" was proverbial) 87 **cheveril** kid leather, easily stretched 88 **ell broad** forty-five inches wide 91 **broad** indecent (?) 96 **natural** idiot 96 **lolling** with tongue hanging out 97 **bauble** trinket (with ribald innuendo) 99–100 **against the hair** against my inclination 102 **large** indecent 105 **occupy the argument** discuss the matter 107 **gear** stuff

*Enter Nurse and her Man [Peter].*

A sail, a sail!

*Mercutio.* Two, two! A shirt and a smock.°

*Nurse.* Peter! 110

*Peter.* Anon.

*Nurse.* My fan, Peter.

*Mercutio.* Good Peter, to hide her face; for her fan's the fairer face.

*Nurse.* God ye good morrow, gentlemen. 115

*Mercutio.* God ye good-den,° fair gentlewoman.

*Nurse.* Is it good-den?

*Mercutio.* 'Tis no less, I tell ye; for the bawdy hand of the dial is now upon the prick° of noon.

*Nurse.* Out upon you! What a man are you! 120

*Romeo.* One, gentlewoman, that God hath made, himself to mar.

*Nurse.* By my troth, it is well said. "For himself to mar," quoth 'a?° Gentlemen, can any of you tell me where I may find the young Romeo? 125

*Romeo.* I can tell you; but young Romeo will be older when you have found him than he was when you sought him. I am the youngest of that name, for fault of a worse.°

*Nurse.* You say well. 130

*Mercutio.* Yea, is the worst well? Very well took,° i' faith! Wisely, wisely.

*Nurse.* If you be he, sir, I desire some confidence° with you.

109 **A shirt and a smock** i.e., a man and a woman   116 **good-den** good evening (i.e., afternoon)   119 **prick** point on the dial of a clock (with bawdy innuendo)   124 **quoth 'a** indeed (literally, "said he") 128–29 **for fault of a worse** (mock-modestly parodying "for want of a better")   131 **took** understood   133 **confidence** conference (possibly a malapropism)

135 *Benvolio.* She will endite° him to some supper.

*Mercutio.* A bawd, a bawd, a bawd! So ho!°

*Romeo.* What hast thou found?

*Mercutio.* No hare,° sir; unless a hare, sir, in a lenten
140     pie,° that is something stale and hoar° ere it be
    spent.

[*He walks by them and sings.*]

An old hare hoar,
And an old hare hoar,
Is very good meat in Lent;
But a hare that is hoar
145      Is too much for a score
When it hoars ere it be spent.

Romeo, will you come to your father's? We'll to
dinner thither.

*Romeo.* I will follow you.

150 *Mercutio.* Farewell, ancient lady. Farewell, [*singing*]
    "Lady, lady, lady."°   *Exeunt* [*Mercutio, Benvolio*].

*Nurse.* I pray you, sir, what saucy merchant was this
    that was so full of his ropery?°

*Romeo.* A gentleman, nurse, that loves to hear himself
155     talk and will speak more in a minute than he will
    stand to in a month.

*Nurse.* And 'a speak anything against me, I'll take him
    down, and 'a were lustier than he is, and twenty
    such Jacks; and if I cannot, I'll find those that shall.
160     Scurvy knave! I am none of his flirt-gills;° I am

---

135 **endite** invite (Benvolio's intentional malapropism?)   136 **So ho!**
(cry on sighting a quarry)   138 **hare** prostitute   138–39 **lenten pie**
rabbit pie (eaten sparingly and hence stale)   139 **hoar** gray-haired,
moldy (wordplay on "hare" and "whore")   151 **Lady, lady, lady** (ballad
refrain from "Chaste Susanna")   153 **ropery** rascally talk   160 **flirt-
gills** flirting wenches

none of his skainsmates.° And thou must stand
by too, and suffer every knave to use me at his
pleasure!

*Peter.* I saw no man use you at his pleasure. If I had,
my weapon should quickly have been out, I warrant    165
you. I dare draw as soon as another man, if I see
occasion in a good quarrel, and the law on my side.

*Nurse.* Now, afore God, I am so vexed that every part
about me quivers. Scurvy knave! Pray you, sir, a
word; and, as I told you, my young lady bid me    170
inquire you out. What she bid me say, I will keep
to myself; but first let me tell ye, if ye should lead
her in a fool's paradise,° as they say, it were a very
gross kind of behavior, as they say; for the gentlewoman is young; and therefore, if you should deal    175
double with her, truly it were an ill thing to be
off'red to any gentlewoman, and very weak° dealing.

*Romeo.* Nurse, commend me to thy lady and mistress.
I protest unto thee—

*Nurse.* Good heart, and i' faith I will tell her as much.    180
Lord, Lord, she will be a joyful woman.

*Romeo.* What wilt thou tell her, nurse? Thou dost not
mark me.

*Nurse.* I will tell her, sir, that you do protest, which,
as I take it, is a gentlemanlike offer.    185

*Romeo.* Bid her devise
Some means to come to shrift this afternoon;
And there she shall at Friar Lawrence' cell
Be shrived and married. Here is for thy pains.

*Nurse.* No, truly, sir; not a penny.    190

*Romeo.* Go to! I say you shall.

*Nurse.* This afternoon, sir? Well, she shall be there.

---

161 **skainsmates** harlots (?) daggers' mates (i.e., outlaws' mates)
173 **fool's paradise** seduction    177 **weak** unmanly, unscrupulous

*Romeo.* And stay, good nurse, behind the abbey wall.
   Within this hour my man shall be with thee
195 And bring thee cords made like a tackled stair,°
   Which to the high topgallant° of my joy
   Must be my convoy° in the secret night.
   Farewell. Be trusty, and I'll quit° thy pains.
   Farewell. Commend me to thy mistress.

200 *Nurse.* Now God in heaven bless thee! Hark you, sir.

*Romeo.* What say'st thou, my dear nurse?

*Nurse.* Is your man secret? Did you ne'er hear say,
   Two may keep counsel, putting one away?

*Romeo.* Warrant thee my man's as true as steel.

205 *Nurse.* Well, sir, my mistress is the sweetest lady. Lord,
   Lord! When 'twas a little prating thing— O, there is
   a nobleman in town, one Paris, that would fain lay
   knife aboard;° but she, good soul, had as lieve° see
   a toad, a very toad, as see him. I anger her some-
210 times, and tell her that Paris is the properer man;
   but I'll warrant you, when I say so, she looks as
   pale as any clout° in the versal world.° Doth not
   rosemary and Romeo begin both with a letter?

*Romeo.* Ay, nurse; what of that? Both with an *R*.

215 *Nurse.* Ah, mocker! That's the dog's name.° *R* is for
   the— No; I know it begins with some other letter;
   and she hath the prettiest sententious° of it, of you
   and rosemary, that it would do you good to hear it.

*Romeo.* Commend me to thy lady.

220 *Nurse.* Ay, a thousand times. [*Exit Romeo.*] Peter!

*Peter.* Anon.

*Nurse.* Before, and apace.          *Exit* [*after Peter*].

---

195 **tackled stair** rope ladder   196 **topgallant** summit (mast above the
topmast)   197 **convoy** conveyance   198 **quit** reward   207–08 **lay knife
aboard** take a slice   208 **had as lieve** would rather   212 **clout** cloth
212 **versal world** universe   215 **dog's name** (the *R* sound suggests a
dog's growl)   217 **sententious** sentences, pithy sayings

[Scene 5. *Capulet's orchard.*]

*Enter Juliet.*

*Juliet.* The clock struck nine when I did send the
    nurse;
  In half an hour she promised to return.
  Perchance she cannot meet him. That's not so.
  O, she is lame! Love's heralds should be thoughts,
  Which ten times faster glides than the sun's beams          5
  Driving back shadows over low'ring hills.
  Therefore do nimble-pinioned doves° draw Love,
  And therefore hath the wind-swift Cupid wings.
  Now is the sun upon the highmost hill
  Of this day's journey, and from nine till twelve          10
  Is three long hours; yet she is not come.
  Had she affections and warm youthful blood,
  She would be as swift in motion as a ball;
  My words would bandy her° to my sweet love,
  And his to me.                                            15
  But old folks, many feign as they were dead°—
  Unwieldy, slow, heavy and pale as lead.

*Enter Nurse [and Peter].*

  O God, she comes! O honey nurse, what news?
  Hast thou met with him? Send thy man away.

*Nurse.* Peter, stay at the gate.              [*Exit Peter.*]    20

*Juliet.* Now, good sweet nurse—O Lord, why lookest
    thou sad?
  Though news be sad, yet tell them merrily;

---

2.5.7 **nimble-pinioned doves** swift-winged doves (sacred to Venus)
14 **bandy her** speed her   16 **old . . . dead** i.e., many old people move
about as if they were almost dead

If good, thou shamest the music of sweet news
By playing it to me with so sour a face.

*Nurse.* I am aweary, give me leave awhile.
Fie, how my bones ache! What a jaunce° have I!

*Juliet.* I would thou hadst my bones, and I thy news.
Nay, come, I pray thee speak. Good, good nurse,
speak.

*Nurse.* Jesu, what haste! Can you not stay° awhile?
Do you not see that I am out of breath?

*Juliet.* How art thou out of breath when thou hast
breath
To say to me that thou art out of breath?
The excuse that thou dost make in this delay
Is longer than the tale thou dost excuse.
Is thy news good or bad? Answer to that.
Say either, and I'll stay the circumstance.°
Let me be satisfied, is't good or bad?

*Nurse.* Well, you have made a simple° choice; you
know not how to choose a man. Romeo? No, not
he. Though his face be better than any man's, yet
his leg excels all men's; and for a hand and a foot,
and a body, though they be not to be talked on,
yet they are past compare. He is not the flower of
courtesy, but, I'll warrant him, as gentle as a lamb.
Go thy ways, wench; serve God. What, have you
dined at home?

*Juliet.* No, no. But all this did I know before.
What says he of our marriage? What of that?

*Nurse.* Lord, how my head aches! What a head have I!
It beats as it would fall in twenty pieces.
My back a° t' other side—ah, my back, my back!
Beshrew° your heart for sending me about
To catch my death with jauncing up and down!

26 **jaunce** jaunt, fatiguing walk   29 **stay** wait   36 **stay the circumstance**
wait for the details   38 **simple** foolish   51 **a** on   52 **Beshrew** curse (in
the sense of "shame on")

*Juliet.* I' faith, I am sorry that thou art not well.
Sweet, sweet, sweet nurse, tell me, what says my
   love?  55

*Nurse.* Your love says, like an honest gentleman, and
a courteous, and a kind, and a handsome, and, I
warrant, a virtuous— Where is your mother?

*Juliet.* Where is my mother? Why, she is within.
Where should she be? How oddly thou repliest!  60
"Your love says, like an honest gentleman,
'Where is your mother?' "

*Nurse.*                              O God's Lady dear!
Are you so hot?° Marry come up, I trow.°
Is this the poultice for my aching bones?
Henceforward do your messages yourself.  65

*Juliet.* Here's such a coil!° Come, what says Romeo?

*Nurse.* Have you got leave to go to shrift today?

*Juliet.* I have.

*Nurse.* Then hie you hence to Friar Lawrence' cell;
There stays a husband to make you a wife.  70
Now comes the wanton blood up in your cheeks:
They'll be in scarlet straight° at any news.
Hie you to church; I must another way,
To fetch a ladder, by the which your love
Must climb a bird's nest soon when it is dark.  75
I am the drudge, and toil in your delight;
But you shall bear the burden soon at night.
Go; I'll to dinner; hie you to the cell.

*Juliet.* Hie to high fortune! Honest nurse, farewell.
                                   *Exeunt.*

---

63 **hot** angry   63 **Marry … trow** indeed, come now, by the Virgin
66 **coil** disturbance   72 **straight** straightway

[Scene 6. *Friar Lawrence's cell.*]

*Enter Friar [Lawrence] and Romeo.*

*Friar.* So smile the heavens upon this holy act
   That afterhours with sorrow chide us not!

*Romeo.* Amen, amen! But come what sorrow can,
   It cannot countervail° the exchange of joy
5   That one short minute gives me in her sight.
   Do thou but close our hands with holy words,
   Then love-devouring death do what he dare—
   It is enough I may but call her mine.

*Friar.* These violent delights have violent ends
10   And in their triumph die, like fire and powder,
   Which, as they kiss, consume. The sweetest honey
   Is loathsome in his own deliciousness
   And in the taste confounds° the appetite.
   Therefore love moderately: long love doth so;
15   Too swift arrives as tardy as too slow.

*Enter Juliet.*

   Here comes the lady. O, so light a foot
   Will ne'er wear out the everlasting flint.°
   A lover may bestride the gossamers°
   That idles in the wanton° summer air,
20   And yet not fall; so light is vanity.°

*Juliet.* Good even to my ghostly confessor.

*Friar.* Romeo shall thank thee, daughter, for us both.

---

2.6.4 **countervail** equal    13 **confounds** destroys    17 **Will . . . flint** i.e.,
Juliet's feet are lighter than waterdrops, which are proverbially said to
wear away stones    18 **gossamers** spiders' webs    19 **wanton** capricious
20 **vanity** a transitory thing (an earthly lover and his love)

*Juliet.* As much to him,° else is his thanks too much.

*Romeo.* Ah, Juliet, if the measure of thy joy
  Be heaped like mine, and that thy skill be more     25
  To blazon it,° then sweeten with thy breath
  This neighbor air, and let rich music's tongue
  Unfold the imagined happiness that both
  Receive in either by this dear encounter.

*Juliet.* Conceit, more rich in matter than in words,     30
  Brags of his substance, not of ornament.°
  They are but beggars that can count their worth;
  But my true love is grown to such excess
  I cannot sum up sum of half my wealth.

*Friar.* Come, come with me, and we will make short
    work;     35
  For, by your leaves, you shall not stay alone
  Till Holy Church incorporate two in one. [*Exeunt.*]

23 **As much to him** i.e., the same greeting to Romeo   25–26 **thy skill
... blazon it** you are better able to set it forth   30–31 **Conceit ...
ornament** i.e., true understanding is its own proud manifestation and
does not need words

# [ACT 3

## Scene 1. *A public place.*]

*Enter Mercutio, Benvolio, and Men.*

*Benvolio.* I pray thee, good Mercutio, let's retire.
  The day is hot, the Capels are abroad,
  And, if we meet, we shall not 'scape a brawl,
  For now, these hot days, is the mad blood stirring.

5  *Mercutio.* Thou art like one of these fellows that,
   when he enters the confines of a tavern, claps me
   his sword upon the table and says, "God send me
   no need of thee!" and by the operation of the
   second cup draws him on the drawer,° when indeed
10 there is no need.

*Benvolio.* Am I like such a fellow?

*Mercutio.* Come, come, thou art as hot a Jack in thy
   mood as any in Italy; and as soon moved to be
   moody,° and as soon moody to be moved.°

15 *Benvolio.* And what to?

*Mercutio.* Nay, and there were two such, we should
   have none shortly, for one would kill the other.
   Thou! Why, thou wilt quarrel with a man that hath

3.1.9 **draws him on the drawer** draws his sword on the waiter  14 **moody**
angry  14 **moody to be moved** quick-tempered

a hair more or a hair less in his beard than thou
hast. Thou wilt quarrel with a man for cracking    20
nuts, having no other reason but because thou hast
hazel eyes. What eye but such an eye would spy
out such a quarrel? Thy head is as full of quarrels
as an egg is full of meat; and yet thy head hath
been beaten as addle as an egg for quarreling. Thou    25
has quarreled with a man for coughing in the street,
because he hath wakened thy dog that hath lain
asleep in the sun. Didst thou not fall out with a
tailor for wearing his new doublet° before Easter?
With another for tying his new shoes with old    30
riband?° And yet thou wilt tutor me from quarreling!

*Benvolio.* And I were so apt to quarrel as thou art, any
man should buy the fee simple° of my life for an
hour and a quarter.°

*Mercutio.* The fee simple? O simple!°    35

    *Enter Tybalt, Petruchio,° and others.*

*Benvolio.* By my head, here comes the Capulets.

*Mercutio.* By my heel, I care not.

*Tybalt.* Follow me close, for I will speak to them.
Gentlemen, good-den.° A word with one of you.

*Mercutio.* And but one word with one of us? Couple    40
it with something; make it a word and a blow.

*Tybalt.* You shall find me apt enough to that, sir, and
you will give me occasion.

*Mercutio.* Could you not take some occasion without
giving?    45

*Tybalt.* Mercutio, thou consortest with Romeo.

---

29 **doublet** jacket   31 **riband** ribbon   33 **fee simple** absolute possession   33–34 **for an hour and a quarter** i.e., the life expectancy of
one with Mercutio's penchant for quarreling   35 **O simple** O stupid
35 **Petruchio** (in 1.5 he was one of Capulet's guests, but he has no
lines)   39 **good-den** good evening (i.e., afternoon)

*Mercutio.* Consort?° What, dost thou make us minstrels? And thou make minstrels of us, look to hear
nothing but discords. Here's my fiddlestick;° here's
50  that shall make you dance. Zounds,° consort!

*Benvolio.* We talk here in the public haunt of men.
Either withdraw unto some private place,
Or reason coldly of your grievances,
Or else depart. Here all eyes gaze on us.

*Mercutio.* Men's eyes were made to look, and let them
55      gaze.
I will not budge for no man's pleasure, I.

*Enter Romeo.*

*Tybalt.* Well, peace be with you, sir. Here comes my
man.°

*Mercutio.* But I'll be hanged, sir, if he wear your
livery.°
Marry, go before the field,° he'll be your follower!
60  Your worship in that sense may call him man.

*Tybalt.* Romeo, the love I bear thee can afford
No better term than this: thou art a villain.°

*Romeo.* Tybalt, the reason that I have to love thee
Doth much excuse the appertaining° rage
65  To such a greeting. Villain am I none.
Therefore farewell. I see thou knowest me not.

*Tybalt.* Boy, this shall not excuse the injuries
That thou hast done me; therefore turn and draw.

*Romeo.* I do protest I never injured thee,
70  But love thee better than thou canst devise°
Till thou shalt know the reason of my love;
And so, good Capulet, which name I tender°
As dearly as mine own, be satisfied.

---

47 **Consort** (1) to keep company with (2) company of musicians
49 **fiddlestick** i.e., sword  50 **Zounds** by God's wounds  57 **man**
(Mercutio takes this to mean "manservant")  58 **livery** servant's uniform  59 **field** dueling field  62 **villain** low fellow  64 **appertaining**
appropriate  70 **devise** imagine  72 **tender** value

*Mercutio.* O calm, dishonorable, vile submission!
    *Alla stoccata*° carries it away.     [*Draws.*]   75
    Tybalt, you ratcatcher, will you walk?°

*Tybalt.* What wouldst thou have with me?

*Mercutio.* Good King of Cats, nothing but one of your
    nine lives. That I mean to make bold withal,° and,
    as you shall use me hereafter, dry-beat° the rest of   80
    the eight. Will you pluck your sword out of his
    pilcher° by the ears? Make haste, lest mine be about
    your ears ere it be out.

*Tybalt.* I am for you.               [*Draws.*]

*Romeo.* Gentle Mercutio, put thy rapier up.   85

*Mercutio.* Come, sir, your *passado!*°   [*They fight.*]

*Romeo.* Draw, Benvolio; beat down their weapons.
    Gentlemen, for shame! Forbear this outrage!
    Tybalt, Mercutio, the Prince expressly hath
    Forbid this bandying° in Verona streets.   90
    Hold, Tybalt! Good Mercutio!
              [*Tybalt under Romeo's arm thrusts*
                     *Mercutio in, and flies.*]

*Mercutio.*               I am hurt.
    A plague a° both houses! I am sped.°
    Is he gone and hath nothing?

*Benvolio.*               What, art thou hurt?

*Mercutio.* Ay, ay, a scratch, a scratch. Marry, 'tis
    enough.
    Where is my page? Go, villain, fetch a surgeon.   95
                        [*Exit Page.*]

*Romeo.* Courage, man. The hurt cannot be much.

*Mercutio.* No, 'tis not so deep as a well, nor so wide

---

75 **Alla stoccata** (a term in fencing, "At the thrust," which Mercutio
uses contemptuously as a nickname for Tybalt)   76 **walk** step aside
79 **make bold withal** make bold with, take   80 **dry-beat** thrash
82 **pilcher** scabbard   86 **passado** lunge   90 **bandying** brawling   92 **a**
on   92 **sped** wounded

as a church door; but 'tis enough, 'twill serve. Ask
for me tomorrow, and you shall find me a grave°
100 man. I am peppered,° I warrant, for this world. A
plague a both your houses! Zounds, a dog, a rat, a
mouse, a cat, to scratch a man to death! A braggart,
a rogue, a villain, that fights by the book of arith-
metic!° Why the devil came you between us? I was
105 hurt under your arm.

*Romeo.* I thought all for the best.

*Mercutio.* Help me into some house, Benvolio,
  Or I shall faint. A plague a both your houses!
  They have made worms' meat of me. I have it,°
110 And soundly too. Your houses!
                    *Exit* [*Mercutio and Benvolio*].

*Romeo.* This gentleman, the Prince's near ally,°
  My very° friend, hath got this mortal hurt
  In my behalf—my reputation stained
  With Tybalt's slander—Tybalt, that an hour
115 Hath been my cousin. O sweet Juliet,
  Thy beauty hath made me effeminate
  And in my temper soft'ned valor's steel!°

                    *Enter Benvolio.*

*Benvolio.* O Romeo, Romeo, brave Mercutio is dead!
  That gallant spirit hath aspired° the clouds,
120 Which too untimely here did scorn the earth.

*Romeo.* This day's black fate on moe° days doth
    depend;°
  This but begins the woe others must end.

                    [*Enter Tybalt.*]

*Benvolio.* Here comes the furious Tybalt back again.

*Romeo.* Alive in triumph, and Mercutio slain?

99 **grave** (1) extremely serious (2) ready for the grave   100 **am peppered** have been given a deathblow   103–04 **by the book of arith-
metic** by formal rules   109 **I have it** i.e., I have received my deathblow
111 **ally** relative   112 **very** true   117 **in ... steel** softened the val-
orous part of my character   119 **aspired** climbed to   121 **moe** more
121 **depend** hang over

Away to heaven respective lenity,°                              *125*
And fire-eyed fury be my conduct° now!
Now, Tybalt, take the "villain" back again
That late thou gavest me; for Mercutio's soul
Is but a little way above our heads,
Staying for thine to keep him company.                         *130*
Either thou or I, or both, must go with him.

*Tybalt.* Thou, wretched boy, that didst consort him
    here,
  Shalt with him hence.

*Romeo.*                    This shall determine that.
                    *They fight. Tybalt falls.*

*Benvolio.* Romeo, away, be gone!
  The citizens are up, and Tybalt slain.                       *135*
  Stand not amazed. The Prince will doom thee death
  If thou art taken. Hence, be gone, away!

*Romeo.* O, I am fortune's fool!°

*Benvolio.*                    Why dost thou stay?
                      *Exit Romeo.*

        *Enter Citizens.*

*Citizen.* Which way ran he that killed Mercutio?
  Tybalt, that murderer, which way ran he?                     *140*

*Benvolio.* There lies that Tybalt.

*Citizen.*                    Up, sir, go with me.
  I charge thee in the Prince's name obey.

  *Enter Prince, old Montague, Capulet, their Wives,*
          *and all.*

*Prince.* Where are the vile beginners of this fray?

*Benvolio.* O noble Prince, I can discover° all
  The unlucky manage° of this fatal brawl.                     *145*

---

125 **respective lenity** discriminating mercifulness   126 **conduct** guide
138 **fool** plaything, dupe   144 **discover** reveal   145 **manage** course

There lies the man, slain by young Romeo,
That slew thy kinsman, brave Mercutio.

*Lady Capulet.* Tybalt, my cousin! O my brother's child!
   O Prince! O cousin! Husband! O, the blood is
   spilled
150 Of my dear kinsman! Prince, as thou art true,
For blood of ours shed blood of Montague.
O cousin, cousin!

*Prince.* Benvolio, who began this bloody fray?

*Benvolio.* Tybalt, here slain, whom Romeo's hand did
   slay.
155 Romeo, that spoke him fair, bid him bethink
How nice° the quarrel was, and urged° withal
Your high displeasure. All this—utterèd
With gentle breath, calm look, knees humbly
   bowed—
Could not take truce with the unruly spleen°
160 Of Tybalt deaf to peace, but that he tilts°
With piercing steel at bold Mercutio's breast;
Who, all as hot, turns deadly point to point,
And, with a martial scorn, with one hand beats
Cold death aside and with the other sends
165 It back to Tybalt, whose dexterity
Retorts it. Romeo he cries aloud,
"Hold, friends! Friends, part!" and swifter than his
   tongue,
His agile arm beats down their fatal points,
And 'twixt them rushes; underneath whose arm
170 An envious° thrust from Tybalt hit the life
Of stout Mercutio, and then Tybalt fled;
But by and by comes back to Romeo,
Who had but newly entertained° revenge,
And to't they go like lightning; for, ere I
175 Could draw to part them, was stout Tybalt slain;
And, as he fell, did Romeo turn and fly.
This is the truth, or let Benvolio die.

---

156 **nice** trivial   156 **urged** mentioned   159 **spleen** ill nature   160 **tilts**
thrusts   170 **envious** full of enmity   173 **entertained** contemplated

*Lady Capulet.* He is a kinsman to the Montague;
  Affection makes him false, he speaks not true.
  Some twenty of them fought in this black strife,          *180*
  And all those twenty could but kill one life.
  I beg for justice, which thou, Prince, must give.
  Romeo slew Tybalt; Romeo must not live.

*Prince.* Romeo slew him; he slew Mercutio.
  Who now the price of his dear blood doth owe?          *185*

*Capulet.* Not Romeo, Prince; he was Mercutio's friend;
  His fault concludes but what the law should end,
  The life of Tybalt.

*Prince.*                    And for that offense
  Immediately we do exile him hence.
  I have an interest in your hate's proceeding,          *190*
  My blood° for your rude brawls doth lie a-bleeding;
  But I'll amerce° you with so strong a fine
  That you shall all repent the loss of mine.
  I will be deaf to pleading and excuses;
  Nor tears nor prayers shall purchase out abuses.          *195*
  Therefore use none. Let Romeo hence in haste,
  Else, when he is found, that hour is his last.
  Bear hence this body and attend our will.°
  Mercy but murders, pardoning those that kill.
                              *Exit [with others].*


[Scene 2. *Capulet's orchard.*]


*Enter Juliet alone.*

*Juliet.* Gallop apace, you fiery-footed steeds,°
  Towards Phoebus' lodging!° Such a wagoner

191 **My blood** (Mercutio was the Prince's relative)   192 **amerce**
punish by fine   198 **attend our will** respect my decision   3.2.1 **fiery-
footed steeds** horses of the sun god, Phoebus   2 **Towards Phoebus'
lodging** i.e., beneath the horizon

As Phaëton° would whip you to the west
And bring in cloudy night immediately.
Spread thy close curtain, love-performing night,
That runaways'° eyes may wink,° and Romeo
Leap to these arms untalked of and unseen.
Lovers can see to do their amorous rites,
And by their own beauties; or, if love be blind,
It best agrees with night. Come, civil night,
Thou sober-suited matron all in black,
And learn me how to lose a winning match,
Played for a pair of stainless maidenhoods.
Hood° my unmanned° blood, bating° in my cheeks,
With thy black mantle till strange° love grow bold,
Think true love acted simple modesty.
Come, night; come, Romeo; come, thou day in
    night;
For thou wilt lie upon the wings of night
Whiter than new snow upon a raven's back.
Come, gentle night; come, loving, black-browed
    night;
Give me my Romeo; and, when I shall die,
Take him and cut him out in little stars,
And he will make the face of heaven so fine
That all the world will be in love with night
And pay no worship to the garish sun.
O, I have bought the mansion of a love,
But not possessed it; and though I am sold,
Not yet enjoyed. So tedious is this day
As is the night before some festival
To an impatient child that hath new robes
And may not wear them. O, here comes my nurse,

*Enter Nurse, with cords.*

And she brings news; and every tongue that speaks
But Romeo's name speaks heavenly eloquence.

---

3 **Phaëton** Phoebus' son, who mismanaged the horses and let them run
away   6 **runaways'** of the horses (?)   6 **wink** shut   14 **Hood** i.e., cover
with a hood, as in falconry   14 **unmanned** (1) untamed (2) unmated
14 **bating** fluttering   15 **strange** unfamiliar

Now, nurse, what news? What hast thou there, the
  cords
That Romeo bid thee fetch?

*Nurse.*                                        Ay, ay, the cords.          *35*

*Juliet.* Ay me! What news? Why dost thou wring thy
  hands?

*Nurse.* Ah, weraday!° He's dead, he's dead, he's dead!
  We are undone, lady, we are undone!
  Alack the day! He's gone, he's killed, he's dead!

*Juliet.* Can heaven be so envious?

*Nurse.*                                        Romeo can,          *40*
  Though heaven cannot. O Romeo, Romeo!
  Who ever would have thought it? Romeo!

*Juliet.* What devil art thou that dost torment me thus?
  This torture should be roared in dismal hell.
  Hath Romeo slain himself? Say thou but "Ay,"          *45*
  And that bare vowel "I" shall poison more
  Than the death-darting eye of cockatrice.°
  I am not I, if there be such an "Ay,"°
  Or those eyes' shot° that makes thee answer "Ay."
  If he be slain, say "Ay"; or if not, "No."          *50*
  Brief sounds determine of my weal or woe.

*Nurse.* I saw the wound, I saw it with mine eyes,
  (God save the mark!°) here on his manly breast.
  A piteous corse,° a bloody piteous corse;
  Pale, pale as ashes, all bedaubed in blood,          *55*
  All in gore-blood. I sounded° at the sight.

*Juliet.* O, break, my heart! Poor bankrout,° break at
  once!
  To prison, eyes; ne'er look on liberty!

---

37 **weraday** wellaway, alas   47 **cockatrice** basilisk (a serpent fabled to
have a killing glance)   48 **Ay** (1) I (2) eye   49 **eyes' shot** i.e., the
Nurse's glance   53 **God save the mark** God avert the bad omen
54 **corse** corpse   56 **sounded** swooned   57 **bankrout** bankrupt

Vile earth,° to earth resign° end motion here,
60    And thou and Romeo press one heavy bier!

*Nurse.* O Tybalt, Tybalt, the best friend I had!
    O courteous Tybalt! Honest gentleman!
    That ever I should live to see thee dead!

*Juliet.* What storm is this that blows so contrary?
65    Is Romeo slaught'red, and is Tybalt dead?
    My dearest cousin, and my dearer lord?
    Then, dreadful trumpet, sound the general doom!°
    For who is living, if those two are gone?

*Nurse.* Tybalt is gone, and Romeo banishèd;
70    Romeo that killed him, he is banishèd.

*Juliet.* O God! Did Romeo's hand shed Tybalt's
    blood?

*Nurse.* It did, it did! Alas the day, it did!

*Juliet.* O serpent heart, hid with a flow'ring face!
    Did ever dragon keep so fair a cave?
75    Beautiful tyrant! Fiend angelical!
    Dove-feathered raven! Wolvish-ravening lamb!
    Despisèd substance of divinest show!
    Just opposite to what thou justly seem'st—
    A damnèd saint, an honorable villain!
80    O nature, what hadst thou to do in hell
    When thou didst bower the spirit of a fiend
    In mortal paradise of such sweet flesh?
    Was ever book containing such vile matter
    So fairly bound? O, that deceit should dwell
    In such a gorgeous palace!

85    *Nurse.*                    There's no trust,
    No faith, no honesty in men; all perjured,
    All forsworn, all naught, all dissemblers.
    Ah, where's my man? Give me some *aqua vitae.*°
    These griefs, these woes, these sorrows make me
    old.

59 **vile earth** referring to her own body   59 **resign** return   67 **dreadful . . . doom** i.e., sound the trumpet of Doomsday   88 **aqua vitae** spirits

Shame come to Romeo!

*Juliet*                    Blistered be thy tongue   *90*
For such a wish! He was not born to shame.
Upon his brow shame is ashamed to sit;
For 'tis a throne where honor may be crowned
Sole monarch of the universal earth.
O, what a beast was I to chide at him!   *95*

*Nurse.* Will you speak well of him that killed your
   cousin?

*Juliet.* Shall I speak ill of him that is my husband?
Ah, poor my lord, what tongue shall smooth thy
   name
When I, thy three-hours wife, have mangled it?
But wherefore, villain, didst thou kill my cousin?   *100*
That villain cousin would have killed my husband.
Back, foolish tears, back to your native spring!
Your tributary° drops belong to woe,
Which you, mistaking, offer up to joy.
My husband lives, that Tybalt would have slain;   *105*
And Tybalt's dead, that would have slain my hus-
   band.
All this is comfort; wherefore weep I then?
Some word there was, worser than Tybalt's death,
That murd'red me. I would forget it fain;
But O, it presses to my memory   *110*
Like damnèd guilty deeds to sinners' minds!
"Tybalt is dead, and Romeo—banishèd."
That "banishèd," that one word "banishèd,"
Hath slain ten thousand Tybalts. Tybalt's death
Was woe enough, if it had ended there;   *115*
Or, if sour woe delights in fellowship
And needly will be ranked with° other griefs,
Why followed not, when she said "Tybalt's dead,"

---

103 **tributary** contributed   117 **needly ... with** must be accompanied by

Thy father, or thy mother, nay, or both,
120    Which modern° lamentation might have moved?
But with a rearward° following Tybalt's death,
"Romeo is banishèd"—to speak that word
Is father, mother, Tybalt, Romeo, Juliet,
All slain, all dead. "Romeo is banishèd"—
125    There is no end, no limit, measure, bound,
In that word's death; no words can that woe sound.
Where is my father and my mother, nurse?

*Nurse.* Weeping and wailing over Tybalt's corse.
Will you go to them? I will bring you thither.

*Juliet.* Wash they his wounds with tears? Mine shall be
130    spent,
When theirs are dry, for Romeo's banishment.
Take up those cords. Poor ropes, you are beguiled,
Both you and I, for Romeo is exiled.
He made you for a highway to my bed;
135    But I, a maid, die maiden-widowèd.
Come, cords; come, nurse. I'll to my wedding bed;
And death, not Romeo, take my maidenhead!

*Nurse.* Hic to your chamber. I'll find Romeo
To comfort you. I wot° well where he is.
140    Hark ye, your Romeo will be here at night.
I'll to him; he is hid at Lawrence' cell.

*Juliet.* O, find him! Give this ring to my true knight
And bid him come to take his last farewell.
                              *Exit [with Nurse].*


[Scene 3. *Friar Lawrence's cell.*]

*Enter Friar [Lawrence].*

*Friar.* Romeo, come forth; come forth, thou fearful°
man.
Affliction is enamored of thy parts,°
And thou art wedded to calamity.

120 **modern** ordinary  121 **rearward** rear guard  139 **wot** know
3.3.1 **fearful** frightened  2 **Affliction ... parts** affliction is in love
with your attractive qualities

[*Enter Romeo.*]

*Romeo.* Father, what news? What is the Prince's doom?°
　What sorrow craves acquaintance at my hand
　That I yet know not?　　　　　　　　　　　　　　*5*

*Friar.*　　　　　　　Too familiar
　Is my dear son with such sour company.
　I bring thee tidings of the Prince's doom.

*Romeo.* What less than doomsday° is the Prince's
　doom?

*Friar.* A gentler judgment vanished° from his lips—　*10*
　Not body's death, but body's banishment.

*Romeo.* Ha, banishment? Be merciful, say "death";
　For exile hath more terror in his look,
　Much more than death. Do not say "banishment."

*Friar.* Here from Verona art thou banishèd.　　　*15*
　Be patient, for the world is broad and wide.

*Romeo.* There is no world without Verona walls,
　But purgatory, torture, hell itself.
　Hence banishèd is banished from the world,
　And world's exile is death. Then "banishèd"
　Is death mistermed. Calling death "banishèd,"　　*20*
　Thou cut'st my head off with a golden ax
　And smilest upon the stroke that murders me.

*Friar.* O deadly sin! O rude unthankfulness!
　Thy fault our law calls death; but the kind Prince,　*25*
　Taking thy part, hath rushed° aside the law,
　And turned that black word "death" to "banish-
　　ment."
　This is dear mercy, and thou seest it not.

*Romeo.* 'Tis torture, and not mercy. Heaven is here,
　Where Juliet lives; and every cat and dog
　And little mouse, every unworthy thing,　　　　*30*
　Live here in heaven and may look on her;
　But Romeo may not. More validity,°

4 **doom** final decision　9 **doomsday** i.e., my death　10 **vanished** escaped
26 **rushed** pushed　33 **validity** value

More honorable state, more courtship° lives
35    In carrion flies than Romeo. They may seize
On the white wonder of dear Juliet's hand
And steal immortal blessing from her lips,
Who, even in pure and vestal° modesty,
Still blush, as thinking their own kisses sin;°
40    But Romeo may not, he is banishèd.
Flies may do this but I from this must fly;
They are freemen, but I am banishèd.
And sayest thou yet that exile is not death?
Hadst thou no poison mixture, no sharp-ground
    knife,
45    No sudden mean of death, though ne'er so mean,°
But "banishèd" to kill me—"banishèd"?
O friar, the damnèd use that word in hell;
Howling attends it! How hast thou the heart,
Being a divine, a ghostly confessor,
50    A sin-absolver, and my friend professed,
To mangle me with that word "banishèd"?

*Friar.* Thou fond° mad man, hear me a little speak.

*Romeo.* O, thou wilt speak again of banishment.

*Friar.* I'll give thee armor to keep off that word;
55    Adversity's sweet milk, philosophy,
To comfort thee, though thou art banishèd.

*Romeo.* Yet° "banishèd"? Hang up philosophy!
Unless philosophy can make a Juliet,
Displant a town, reverse a prince's doom,
60    It helps not, it prevails not. Talk no more.

*Friar.* O, then I see that madmen have no ears.

*Romeo.* How should they, when that wise men have
    no eyes?

*Friar.* Let me dispute° with thee of thy estate.°

---

34 **courtship** opportunity for courting   38 **vestal** virgin   39 **their own
kisses sin** i.e., sin when they touch each other   45 **mean ... mean**
method ... lowly   52 **fond** foolish   57 **Yet** still   63 **dispute** discuss
63 **estate** situation

*Romeo.* Thou canst not speak of that thou dost not
  feel.
  Wert thou as young as I, Juliet thy love,                        65
  An hour but married, Tybalt murderèd,
  Doting like me, and like me banishèd,
  Then mightst thou speak, then mightst thou tear thy
  hair,
  And fall upon the ground, as I do now,
  Taking the measure° of an unmade grave.                        70

                              *Enter Nurse and knock.*

*Friar.* Arise, one knocks. Good Romeo, hide thyself.

*Romeo.* Not I; unless the breath of heartsick groans
  Mistlike infold me from the search of eyes. [*Knock.*]

*Friar.* Hark, how they knock! Who's there? Romeo,
  arise;
  Thou wilt be taken.—Stay awhile!—Stand up;           75
                                               [*Knock.*]
  Run to my study.—By and by!°—God's will,
  What simpleness° is this.—I come, I come! *Knock.*
  Who knocks so hard? Whence come you? What's
  your will?

                              *Enter Nurse.*

*Nurse.* Let me come in, and you shall know my er-
  rand.
  I come from Lady Juliet.

*Friar.*                        Welcome then.                        80

*Nurse.* O holy friar, O, tell me, holy friar,
  Where is my lady's lord, where's Romeo?

*Friar.* There on the ground, with his own tears made
  drunk.

*Nurse.* O, he is even in my mistress' case,°

70 **Taking the measure** i.e., measuring by my outstretched body
76 **By and by** in a moment (said to the person knocking)    77 **simple-
ness** silly behavior (Romeo refuses to rise)    84 **case** (with bawdy innuendo complementing "stand," "rise," etc. But the Nurse is unaware of
this possible interpretation)

85      Just in her case! O woeful sympathy!
        Piteous predicament! Even so lies she,
        Blubb'ring and weeping, weeping and blubb'ring.
        Stand up, stand up! Stand, and you be a man.
        For Juliet's sake, for her sake, rise and stand!
90      Why should you fall into so deep an O?°

*Romeo.* [*Rises.*] Nurse—

*Nurse.* Ah sir, ah sir! Death's the end of all.

*Romeo.* Spakest thou of Juliet? How is it with her?
        Doth not she think me an old murderer,
95      Now I have stained the childhood of our joy
        With blood removed but little from her own?
        Where is she? And how doth she! And what says
        My concealed lady to our canceled° love?

*Nurse.* O, she says nothing, sir, but weeps and weeps;
100     And now falls on her bed, and then starts up,
        And Tybalt calls; and then on Romeo cries,
        And then down falls again.

*Romeo.*                         As if that name,
        Shot from the deadly level° of a gun,
        Did murder her; as that name's cursèd hand
105     Murdered her kinsman. O, tell me, friar, tell me,
        In what vile part of this anatomy
        Doth my name lodge? Tell me, that I may sack°
        The hateful mansion.
                    [*He offers to stab himself, and Nurse
                        snatches the dagger away.*]

*Friar.*                    Hold thy desperate hand.
        Art thou a man? Thy form cries out thou art;
110     Thy tears are womanish, thy wild acts denote
        The unreasonable° fury of a beast.
        Unseemly° woman in a seeming man!
        And ill-beseeming beast in seeming both!°

90 **so deep an O** such a fit of moaning    98 **canceled** invalidated
103 **level** aim    107 **sack** plunder    111 **unreasonable** irrational    112 **Unseemly** indecorous    113 **ill-beseeming . . . both** i.e., inappropriate even
to a beast in being both man and woman

Thou hast amazed me. By my holy order,
I thought thy disposition better tempered.                         *115*
Hast thou slain Tybalt? Wilt thou slay thyself?
And slay thy lady that in thy life lives,
By doing damnèd hate upon thyself?
Why railest thou on thy birth, the heaven, and
   earth?
Since birth and heaven and earth,° all three do meet   *120*
In thee at once; which thou at once wouldst lose.°
Fie, fie, thou shamest thy shape, thy love, thy wit,°
Which,° like a usurer, abound'st in all,
And usest none in that true use indeed
Which should bedeck° thy shape, thy love, thy wit.   *125*
Thy noble shape is but a form of wax,
Digressing from the valor of a man;°
Thy dear love sworn but hollow perjury,
Killing that love which thou hast vowed to cherish;
Thy wit, that ornament to shape and love,              *130*
Misshapen in the conduct° of them both,
Like powder in a skilless soldier's flask,°
Is set afire by thine own ignorance,
And thou dismemb'red with thine own defense.°
What, rouse thee, man! Thy Juliet is alive,            *135*
For whose dear sake thou wast but lately dead.°
There are thou happy.° Tybalt would kill thee,
But thou slewest Tybalt. There art thou happy.
The law, that threat'ned death, becomes thy friend
And turns it to exile. There art thou happy.           *140*
A pack of blessings light upon thy back;
Happiness courts thee in her best array;
But, like a misbehaved and sullen wench,
Thou puts up thy fortune and thy love.
Take heed, take heed, for such die miserable.          *145*

---

**120 birth and heaven and earth** family origin, soul, and body    **121 lose**
abandon    **122 wit** intellect    **123 Which** who    **125 bedeck** do honor to
**127 valor of a man** i.e., his manly qualities    **131 conduct** management
**132 flask** powder flask    **134 dismemb'red ... defense** (i.e., your intellect, properly the defender of shape and love, is set off independently
and destroys all)    **136 dead** i.e., declaring yourself dead    **137 happy**
fortunate

Go get thee to thy love, as was decreed,
Ascend her chamber, hence and comfort her.
But look thou stay not till the watch be set,
For then thou canst not pass to Mantua,
150   Where thou shalt live till we can find a time
To blaze° your marriage, reconcile your friends,
Beg pardon of the Prince, and call thee back
With twenty hundred thousand times more joy
Than thou went'st forth in lamentation.
155   Go before, nurse. Commend me to thy lady,
And bid her hasten all the house to bed,
Which heavy sorrow makes them apt unto.
Romeo is coming.

*Nurse.* O Lord, I could have stayed here all the night
160   To hear good counsel. O, what learning is!
My lord, I'll tell my lady you will come.

*Romeo.* Do so, and bid my sweet prepare to chide.
           [*Nurse offers to go in and turns again.*]

*Nurse.* Here, sir, a ring she bid me give you, sir.
Hie you, make haste, for it grows very late. [*Exit.*]

165  *Romeo.* How well my comfort is revived by this!

*Friar.* Go hence; good night; and here stands all your
state:°
Either be gone before the watch be set,
Or by the break of day disguised from hence.
Sojourn in Mantua. I'll find out your man,
170   And he shall signify from time to time
Every good hap to you that chances here.
Give me thy hand. 'Tis late. Farewell; good night.

*Romeo.* But that a joy past joy calls out on me,
It were a grief so brief to part with thee.
175   Farewell.                                    *Exeunt.*

151 **blaze** announce publicly   166 **here . . . state** this is your situation

[Scene 4. *A room in Capulet's house.*]

*Enter old Capulet, his Wife, and Paris.*

*Capulet.* Things have fall'n out, sir, so unluckily
 That we have had no time to move° our daughter.
 Look you, she loved her kinsman Tybalt dearly,
 And so did I. Well, we were born to die.
 'Tis very late; she'll not come down tonight.                    5
 I promise° you, but for your company,
 I would have been abed an hour ago.

*Paris.* These times of woe afford no times to woo.
 Madam, good night. Commend me to your daughter.

*Lady Capulet.* I will, and know her mind early tomorrow;    10
 Tonight she's mewed up to her heaviness.°

*Capulet.* Sir Paris, I will make a desperate tender°
 Of my child's love. I think she will be ruled
 In all respects by me; nay more, I doubt it not.
 Wife, go you to her ere you go to bed;                           15
 Acquaint her here of my son Paris' love
 And bid her (mark you me?) on Wednesday next—
 But soft! What day is this?

*Paris.*                                Monday, my lord.

*Capulet.* Monday! Ha, ha! Well, Wednesday is too
    soon.
 A° Thursday let it be—a Thursday, tell her,                     20
 She shall be married to this noble earl.
 Will you be ready? Do you like this haste?
 We'll keep no great ado—a friend or two;
 For hark you, Tybalt being slain so late,

3.4.2 **move** discuss the matter with   6 **promise** assure   11 **mewed . . .
heaviness** shut up with her grief ·  12 **make . . . tender** risk an offer
20 **A** on

25      It may be thought we held him carelessly,
        Being our kinsman, if we revel much.
        Therefore we'll have some half a dozen friends,
        And there an end. But what say you to Thursday?

*Paris.* My lord, I would that Thursday were tomorrow.

30   *Capulet.* Well, get you gone. A Thursday be it then.
        Go you to Juliet ere you go to bed;
        Prepare her, wife, against° this wedding day.
        Farewell, my lord.—Light to my chamber, ho!
        Afore me,° it is so very late
35      That we may call it early by and by.°
        Good night                                    *Exeunt.*


[Scene 5. *Capulet's orchard.*]


*Enter Romeo and Juliet aloft.*


*Juliet.* Wilt thou be gone? It is not yet near day.
        It was the nightingale, and not the lark,
        That pierced the fearful° hollow of thine ear.
        Nightly she sings on yond pomegranate tree.
5       Believe me, love, it was the nightingale.

*Romeo.* It was the lark, the herald of the morn;
        No nightingale. Look, love, what envious streaks
        Do lace the severing clouds in yonder East.
        Night's candles are burnt out, and jocund day
10      Stands tiptoe on the misty mountaintops.
        I must be gone and live, or stay and die.

*Juliet.* Yond light is not daylight; I know it, I.
        It is some meteor that the sun exhales°
        To be to thee this night a torchbearer
15      And light thee on thy way to Mantua.


32 **against** in preparation for   34 **Afore me** indeed (a light oath)   35 **by
and by** soon   3.5.3 **fearful** fearing   13 **exhales** gives out

Therefore stay yet; thou need'st not to be gone.

*Romeo.* Let me be ta'en, let me be put to death.
I am content, so thou wilt have it so.
I'll say yon gray is not the morning's eye,
'Tis but the pale reflex of Cynthia's brow;°          20
Nor that is not the lark whose notes do beat
The vaulty heaven so high above our heads.
I have more care to stay than will to go.
Come, death, and welcome! Juliet wills it so.
How is't, my soul? Let's talk; it is not day.          25

*Juliet.* It is, it is! Hie hence, be gone, away!
It is the lark that sings so out of tune,
Straining harsh discords and unpleasing sharps.
Some say the lark makes sweet division;°
This doth not so, for she divideth us.          30
Some say the lark and loathèd toad change eyes;
O, now I would they had changed voices too,
Since arm from arm that voice doth us affray,°
Hunting thee hence with hunt's-up° to the day.
O, now be gone! More light and light it grows.          35

*Romeo.* More light and light—more dark and dark
our woes.

                    *Enter Nurse.*

*Nurse.* Madam!

*Juliet.* Nurse?

*Nurse.* Your lady mother is coming to your chamber.
The day is broke; be wary, look about.          [*Exit.*]          40

*Juliet.* Then, window, let day in, and let life out.

*Romeo.* Farewell, farewell! One kiss, and I'll descend.
                                        [*He goeth down.*]

*Juliet.* Art thou gone so, love-lord, ay husband-friend?°

---

20 **reflex of Cynthia's brow** reflection of the edge of the moon     29 **division** melody (i.e., a division of notes)     33 **affray** frighten     34 **hunt's-up** morning song (for hunters)     43 **husband-friend** husband-lover

I must hear from thee every day in the hour,
45 For in a minute there are many days.
O, by this count I shall be much in years°
Ere I again behold my Romeo!

*Romeo.* Farewell!
I will omit no opportunity
50 That may convey my greetings, love, to thee.

*Juliet.* O, think'st thou we shall ever meet again?

*Romeo.* I doubt it not; and all these woes shall serve
For sweet discourses in our times to come.

*Juliet.* O God, I have an ill-divining° soul!
55 Methinks I see thee, now thou art so low,
As one dead in the bottom of a tomb.
Either my eyesight fails, or thou lookest pale.

*Romeo.* And trust me, love, in my eye so do you.
Dry° sorrow drinks our blood. Adieu, adieu! *Exit.*

60 *Juliet.* O Fortune, Fortune! All men call thee fickle.
If thou art fickle, what dost thou° with him
That is renowned for faith? Be fickle, Fortune,
For then I hope thou wilt not keep him long
But send him back.

*Enter Mother.*

65 *Lady Capulet.* Ho, daughter! Are you up?

*Juliet.* Who is't that calls? It is my lady mother.
Is she not down so late,° or up so early?
What unaccustomed cause procures her hither?

*Lady Capulet.* Why, how now, Juliet?

*Juliet.*        Madam, I am not well.

*Lady Capulet.* Evermore weeping for your cousin's
70 death?

---

46 **much in years** much older 54 **ill-divining** foreseeing evil 59 **Dry**
thirsty (as grief was thought to be) 61 **what dost thou** what business
have you 67 **not down so late** so late getting to bed

What, wilt thou wash him from his grave with tears?
And if thou couldst, thou couldst not make him live.
Therefore have done. Some grief shows much of
    love;
But much of grief shows still some want of wit.

*Juliet.* Yet let me weep for such a feeling loss.° 75

*Lady Capulet.* So shall you feel the loss, but not the
    friend
Which you weep for.

*Juliet.*                          Feeling so the loss,
I cannot choose but ever weep the friend.

*Lady Capulet.* Well, girl, thou weep'st not so much for
    his death
As that the villain lives which slaughtered him. 80

*Juliet.* What villain, madam?

*Lady Capulet.*                          That same villain Romeo.

*Juliet.* [*Aside*] Villain and he be many miles asunder.—
God pardon him! I do, with all my heart;
And yet no man like he doth grieve my heart.

*Lady Capulet.* That is because the traitor murderer
    lives. 85

*Juliet.* Ay, madam, from the reach of these my hands.
Would none but I might venge my cousin's death!

*Lady Capulet.* We will have vengeance for it, fear
    thou not.
Then weep no more. I'll send to one in Mantua,
Where that same banished runagate° doth live, 90
Shall give him such an unaccustomed dram
That he shall soon keep Tybalt company;
And then I hope thou wilt be satisfied.

*Juliet.* Indeed I never shall be satisfied
With Romeo till I behold him—dead°— 95

75 **feeling loss** loss to be felt   90 **runagate** renegade   95 **dead** (Lady
Capulet takes this to refer to "him"; Juliet takes it to refer to "heart")

Is my poor heart so for a kinsman vexed.
Madam, if you could find out but a man
To bear a poison, I would temper° it;
That Romeo should, upon receipt thereof,
100 Soon sleep in quiet. O, how my heart abhors
To hear him named and cannot come to him,
To wreak° the love I bore my cousin
Upon his body that hath slaughtered him!

*Lady Capulet.* Find thou the means, and I'll find such
a man.
105 But now I'll tell thee joyful tidings, girl.

*Juliet.* And joy comes well in such a needy time.
What are they, beseech your ladyship?

*Lady Capulet.* Well, well, thou hast a careful° father,
child;
One who, to put thee from thy heaviness,
110 Hath sorted out° a sudden day of joy
That thou expects not nor I looked not for.

*Juliet.* Madam, in happy time!° What day is that?

*Lady Capulet.* Marry, my child, early next Thursday
morn
The gallant, young, and noble gentleman,
115 The County Paris, at Saint Peter's Church,
Shall happily make thee there a joyful bride.

*Juliet.* Now by Saint Peter's Church, and Peter too,
He shall not make me there a joyful bride!
I wonder at this haste, that I must wed
120 Ere he that should be husband comes to woo.
I pray you tell my lord and father, madam,
I will not marry yet; and when I do, I swear
It shall be Romeo, whom you know I hate,
Rather than Paris. These are news indeed!

---

98 **temper** (1) mix (2) weaken
sion to   108 **careful** solicitous
**time** most opportunely   102 **wreak** (1) avenge (2) give expres-
110 **sorted out** selected   112 **in happy**

*Lady Capulet.* Here comes your father. Tell him so
    yourself,                                  *125*
    And see how he will take it at your hands.

          *Enter Capulet and Nurse.*

*Capulet.* When the sun sets the earth doth drizzle dew,
    But for the sunset of my brother's son
    It rains downright.
    How now? A conduit,° girl? What, still in tears?    *130*
    Evermore show'ring? In one little body
    Thou counterfeits a bark, a sea, a wind:
    For still thy eyes, which I may call the sea,
    Do ebb and flow with tears; the bark thy body is,
    Sailing in this salt flood; the winds, thy sighs,    *135*
    Who, raging with thy tears and they with them,
    Without a sudden° calm will overset
    Thy tempest-tossèd body. How now, wife?
    Have you delivered to her our decree?

*Lady Capulet.* Ay, sir; but she will none, she gives
    you thanks.°                                *140*
    I would the fool were married to her grave!

*Capulet.* Soft! Take me with you,° take me with you,
    wife.
    How? Will she none? Doth she not give us thanks?
    Is she not proud? Doth she not count her blest,
    Unworthy as she is, that we have wrought°    *145*
    So worthy a gentleman to be her bride?

*Juliet.* Not proud° you have, but thankful that you
    have.
    Proud can I never be of what I hate,
    But thankful even for hate that is meant love.

*Capulet.* How, how, how, how, chopped-logic?° What
    is this?                                   *150*

---

130 **conduit** water pipe   137 **sudden** unanticipated, immediate   140 **she
gives you thanks** she'll have none of it, thank you   142 **Soft ... you**
Wait! Help me to understand you   145 **wrought** arranged   147 **proud**
highly pleased   150 **chopped-logic** chop logic, sophistry

"Proud"—and "I thank you"—and "I thank you
  not"—
And yet "not proud"? Mistress minion° you,
Thank me no thankings, nor proud me no prouds,
But fettle° your fine joints 'gainst Thursday next
To go with Paris to Saint Peter's Church,
Or I will drag thee on a hurdle° thither.
Out, you greensickness° carrion! Out, you baggage!°
You tallow-face!

*Lady Capulet.*      Fie, fie! What, are you mad?

*Juliet.* Good father, I beseech you on my knees,
Hear me with patience but to speak a word.

*Capulet.* Hang thee, young baggage! Disobedient
  wretch!
I tell thee what—get thee to church a Thursday
Or never after look me in the face.
Speak not, reply not, do not answer me!
My fingers itch. Wife, we scarce thought us blest
That God had lent us but this only child;
But now I see this one is one too much,
And that we have a curse in having her.
Out on her, hilding!°

*Nurse.*          God in heaven bless her!
You are to blame, my lord, to rate° her so.

*Capulet.* And why, my Lady Wisdom? Hold your
  tongue,
Good Prudence. Smatter with your gossips,° go!

*Nurse.* I speak no treason.

*Capulet.*         O, God-i-god-en!°

*Nurse.* May not one speak?

---

152 **minion** minx   154 **fettle** make ready   156 **hurdle** sledge on which
traitors were taken to execution   157 **greensickness** anemic, after the
fashion of young girls   157 **baggage** strumpet   169 **hilding** worthless
person   170 **rate** scold   172 **Smatter with your gossips** save your
chatter for your cronies   173 **God-i-god-en** God give you good even
(here equivalent to "Get on with you!")

*Capulet.*                    Peace, you mumbling fool!
  Utter your gravity o'er a gossip's bowl,                    *175*
  For here we need it not.

*Lady Capulet.*              You are too hot.

*Capulet.* God's bread!° It makes me mad.
  Day, night; hour, tide, time; work, play;
  Alone, in company; still my care hath been
  To have her matched; and having now provided                    *180*
  A gentleman of noble parentage,
  Of fair demesnes,° youthful, and nobly trained,
  Stuffed, as they say, with honorable parts,
  Proportioned as one's thought would wish a man—
  And then to have a wretched puling° fool,                    *185*
  A whining mammet,° in her fortune's tender,°
  To answer "I'll not wed, I cannot love;
  I am too young, I pray you pardon me"!
  But, and you will not wed, I'll pardon you!°
  Graze where you will, you shall not house with me.                    *190*
  Look to't, think on't; I do not use to jest.°
  Thursday is near; lay hand on heart, advise:°
  And you be mine, I'll give you to my friend;
  And you be not, hang, beg, starve, die in the streets,
  For, by my soul, I'll ne'er acknowledge thee,                    *195*
  Nor what is mine shall never do thee good.
  Trust to't. Bethink you. I'll not be forsworn.      *Exit.*

*Juliet.* Is there no pity sitting in the clouds
  That sees into the bottom of my grief?
  O sweet my mother, cast me not away!                    *200*
  Delay this marriage for a month, a week;
  Or if you do not, make the bridal bed
  In that dim monument where Tybalt lies.

*Lady Capulet.* Talk not to me, for I'll not speak a
  word.

---

177 **God's bread** by the sacred host   182 **demesnes** domains
185 **puling** whining   186 **mammet** puppet   186 **in her fortune's tender** (1) on good fortune's offer (2) subject to fortuitous circumstance (?)
189 **I'll pardon you** i.e., in a way you don't expect   191 **do not use to jest** am not in the habit of joking   192 **advise** consider

205     Do as thou wilt, for I have done with thee.     *Exit.*

*Juliet.* O God!—O nurse, how shall this be prevented?
My husband is on earth, my faith in heaven.°
How shall that faith return again to earth
Unless that husband send it me from heaven
210     By leaving earth?° Comfort me, counsel me.
Alack, alack, that heaven should practice stratagems
Upon so soft a subject as myself!
What say'st thou? Hast thou not a word of joy?
Some comfort, nurse.

*Nurse.*                    Faith, here it is.
215     Romeo is banished; and all the world to nothing°
That he dares ne'er come back to challenge you;
Or if he do, it needs must be by stealth.
Then, since the case so stands as now it doth,
I think it best you married with the County.
220     O, he's a lovely gentleman!
Romeo's a dishclout° to him. An eagle, madam,
Hath not so green, so quick, so fair an eye
As Paris hath. Beshrew° my very heart,
I think you are happy in this second match,
225     For it excels your first; or if it did not,
Your first is dead—or 'twere as good he were
As living here and you no use of him.

*Juliet.* Speak'st thou from thy heart?

*Nurse.* And from my soul too; else beshrew them both.

230     *Juliet.* Amen!

*Nurse.* What?

*Juliet.* Well, thou hast comforted me marvelous much.
Go in; and tell my lady I am gone,
Having displeased my father, to Lawrence' cell,
235     To make confession and to be absolved.

207 **my faith in heaven** my vow is recorded in heaven   210 **By leaving earth** i.e., by dying   215 **all the world to nothing** (the Nurse advises a safe bet)   221 **dishclout** dishcloth   223 **Beshrew** curse (used in light oaths)

*Nurse.* Marry, I will; and this is wisely done.   [*Exit.*]

*Juliet.* Ancient damnation!° O most wicked fiend!
  Is it more sin to wish me thus forsworn,°
  Or to dispraise my lord with that same tongue
  Which she hath praised him with above compare    240
  So many thousand times? Go, counselor!
  Thou and my bosom henceforth shall be twain.°
  I'll to the friar to know his remedy.
  If all else fail, myself have power to die.         *Exit.*

---

237 **Ancient damnation** (1) damned old woman (2) ancient devil (note
the term "wicked fiend" immediately following)   238 **forsworn** guilty
of breaking a vow   242 **Thou ... twain** i.e., you shall henceforth be
separated from my trust

# [ACT 4

### Scene 1. *Friar Lawrence's cell.*]

*Enter Friar [Lawrence] and County Paris.*

*Friar.* On Thursday, sir? The time is very short.

*Paris.* My father Capulet will have it so,
And I am nothing slow to slack his haste.°

*Friar.* You say you do not know the lady's mind.
5      Uneven° is the course; I like it not.

*Paris.* Immoderately she weeps for Tybalt's death,
And therefore have I little talked of love;
For Venus smiles not in a house of tears.
Now, sir, her father counts it dangerous
10    That she do give her sorrow so much sway,
And in his wisdom hastes our marriage
To stop the inundation of her tears,
Which, too much minded° by herself alone,°
May be put from her by society.
15    Now do you know the reason of this haste.

*Friar.* [*Aside*] I would I knew not why it should be
      slowed.—
Look, sir, here comes the lady toward my cell.

---

4.1.3 **I . . . haste** i.e., I shall not check his haste by being slow myself
5 **Uneven** irregular   13 **minded** thought about   13 **by herself alone**
when she is alone

*Enter Juliet.*

*Paris.* Happily met, my lady and my wife!

*Juliet.* That may be, sir, when I may be a wife.

*Paris.* That "may be" must be, love, on Thursday next. 20

*Juliet.* What must be shall be.

*Friar.* That's a certain text.

*Paris.* Come you to make confession to this father?

*Juliet.* To answer that, I should confess to you.

*Paris.* Do not deny to him that you love me.

*Juliet.* I confess to you that I love him. 25

*Paris.* So will ye, I am sure, that you love me.

*Juliet.* If I do so, it will be of more price,
Being spoke behind your back, than to your face.

*Paris.* Poor soul, thy face is much abused with tears.

*Juliet.* The tears have got small victory by that, 30
For it was bad enough before their spite.°

*Paris.* Thou wrong'st it more than tears with that
report.

*Juliet.* That is no slander, sir, which is a truth;
And what I spake, I spake it to my face.

*Paris.* Thy face is mine, and thou hast sland'red it. 35

*Juliet.* It may be so, for it is not mine own.
Are you at leisure, holy father, now,
Or shall I come to you at evening mass?°

*Friar.* My leisure serves me, pensive daughter, now.
My lord, we must entreat the time alone.° 40

---

31 **before their spite** before they marred it    38 **evening mass** (evening
mass was still said occasionally in Shakespeare's time)    40 **entreat the
time alone** ask to have this time to ourselves

*Paris.* God shield° I should disturb devotion!
    Juliet, on Thursday early will I rouse ye.
    Till then, adieu, and keep this holy kiss.    *Exit.*

*Juliet.* O, shut the door, and when thou hast done so,
    Come weep with me—past hope, past care, past
45    help!

*Friar.* O Juliet, I already know thy grief;
    It strains me past the compass of my wits.
    I hear thou must, and nothing may prorogue° it,
    On Thursday next be married to this County.

50 *Juliet.* Tell me not, friar, that thou hearest of this,
    Unless thou tell me how I may prevent it.
    If in thy wisdom thou canst give no help,
    Do thou but call my resolution wise
    And with this knife I'll help it presently.°
55    God joined my heart and Romeo's, thou our hands;
    And ere this hand, by thee to Romeo's sealed,
    Shall be the label° to another deed,°
    Or my true heart with treacherous revolt
    Turn to another, this shall slay them both.
60    Therefore, out of thy long-experienced time,
    Give me some present counsel; or, behold,
    'Twixt my extremes and me this bloody knife
    Shall play the umpire, arbitrating that
    Which the commission° of thy years and art
65    Could to no issue of true honor bring.
    Be not so long to speak. I long to die
    If what thou speak'st speak not of remedy.

*Friar.* Hold, daughter. I do spy a kind of hope,
    Which craves as desperate an execution
70    As that is desperate which we would prevent.
    If, rather than to marry County Paris,
    Thou hast the strength of will to slay thyself,
    Then is it likely thou wilt undertake

41 **God shield** God forbid   48 **prorogue** delay   54 **presently** at once
57 **label** bearer of the seal   57 **deed** (1) act (2) legal document   64 **com-
mission** authority

A thing like death to chide away this shame,
That cop'st° with death himself to scape from it;     75
And, if thou darest, I'll give thee remedy.

*Juliet.* O, bid me leap, rather than marry Paris,
From off the battlements of any tower,
Or walk in thievish° ways, or bid me lurk
Where serpents are; chain me with roaring bears,     80
Or hide me nightly in a charnel house,°
O'ercovered quite with dead men's rattling bones,
With reeky° shanks and yellow chapless° skulls;
Or bid me go into a new-made grave
And hide me with a dead man in his shroud—     85
Things that, to hear them told, have made me
    tremble—
And I will do it without fear or doubt,
To live an unstained wife to my sweet love.

*Friar.* Hold, then. Go home, be merry, give consent
To marry Paris. Wednesday is tomorrow.     90
Tomorrow night look that thou lie alone;
Let not the nurse lie with thee in thy chamber.
Take thou this vial, being then in bed,
And this distilling° liquor drink thou off;
When presently through all thy veins shall run     95
A cold and drowsy humor;° for no pulse
Shall keep his native° progress, but surcease;°
No warmth, no breath, shall testify thou livest;
The roses in thy lips and cheeks shall fade
To wanny° ashes, thy eyes' windows° fall     100
Like death when he shuts up the day of life;
Each part, deprived of supple government,°
Shall, stiff and stark and cold, appear like death;
And in this borrowed likeness of shrunk death
Thou shalt continue two-and-forty hours,     105
And then awake as from a pleasant sleep.

---

75 **cop'st** negotiates  79 **thievish** infested with thieves  81 **charnel house** vault for old bones  83 **reeky** damp  83 **chapless** jawless  94 **distilling** infusing  96 **humor** fluid  97 **native** natural  97 **surcease** stop  100 **wanny** pale  100 **windows** lids  102 **supple government** i.e., faculty for maintaining motion

Now, when the bridegroom in the morning comes
To rouse thee from thy bed, there art thou dead.
Then, as the manner of our country is,
110 In thy best robes uncovered on the bier
Thou shalt be borne to that same ancient vault
Where all the kindred of the Capulets lie.
In the meantime, against° thou shalt awake,
Shall Romeo by my letters know our drift;°
115 And hither shall he come; and he and I
Will watch thy waking, and that very night
Shall Romeo bear thee hence to Mantua.
And this shall free thee from this present shame,
If no inconstant toy° nor womanish fear
120 Abate thy valor in the acting it.

*Juliet.* Give me, give me! O, tell not me of fear!

*Friar.* Hold! Get you gone, be strong and prosperous
In this resolve. I'll send a friar with speed
To Mantua, with my letters to thy lord.

*Juliet.* Love give me strength, and strength shall help
125     afford.
Farewell, dear father.                    *Exit [with Friar].*



[Scene 2. *Hall in Capulet's house.*]


*Enter Father Capulet, Mother, Nurse, and
Servingmen, two or three.*

*Capulet.* So many guests invite as here are writ.
                    [*Exit a Servingman.*]
Sirrah, go hire me twenty cunning° cooks.

*Servingman.* You shall have none ill, sir; for I'll try°
if they can lick their fingers.

---

113 **against** before   114 **drift** purpose   119 **inconstant toy** whim
4.2.2 **cunning** skillful   3 **try** test

*Capulet.* How canst thou try them so?                              5

*Servingman.* Marry, sir, 'tis an ill cook that cannot
  lick his own fingers.° Therefore he that cannot lick
  his fingers goes not with me.

*Capulet.* Go, begone.                    [*Exit Servingman.*]
  We shall be much unfurnished° for this time.                     10
  What, is my daughter gone to Friar Lawrence?

*Nurse.* Ay, forsooth.

*Capulet.* Well, he may chance to do some good on her.
  A peevish self-willed harlotry it is.°

                    *Enter Juliet.*

*Nurse.* See where she comes from shrift with merry
  look.                                                            15

*Capulet.* How now, my headstrong? Where have you
  been gadding?

*Juliet.* Where I have learnt me to repent the sin
  Of disobedient opposition
  To you and your behests, and am enjoined
  By holy Lawrence to fall prostrate here                          20
  To beg your pardon. Pardon, I beseech you!
  Henceforward I am ever ruled by you.

*Capulet.* Send for the County. Go tell him of this.
  I'll have this knot knit up tomorrow morning.

*Juliet.* I met the youthful lord at Lawrence' cell                25
  And gave him what becomèd° love I might,
  Not stepping o'er the bounds of modesty.

*Capulet.* Why, I am glad on't. This is well. Stand up.
  This is as't should be. Let me see the County.
  Ay, marry, go, I say, and fetch him hither.                      30
  Now, afore God, this reverend holy friar,
  All our whole city is much bound to him.

---

6–7 **cannot lick his own fingers** i.e., cannot taste his own cooking
10 **unfurnished** unprovisioned   14 **A peevish self-willed harlotry it is**
she's a silly good-for-nothing   26 **becomèd** proper

*Juliet.* Nurse, will you go with me into my closet°
    To help me sort such needful ornaments
35  As you think fit to furnish me tomorrow?

*Lady Capulet.* No, not till Thursday. There is time
    enough.

*Capulet.* Go, nurse, go with her. We'll to church
    tomorrow.                    *Exeunt [Juliet and Nurse].*

*Lady Capulet.* We shall be short in our provision.
    'Tis now near night.

*Capulet.*                    Tush, I will stir about,
40  And all things shall be well, I warrant thee, wife.
    Go thou to Juliet, help to deck up her.
    I'll not to bed tonight; let me alone.
    I'll play the housewife for this once. What, ho!
    They are all forth; well, I will walk myself
45  To County Paris, to prepare up him
    Against° tomorrow. My heart is wondrous light,
    Since this same wayward girl is so reclaimed.
                            *Exit [with Mother].*

[Scene 3. *Juliet's chamber.*]

*Enter Juliet and Nurse.*

*Juliet.* Ay, those attires are best; but, gentle nurse,
    I pray thee leave me to myself tonight;
    For I have need of many orisons°
    To move the heavens to smile upon my state,°
5  Which, well thou knowest, is cross° and full of sin.

*Enter Mother.*

*Lady Capulet.* What, are you busy, ho? Need you my
    help?

33 **closet** private chamber   46 **Against** in anticipation of   4.3.3 **orisons**
prayers   4 **state** condition   5 **cross** perverse

*Juliet.* No, madam; we have culled such necessaries
    As arc behoveful° for our state° tomorrow.
    So please you, let me now be left alone,
    And let the nurse this night sit up with you;                    *10*
    For I am sure you have your hands full all
    In this so sudden business.

*Lady Capulet.*              Good night.
    Get thee to bed, and rest; for thou hast need.
                            *Exeunt [Mother and Nurse].*

*Juliet.* Farewell! God knows when we shall meet again.
    I have a faint° cold fear thrills through my veins            *15*
    That almost freezes up the heat of life.
    I'll call them back again to comfort me.
    Nurse!—What should she do here?
    My dismal scene I needs must act alone.
    Come, vial.                                                        *20*
    What if this mixture do not work at all?
    Shall I be married then tomorrow morning?
    No; no! This shall forbid it. Lie thou there.
                    *[Lays down a dagger.]*
    What if it be a poison which the friar
    Subtly hath minist'red° to have me dead,                        *25*
    Lest in this marriage he should be dishonored
    Because he married me before to Romeo?
    I fear it is; and yet methinks it should not,
    For he hath still° been tried° a holy man.
    How if, when I am laid into the tomb,                           *30*
    I wake before the time that Romeo
    Come to redeem me? There's a fearful point!
    Shall I not then be stifled in the vault,
    To whose foul mouth no healthsome air breathes in,
    And there die strangled ere my Romeo comes?                    *35*
    Or, if I live, is it not very like
    The horrible conceit° of death and night,
    Together with the terror of the place—
    As in a vault, an ancient receptacle

8 **behoveful** expedient  8 **state** pomp  15 **faint** causing  faintness
25 **minist'red** provided  29 **still** always  29 **tried** proved  37 **conceit**
thought

40     Where for this many hundred years the bones
      Of all my buried ancestors are packed;
      Where bloody Tybalt, yet but green in earth,°
      Lies fest'ring in his shroud; where, as they say,
      At some hours in the night spirits resort—
45     Alack, alack, is it not like that I,
      So early waking—what with loathsome smells,
      And shrieks like mandrakes° torn out of the earth,
      That living mortals, hearing them, run mad—
      O, if I wake, shall I not be distraught,°
50     Environèd with all these hideous fears,
      And madly play with my forefathers' joints,
      And pluck the mangled Tybalt from his shroud,
      And, in this rage, with some great kinsman's bone
      As with a club dash out my desp'rate brains?
55     O, look! Methinks I see my cousin's ghost
      Seeking out Romeo, that did spit his body
      Upon a rapier's point. Stay, Tybalt, stay!
      Romeo, Romeo, Romeo, I drink to thee.
               [*She falls upon her bed within the curtains.*]


[Scene 4. *Hall in Capulet's house.*]


*Enter Lady of the House and Nurse.*

*Lady Capulet.* Hold, take these keys and fetch more
    spices, nurse.

*Nurse.* They call for dates and quinces in the pastry.°

            *Enter old Capulet.*

*Capulet.* Come, stir, stir, stir! The second cock hath
    crowed,
    The curfew bell hath rung, 'tis three o'clock.

42 **green in earth** newly entombed   47 **mandrakes** plant with forked
root, resembling the human body (supposed to shriek when uprooted
and drive the hearer mad)   49 **distraught** driven mad   4.4.2 **pastry**
pastry cook's room

Look to the baked meats,° good Angelica;°          5
Spare not for cost.

*Nurse.*                    Go, you cotquean,° go,
  Get you to bed! Faith, you'll be sick tomorrow
  For this night's watching.°

*Capulet.* No, not a whit. What, I have watched ere now
  All night for lesser cause, and ne'er been sick.          10

*Lady Capulet.* Ay, you have been a mouse hunt° in
    your time;
  But I will watch you from such watching now.
                        *Exit Lady and Nurse.*

*Capulet.* A jealous hood,° a jealous hood!

    *Enter three or four [Fellows] with spits and
              logs and baskets.*

                        Now, fellow,
  What is there?

*First Fellow.* Things for the cook, sir; but I know not
    what.          15

*Capulet.* Make haste, make haste. [*Exit first Fellow.*]
    Sirrah, fetch drier logs.
  Call Peter; he will show thee where they are.

*Second Fellow.* I have a head, sir, that will find out
    logs°
  And never trouble Peter for the matter.

*Capulet.* Mass,° and well said; a merry whoreson,° ha!          20
    Thou shalt be loggerhead.° [*Exit second Fellow,
    with the others.*] Good faith, 'tis day.
  The County will be here with music straight,
  For so he said he would.          *Play music.*

---

5 **baked meats** meat pies    5 **Angelica** (the Nurse's name)    6 **cotquean**
man who does woman's work    8 **watching** staying awake    11 **mouse
hunt** night prowler, woman chaser    13 **A jealous hood** i.e., you wear
the cap of a jealous person    18 **will find out logs** has an affinity for
logs (i.e., is wooden also)    20 **Mass** by the Mass    20 **whoreson** rascal
21 **loggerhead** blockhead

I hear him near.
Nurse! Wife! What, ho! What, nurse, I say!

*Enter Nurse.*

25   Go waken Juliet; go and trim her up.
I'll go and chat with Paris. Hie, make haste,
Make haste! The bridegroom he is come already:
Make haste, I say.                          [*Exit.*]


[Scene 5. *Juliet's chamber.*]


*Nurse.*° Mistress! What, mistress! Juliet! Fast,° I war-
    rant her, she.
Why, lamb! Why, lady! Fie, you slugabed.°
Why, love, I say! Madam; Sweetheart! Why, bride!
What, not a word? You take your pennyworths°
    now;
5   Sleep for a week; for the next night, I warrant,
The County Paris hath set up his rest°
That you shall rest but little. God forgive me!
Marry, and amen. How sound is she asleep!
I needs must wake her. Madam, madam, madam!
10   Ay, let the County take you in your bed;
He'll fright you up, i' faith. Will it not be?
                          [*Draws aside the curtains.*]
What, dressed, and in your clothes, and down°
    again?
I must needs wake you. Lady! Lady! Lady!
Alas, alas! Help, help! My lady's dead!


4.5.1 **Nurse** (at the conclusion of the last scene the nurse presumably
did not go offstage but remained on the forestage, and after Capulet's
departure she now walks to the rear to open the curtains, revealing
Juliet) 1 **Fast** fast asleep 2 **slugabed** sleepyhead 4 **pennyworths**
small portions (i.e., short naps) 6 **set up his rest** firmly resolved (with
bawdy suggestion of having a lance in readiness) 12 **down** gone back
to bed

O weraday° that ever I was born!                                    *15*
Some *aqua vitae,*° ho! My lord! My lady!

[*Enter Mother.*]

*Lady Capulet.* What noise is here?

*Nurse.*                              O lamentable day!

*Lady Capulet.* What is the matter?

*Nurse.*                          Look, look! O heavy day!

*Lady Capulet.* O me, O me! My child, my only life!
Revive, look up, or I will die with thee!                          *20*
Help, help! Call help.

*Enter Father.*

*Capulet.* For shame, bring Juliet forth; her lord is
come.

*Nurse.* She's dead, deceased; she's dead, alack the day!

*Lady Capulet.* Alack the day, she's dead, she's dead,
she's dead!

*Capulet.* Ha! Let me see her. Out alas! She's cold,         *25*
Her blood is settled, and her joints are stiff;
Life and these lips have long been separated.
Death lies on her like an untimely frost.
Upon the sweetest flower of all the field.

*Nurse.* O lamentable day!

*Lady Capulet.*                  O woeful time!                    *30*

*Capulet.* Death, that hath ta'en her hence to make me
wail,
Ties up my tongue and will not let me speak.

*Enter Friar* [*Lawrence*] *and the County* [*Paris,
with Musicians*].

*Friar.* Come, is the bride ready to go to church?

*Capulet.* Ready to go, but never to return.

15 **weraday** welladay, alas   16 **aqua vitae** spirits

35     O son, the night before thy wedding day
       Hath Death lain with thy wife. There she lies,
       Flower as she was, deflowerèd by him.
       Death is my son-in-law, Death is my heir;
       My daughter he hath wedded. I will die
40     And leave him all. Life, living, all is Death's.

       *Paris.* Have I thought, love, to see this morning's face,
       And doth it give me such a sight as this?

       *Lady Capulet.* Accursed, unhappy, wretched, hateful
          day!
       Most miserable hour that e'er time saw
45     In lasting labor of his pilgrimage!
       But one, poor one, one poor and loving child,
       But one thing to rejoice and solace in,
       And cruel Death hath catched it from my sight.

       *Nurse.* O woe! O woeful, woeful, woeful day!
50     Most lamentable day, most woeful day
       That ever ever I did yet behold!
       O day, O day, O day! O hateful day!
       Never was seen so black a day as this.
       O woeful day! O woeful day!

55     *Paris.* Beguiled, divorcèd, wrongèd, spited, slain!
       Most detestable Death, by thee beguiled,
       By cruel, cruel thee quite overthrown.
       O love! O life!—not life, but love in death!

       *Capulet.* Despised, distressèd, hated, martyred, killed!
60     Uncomfortable° time, why cam'st thou now
       To murder, murder our solemnity?
       O child, O child! My soul, and not my child!
       Dead art thou—alack, my child is dead,
       And with my child my joys are burièd!

65     *Friar.* Peace, ho, for shame! Confusion's cure lives not
       In these confusions. Heaven and yourself
       Had part in this fair maid—now heaven hath all,
       And all the better is it for the maid.

60 **Uncomfortable** discomforting

Your part in her you could not keep from death,
But heaven keeps his part in eternal life.            70
The most you sought was her promotion,
For 'twas your heaven she should be advanced;
And weep ye now, seeing she is advanced
Above the clouds, as high as heaven itself?
O, in this love, you love your child so ill            75
That you run mad, seeing that she is well.°
She's not well married that lives married long,
But she's best married that dies married young.
Dry up your tears and stick your rosemary°
On this fair corse, and, as the custom is,            80
And in her best array bear her to church;
For though fond nature° bids us all lament,
Yet nature's tears are reason's merriment.

*Capulet.* All things that we ordainèd festival
Turn from their office to black funeral—            85
Our instruments to melancholy bells,
Our wedding cheer to a sad burial feast;
Our solemn hymns to sullen dirges change;
Our bridal flowers serve for a buried corse;
And all things change them to the contrary.            90

*Friar.* Sir, go you in; and, madam, go with him;
And go, Sir Paris. Everyone prepare
To follow this fair corse unto her grave.
The heavens do low'r° upon you for some ill;
Move them no more by crossing their high will.            95

> *Exeunt* [*casting rosemary on her
> and shutting the curtains*].
> *Manet*° [*the Nurse with Musicians*].

*First Musician.* Faith, we may put up our pipes and
be gone.

*Nurse.* Honest good fellows, ah, put up, put up!
For well you know this is a pitiful case.°      [*Exit.*]

76 **well** i.e., in blessed condition, in heaven   79 **rosemary** an ever-
green, signifying remembrance   82 **fond nature** foolish human nature
94 **low'r** frown   95 s.d. **Manet** remains (Latin)   99 **case** (1) situation
(2) instrument case

*100* *First Musician.* Ay, by my troth, the case may be
   amended.

*Enter [Peter].*

*Peter.* Musicians, O, musicians, "Heart's ease,"
   "Heart's ease"! O, and you will have me live, play
*105* "Heart's ease."

*First Musician.* Why "Heart's ease"?

*Peter.* O, musicians, because my heart itself plays
   "My heart is full." O, play me some merry dump°
   to comfort me.

*First Musician.* Not a dump we! 'Tis no time to play
*110* now.

*Peter.* You will not then?

*First Musician.* No.

*Peter.* I will then give it you soundly.

*First Musician.* What will you give us?

*115* *Peter.* No money, on my faith, but the gleek.° I will
   give you° the minstrel.

*First Musician.* Then will I give you the serving-
   creature.

*Peter.* Then will I lay the serving-creature's dagger
*120* on your pate. I will carry° no crotchets.° I'll *re*
   you, I'll *fa*° you. Do you note° me?

*First Musician.* And you *re* us and *fa* us, you note
   us.°

*Second Musician.* Pray you put up your dagger, and
*125* put out° your wit. Then have at you with my wit!

---

107 **dump** sad tune   115 **gleek** gibe   116 **give you** call you   120 **carry**
endure   120 **crotchets** (1) whims (2) quarter notes   120–21 **re . . . fa**
(musical notes, but used perhaps with puns on "ray," or "bewray"
["befoul"], and "fay" ["polish"]; see H. Kökeritz, *Shakespeare's Pronunciation,* pp. 105–06)   121 **note** understand   122–23 **note us** set us
to music   125 **put out** set out, display

*Peter.* I will dry-beat you with an iron wit, and put up my iron dagger. Answer me like men.

"When griping grief the heart doth wound,
    And doleful dumps the mind oppress,
Then music with her silver sound"° —          130

Why "silver sound"? Why "music with her silver sound"? What say you, Simon Catling?°

*First Musician.* Marry, sir, because silver hath a sweet sound.

*Peter.* Pretty! What say you, Hugh Rebeck?°          135

*Second Musician.* I say "silver sound" because musicians sound for silver.

*Peter.* Pretty too! What say you, James Soundpost?°

*Third Musician.* Faith, I know not what to say.

*Peter.* O, I cry you mercy,° you are the singer. I will          140
say for you. It is "music with her silver sound" because musicians have no gold for sounding.

"Then music with her silver sound
With speedy help doth lend redress."    *Exit.*

*First Musician.* What a pestilent knave is this same!          145

*Second Musician.* Hang him, Jack! Come, we'll in here, tarry for the mourners, and stay dinner.
                            *Exit* [*with others*].

---

128–30 **When . . . sound** (the song is from Richard Edwards' "In Commendation of Music," in *The Paradise of Dainty Devices,* 1576)
132 **Catling** catgut, a lute string    135 **Rebeck** a three-stringed fiddle
138 **Soundpost** peg that gives internal support to a violin    140 **cry you mercy** beg your pardon

# [ACT 5

### Scene 1. *Mantua. A street.*]

*Enter Romeo.*

*Romeo.* If I may trust the flattering° truth of sleep,
My dreams presage some joyful news at hand.
My bosom's lord° sits lightly in his throne,
And all this day an unaccustomed spirit
5    Lifts me above the ground with cheerful thoughts.
I dreamt my lady came and found me dead
(Strange dream that gives a dead man leave to think!)
And breathed such life with kisses in my lips
That I revived and was an emperor.
10    Ah me! How sweet is love itself possessed,
When but love's shadows° are so rich in joy!

*Enter Romeo's Man [Balthasar, booted].*

News from Verona! How now, Balthasar?
Dost thou not bring me letters from the friar?
How doth my lady? Is my father well?
15    How fares my Juliet? That I ask again,
For nothing can be ill if she be well.

*Man.* Then she is well, and nothing can be ill.
Her body sleeps in Capel's monument,°
And her immortal part with angels lives.

---

5.1.1 **flattering** illusory  3 **bosom's lord** i.e., heart  11 **shadows** dreams  18 **monument** tomb

I saw her laid low in her kindred's vault　　　　20
And presently took post° to tell it you.
O, pardon me for bringing these ill news,
Since you did leave it for my office,° sir.

*Romeo.* Is it e'en so? Then I defy you, stars!
Thou knowest my lodging. Get me ink and paper　　25
And hire post horses. I will hence tonight.

*Man.* I do beseech you, sir, have patience.
Your looks are pale and wild and do import°
Some misadventure.

*Romeo.*　　　　　　Tush, thou art deceived.
Leave me and do the thing I bid thee do.
Hast thou no letters to me from the friar?　　　30

*Man.* No, my good lord.

*Romeo.*　　　　　　No matter. Get thee gone.
And hire those horses. I'll be with thee straight.
　　　　　　　　　　　　*Exit* [*Balthasar*].
Well, Juliet, I will lie with thee tonight.
Let's see for means. O mischief, thou art swift　　35
To enter in the thoughts of desperate men!
I do remember an apothecary,
And hereabouts 'a dwells, which late I noted
In tatt'red weeds,° with overwhelming° brows,
Culling of simples.° Meager were his looks,　　　40
Sharp misery had worn him to the bones;
And in his needy shop a tortoise hung,
An alligator stuffed, and other skins
Of ill-shaped fishes; and about his shelves
A beggarly account° of empty boxes,　　　　　　45
Green earthen pots, bladders, and musty seeds,
Remnants of packthread, and old cakes of roses°
Were thinly scatterèd, to make up a show.
Noting this penury, to myself I said,

---

21 **post** post horses　23 **office** duty　28 **import** suggest　39 **weeds** clothes　39 **overwhelming** overhanging　40 **Culling of simples** collecting medicinal herbs　45 **account** number　47 **cakes of roses** pressed rose petals (for perfume)

50    "And if a man did need a poison now
     Whose sale is present death in Mantua,
     Here lives a caitiff° wretch would sell it him."
     O, this same thought did but forerun my need,
     And this same needy man must sell it me.
55    As I remember, this should be the house.
     Being holiday, the beggar's shop is shut.
     What, ho! Apothecary!

*[Enter Apothecary.]*

*Apothecary.*          Who calls so loud?

*Romeo.* Come hither, man. I see that thou art poor.
     Hold, there is forty ducats. Let me have
60    A dram of poison, such soon-speeding gear°
     As will disperse itself through all the veins
     That the life-weary taker may fall dead,
     And that the trunk° may be discharged of breath
     As violently as hasty powder fired
65    Doth hurry from the fatal cannon's womb.

*Apothecary.* Such mortal drugs I have; but Mantua's
     law
     Is death to any he that utters° them.

*Romeo.* Art thou so bare and full of wretchedness
     And fearest to die? Famine is in thy cheeks,
70    Need and oppression starveth° in thy eyes,
     Contempt and beggary hangs upon thy back:
     The world is not thy friend, nor the world's law;
     The world affords no law to make thee rich;
     Then be not poor, but break it and take this.

75 *Apothecary.* My poverty but not my will consents.

*Romeo.* I pay thy poverty and not thy will.

*Apothecary.* Put this in any liquid thing you will
     And drink it off, and if you had the strength
     Of twenty men, it would dispatch you straight.

---

52 **caitiff** miserable    60 **soon-speeding gear** fast-working stuff    63 **trunk** body    67 **utters** dispenses    70 **starveth** stand starving

*Romeo.* There is thy gold—worse poison to men's
 souls,                                                        80
 Doing more murder in this loathsome world,
 Than these poor compounds that thou mayst not
 sell.
 I sell thee poison; thou hast sold me none.
 Farewell. Buy food and get thyself in flesh.
 Come, cordial° and not poison, go with me            85
 To Juliet's grave; for there must I use thee.

                                                *Exeunt.*

[Scene 2. *Friar Lawrence's cell.*]

*Enter Friar John to Friar Lawrence.*

*John.* Holy Franciscan father, brother, ho!

          *Enter [Friar] Lawrence.*

*Lawrence.* This same should be the voice of Friar John.
 Welcome from Mantua. What says Romeo?
 Or, if his mind be writ, give me his letter.

*John.* Going to find a barefoot brother out,            5
 One of our order, to associate° me
 Here in this city visiting the sick,
 And finding him, the searchers° of the town,
 Suspecting that we both were in a house
 Where the infectious pestilence did reign,          10
 Sealed up the doors, and would not let us forth,
 So that my speed to Mantua there was stayed.

*Lawrence.* Who bare my letter, then, to Romeo?

*John.* I could not send it—here it is again—
 Nor get a messenger to bring it thee,                 15
 So fearful were they of infection.

85 **cordial** restorative   5.2.6 **associate** accompany   8 **searchers** health
officers

*Lawrence.* Unhappy fortune! By my brotherhood,°
   The letter was not nice,° but full of charge,°
   Of dear import; and the neglecting it
20    May do much danger. Friar John, go hence,
   Get me an iron crow° and bring it straight
   Unto my cell.

*John.*            Brother, I'll go and bring it thee. *Exit.*

*Lawrence.* Now must I to the monument alone.
   Within this three hours will fair Juliet wake.
25    She will beshrew° me much that Romeo
   Hath had no notice of these accidents;°
   But I will write again to Mantua,
   And keep her at my cell till Romeo come—
Poor living corse, closed in a dead man's tomb!     *Exit.*


[Scene 3. *A churchyard; in it a monument*
*belonging to the Capulets.*]


*Enter Paris and his Page [with flowers and*
*sweet water].*


*Paris.* Give me thy torch, boy. Hence, and stand aloof.
   Yet put it out, for I would not be seen.
   Under yond yew trees lay thee all along,°
   Holding thy ear close to the hollow ground.
5    So shall no foot upon the churchyard tread
   (Being loose, unfirm, with digging up of graves)
   But thou shalt hear it. Whistle then to me,
   As signal that thou hearest something approach.
   Give me those flowers. Do as I bid thee, go.

10 *Page.* [*Aside*] I am almost afraid to stand alone

---

17 **brotherhood** religious order   18 **nice** trivial   18 **charge** importance   21 **crow** crowbar   25 **beshrew** blame   26 **accidents** happenings   5.3.3 **lay thee all along** lie at full length

Here in the churchyard; yet I will adventure.°
[*Retires.*]

*Paris.* Sweet flower, with flowers thy bridal bed I strew
 (O woe! thy canopy is dust and stones)
 Which with sweet° water nightly I will dew;
  Or, wanting that, with tears distilled by moans.  *15*
 The obsequies that I for thee will keep
 Nightly shall be to strew thy grave and weep.
*Whistle Boy.*
 The boy gives warning something doth approach.
 What cursèd foot wanders this way tonight
 To cross° my obsequies and true love's rite?  *20*
 What, with a torch? Muffle° me, night, awhile.
[*Retires.*]

*Enter Romeo, [and Balthasar with a torch, a mattock,
  and a crow of iron].*

*Romeo.* Give me that mattock and the wrenching iron.
 Hold, take this letter. Early in the morning
 See thou deliver it to my lord and father.
 Give me the light. Upon thy life I charge thee,  *25*
 Whate'er thou hearest or seest, stand all aloof
 And do not interrupt me in my course.
 Why I descend into this bed of death
 Is partly to behold my lady's face,
 But chiefly to take thence from her dead finger  *30*
 A precious ring—a ring that I must use.
 In dear employment.° Therefore hence, be gone.
 But if thou, jealous,° dost return to pry
 In what I farther shall intend to do,
 By heaven, I will tear thee joint by joint  *35*
 And strew this hungry churchyard with thy limbs.
 The time and my intents are savage-wild,
 More fierce and more inexorable far
 Than empty tigers or the roaring sea.

---

11 **adventure** risk it   14 **sweet** perfumed   20 **cross** interrupt   21 **Muffle**
hide   32 **dear employment** important business   33 **jealous** curious

40 *Balthasar.* I will be gone, sir, and not trouble ye.

*Romeo.* So shalt thou show me friendship. Take thou
    that.
    Live, and be prosperous; and farewell, good fellow.

*Balthasar.* [*Aside*] For all this same, I'll hide me here-
    about.
    His looks I fear, and his intents I doubt.° [*Retires.*]

45 *Romeo.* Thou detestable maw,° thou womb of death,
    Gorged with the dearest morsel of the earth,
    Thus I enforce thy rotten jaws to open,
    And in despite° I'll cram thee with more food.
                [*Romeo opens the tomb.*]

*Paris.* This is that banished haughty Montague
50    That murd'red my love's cousin—with which grief
    It is supposed the fair creature died—
    And here is come to do some villainous shame
    To the dead bodies. I will apprehend him.
    Stop thy unhallowèd toil, vile Montague!
55    Can vengeance be pursued further than death?
    Condemnèd villain, I do apprehend thee.
    Obey, and go with me; for thou must die.

*Romeo.* I must indeed; and therefore came I hither.
    Good gentle youth, tempt not a desp'rate man.
60    Fly hence and leave me. Think upon these gone;
    Let them affright thee. I beseech thee, youth,
    Put not another sin upon my head
    By urging me to fury. O, be gone!
    By heaven, I love thee better than myself,
65    For I come hither armed against myself.
    Stay not, be gone. Live, and hereafter say
    A madman's mercy bid thee run away.

*Paris.* I do defy thy conjurations.°
    And apprehend thee for a felon here.

70 *Romeo.* Wilt thou provoke me? Then have at thee, boy!
                   [*They fight.*]

44 **doubt** suspect   45 **maw** stomach   48 **in despite** to spite you
68 **conjurations** solemn charges

*Page.* O Lord, they fight! I will go call the watch.
         [*Exit. Paris falls.*]

*Paris.* O, I am slain! If thou be merciful,
 Open the tomb, lay me with Juliet.   [*Dies.*]

*Romeo.* In faith, I will. Let me peruse this face.
 Mercutio's kinsman, noble County Paris!    *75*
 What said my man when my betossèd soul
 Did not attend° him as we rode? I think
 He told me Paris should have married Juliet.
 Said he not so, or did I dream it so?
 Or am I mad, hearing him talk of Juliet,    *80*
 To think it was so? O, give me thy hand,
 One writ with me in sour misfortune's book!
 I'll bury thee in a triumphant grave.
 A grave? O, no, a lanthorn,° slaught'red youth,
 For here lies Juliet, and her beauty makes    *85*
 This vault a feasting presence° full of light.
 Death, lie thou there, by a dead man interred.
       [*Lays him in the tomb.*]
 How oft when men are at the point of death
 Have they been merry! Which their keepers° call
 A lightning before death. O, how may I    *90*
 Call this a lightning? O my love, my wife!
 Death, that hath sucked the honey of thy breath,
 Hath had no power yet upon thy beauty.
 Thou art not conquered. Beauty's ensign° yet
 Is crimson in thy lips and in thy cheeks,    *95*
 And death's pale flag is not advancèd there.
 Tybalt, liest thou there in thy bloody sheet?
 O, what more favor can I do to thee
 Than with that hand that cut thy youth in twain
 To sunder his that was thine enemy?    *100*
 Forgive me, cousin! Ah, dear Juliet,
 Why art thou yet so fair? Shall I believe
 That unsubstantial Death is amorous,

---

77 **attend** give attention to 84 **lanthorn** lantern (a windowed erection on the top of a dome or room to admit light) 86 **feasting presence** festive presence chamber 89 **keepers** jailers 94 **ensign** banner

And that the lean abhorrèd monster keeps
105 Thee here in dark to be his paramour?
For fear of that I still will stay with thee
And never from this pallet of dim night
Depart again. Here, here will I remain
With worms that are thy chambermaids. O, here
110 Will I set up my everlasting rest
And shake the yoke of inauspicious stars
From this world-wearied flesh. Eyes, look your last!
Arms, take your last embrace! And, lips, O you
The doors of breath, seal with a righteous kiss
115 A dateless° bargain to engrossing° death!
Come, bitter conduct;° come, unsavory guide!
Thou desperate pilot,° now at once run on
The dashing rocks thy seasick weary bark!
Here's to my love! [*Drinks.*] O true apothecary!
120 Thy drugs are quick. Thus with a kiss I die. [*Falls.*]

*Enter Friar [Lawrence], with lanthorn, crow,
and spade.*

*Friar.* Saint Francis be my speed!° How oft tonight
Have my old feet stumbled° at graves! Who's there?

*Balthasar.* Here's one, a friend, and one that knows
you well.

*Friar.* Bliss be upon you! Tell me, good my friend,
125 What torch is yond that vainly lends his light
To grubs and eyeless skulls? As I discern,
It burneth in the Capels' monument.

*Balthasar.* It doth so, holy sir; and there's my master,
One that you love.

*Friar.*              Who is it?

*Balthasar.*                        Romeo.

*Friar.* How long hath he been there?

---

115 **dateless** eternal   115 **engrossing** all-buying, all-encompassing
116 **conduct** guide   117 **desperate pilot** i.e., himself   121 **speed** help
122 **stumbled** (a bad omen)

*Balthasar.*                            Full half an hour.    130

*Friar.* Go with me to the vault.

*Balthasar.*                        I dare not, sir.
My master knows not but I am gone hence,
And fearfully did menace me with death
If I did stay to look on his intents.

*Friar.* Stay then; I'll go alone. Fear comes upon me.    135
O, much I fear some ill unthrifty° thing.

*Balthasar.* As I did sleep under this yew tree here,
I dreamt my master and another fought,
And that my master slew him.

*Friar.*                            Romeo!
Alack, alack, what blood is this which stains    140
The stony entrance of this sepulcher?
What mean these masterless and gory swords
To lie discolored by this place of peace?
                        [*Enters the tomb.*]
Romeo! O, pale! Who else? What, Paris too?
And steeped in blood? Ah, what an unkind° hour    145
Is guilty of this lamentable chance!
The lady stirs.                        [*Juliet rises.*]

*Juliet.* O comfortable° friar! Where is my lord?
I do remember well where I should be,
And there I am. Where is my Romeo?    150

*Friar.* I hear some noise. Lady, come from that nest
Of death, contagion, and unnatural sleep.
A greater power than we can contradict
Hath thwarted our intents. Come, come away.
Thy husband in thy bosom there lies dead;    155
And Paris too. Come, I'll dispose of thee
Among a sisterhood of holy nuns.
Stay not to question, for the watch is coming.
Come, go, good Juliet. I dare no longer stay.

___

136 **unthrifty** unlucky   145 **unkind** unnatural   148 **comfortable** comforting

160  *Juliet.* Go, get thee hence, for I will not away.

                                      *Exit [Friar].*

    What's here? A cup, closed in my truelove's hand?
    Poison, I see, hath been his timeless° end.
    O churl!° Drunk all, and left no friendly drop
    To help me after? I will kiss thy lips.

165  Haply some poison yet doth hang on them
    To make me die with a restorative.    [*Kisses him.*]
    Thy lips are warm!

*Chief Watchman.* [*Within*] Lead, boy. Which way?

*Juliet.* Yea, noise? Then I'll be brief. O happy°
    dagger!            [*Snatches Romeo's dagger.*]

170  This is thy sheath; there rust, and let me die.

                  [*She stabs herself and falls.*]

       *Enter [Paris'] Boy and Watch.*

*Boy.* This is the place. There, where the torch doth
    burn.

*Chief Watchman.* The ground is bloody. Search about
    the churchyard.
    Go, some of you; whoe'er you find attach.

              [*Exeunt some of the Watch.*]

    Pitiful sight! Here lies the County slain;

175  And Juliet bleeding, warm, and newly dead,
    Who here hath lain this two days burièd.
    Go, tell the Prince; run to the Capulets;
    Raise up the Montagues; some others search.

             [*Exeunt others of the Watch.*]

    We see the ground whereon these woes do lie,

180  But the true ground° of all these piteous woes
    We cannot without circumstance° descry.

    *Enter [some of the Watch, with] Romeo's Man*
                 *[Balthasar].*

*Second Watchman.* Here's Romeo's man. We found
    him in the churchyard.

---

162 **timeless** untimely   163 **churl** rude fellow   169 **happy** opportune
180 **ground** cause   181 **circumstance** details

*Chief Watchman.* Hold him in safety till the Prince
    come hither.

    *Enter Friar [Lawrence] and another Watchman.*

*Third Watchman.* Here is a friar that trembles, sighs,
    and weeps.
  We took this mattock and this spade from him    *185*
  As he was coming from this churchyard's side.

*Chief Watchman.* A great suspicion! Stay the friar too.

    *Enter the Prince [and Attendants].*

*Prince.* What misadventure is so early up,
  That calls our person from our morning rest?

    *Enter Capulet and his Wife [with others].*

*Capulet.* What should it be, that is so shrieked abroad?  *190*

*Lady Capulet.* O, the people in the street cry "Romeo,"
  Some "Juliet," and some "Paris"; and all run
  With open outcry toward our monument.

*Prince.* What fear is this which startles in your ears?

*Chief Watchman.* Sovereign, here lies the County Paris
    slain;    *195*
  And Romeo dead; and Juliet, dead before,
  Warm and new killed.

*Prince.* Search, seek, and know how this foul murder
    comes.

*Chief Watchman.* Here is a friar, and slaughtered
    Romeo's man,
  With instruments upon them fit to open    *200*
  These dead men's tombs.

*Capulet.* O heavens! O wife, look how our daughter
    bleeds!
  This dagger hath mista'en, for, lo, his house°
  Is empty on the back of Montague,
  And it missheathèd in my daughter's bosom!    *205*

203 **his house** its sheath

*Lady Capulet.* O me, this sight of death is as a bell
    That warns my old age to a sepulcher.

        *Enter Montague [and others].*

*Prince.* Come, Montague; for thou art early up
    To see thy son and heir more early down.

210 *Montague.* Alas, my liege, my wife is dead tonight!
    Grief of my son's exile hath stopped her breath.
    What further woe conspires against mine age?

*Prince.* Look, and thou shalt see.

*Montague.* O thou untaught! What manners is in this,
215     To press before thy father to a grave?

*Prince.* Seal up the mouth of outrage° for a while,
    Till we can clear these ambiguities
    And know their spring, their head, their true
        descent;
    And then will I general of your woes°
220     And lead you even to death. Meantime forbear,
    And let mischance be slave to patience.
    Bring forth the parties of suspicion.

*Friar.* I am the greatest, able to do least,
    Yet most suspected, as the time and place
225     Doth make against me, of this direful murder;
    And here I stand, both to impeach and purge°
    Myself condemnèd and myself excused.

*Prince.* Then say at once what thou dost know in this.

*Friar.* I will be brief, for my short date of breath°
230     Is not so long as is a tedious tale.
    Romeo, there dead, was husband to that Juliet;
    And she, there dead, that's Romeo's faithful wife.
    I married them; and their stol'n marriage day
    Was Tybalt's doomsday, whose untimely death
235     Banished the new-made bridegroom from this city;

---

216 **the mouth of outrage** these violent cries   219 **general of your woes** leader in your sorrowing   226 **impeach and purge** make charges and exonerate   229 **date of breath** term of life

For whom, and not for Tybalt, Juliet pined.
You, to remove that siege of grief from her,
Betrothed and would have married her perforce
To County Paris. Then comes she to me
And with wild looks bid me devise some mean          *240*
To rid her from this second marriage,
Or in my cell there would she kill herself.
Then gave I her (so tutored by my art)
A sleeping potion; which so took effect
As I intended, for it wrought on her          *245*
The form of death. Meantime I writ to Romeo
That he should hither come as° this dire night
To help to take her from her borrowed grave,
Being the time the potion's force should cease.
But he which bore my letter, Friar John,          *250*
Was stayed by accident, and yesternight
Returned my letter back. Then all alone
At the prefixèd hour of her waking
Came I to take her from her kindred's vault;
Meaning to keep her closely° at my cell          *255*
Till I conveniently could send to Romeo.
But when I came, some minute ere the time
Of her awakening, here untimely lay
The noble Paris and true Romeo dead.
She wakes; and I entreated her come forth          *260*
And bear this work of heaven with patience;
But then a noise did scare me from the tomb,
And she, too desperate, would not go with me,
But, as it seems, did violence on herself.
All this I know, and to the marriage          *265*
Her nurse is privy;° and if aught in this
Miscarried by my fault, let my old life
Be sacrificed some hour before his time
Unto the rigor of severest law.

*Prince.* We still° have known thee for a holy man.          *270*
    Where's Romeo's man? What can he say to this?

*Balthasar.* I brought my master news of Juliet's death;

247 **as** on   255 **closely** hidden   266 **privy** accessory   270 **still** always

And then in post he came from Mantua
To this same place, to this same monument.
275 This letter he early bid me give his father,
And threat'ned me with death, going in the vault,
If I departed not and left him there.

*Prince.* Give me the letter. I will look on it.
Where is the County's page that raised the watch?
280 Sirrah, what made your master° in this place?

*Boy.* He came with flowers to strew his lady's grave;
And bid me stand aloof, and so I did.
Anon comes one with light to ope the tomb;
And by and by° my master drew on him;
285 And then I ran away to call the watch.

*Prince.* This letter doth make good the friar's words,
Their course of love, the tidings of her death;
And here he writes that he did buy a poison
Of a poor apothecary and therewithal°
290 Came to this vault to die and lie with Juliet.
Where be these enemies? Capulet, Montague,
See what a scourge is laid upon your hate,
That heaven finds means to kill your joys with love.
And I, for winking at° your discords, too,
295 Have lost a brace° of kinsmen. All are punished.

*Capulet.* O brother Montague, give me thy hand.
This is my daughter's jointure,° for no more
Can I demand.

*Montague.*          But I can give thee more;
For I will raise her statue in pure gold,
300 That whiles Verona by that name is known,
There shall no figure at such rate° be set
As that of true and faithful Juliet.

*Capulet.* As rich shall Romeo's by his lady's lie—
Poor sacrifices of our enmity!

280 **made your master** was your master doing   284 **by and by** soon
289 **therewithal** therewith   294 **winking at** closing eyes to   295 **brace**
pair (i.e., Mercutio and Paris)   297 **jointure** marriage settlement
301 **rate** value

*Prince.* A glooming° peace this morning with it brings.  *305*
    The sun for sorrow will not show his head.
  Go hence, to have more talk of these sad things;
    Some shall be pardoned, and some punishèd;
  For never was a story of more woe
  Than this of Juliet and her Romeo.  *310*
                 [*Exeunt omnes.*]

FINIS

305 **glooming** cloudy

# Textual Note

The First Quarto (Q1) of *Romeo and Juliet* was printed in 1597 without previous entry in the Stationers' Register. It bore the following title page: "An/ EXCELLENT/ conceited Tragedie/ OF/ Romeo and Iuliet./ As it hath been often (with great applause)/ plaid publiquely, by the right Ho-/ nourable the L. of *Hunsdon*/ his Seruants./ LONDON,/ Printed by Iohn Danter./ 1597." Until the present century, editors frequently assumed that this text, curtailed and manifestly corrupt, represented an early draft of the play. Most now agree that Q1, like the other "bad" Shakespeare quartos, is a memorial reconstruction; that is, a version which some of the actors (accusing fingers have been pointed at those who played Romeo and Peter) put together from memory and gave to the printer. The Second Quarto (Q2) was printed in 1599 with the following title page: "THE/ MOST/ EX-/ cellent and lamentable/ Tragedie, of Romeo/ and *Iuliet*./ *Newly corrected, augmented, and/ amended*: As it hath bene sundry times publiquely acted, by the/ right Honourable the Lord Chamberlaine/ his Seruants./ London/ Printed by Thomas Creede, for Cuthbert Burby, and are to/ be sold at his shop neare the Exchange./ 1599." Apparently Q2 derives directly from the same acting version that is imperfectly reflected in the memorially reconstructed Q1, but it is based on a written script of the play rather than on actors' memories. Q2, however, is the product of careless or hasty printing and does not inspire complete confidence. Lines that the author doubtless had canceled are sometimes printed along with the lines intended to replace them, and occasionally notes about staging appear which are probably the prompter's, or possibly Shakespeare's.

Vexing matters like these, together with the fact that some
speeches in Q2 are clearly based on Q1 (possibly the
manuscript that provided the copy for most of Q2 was
illegible in places), have caused editors to make at least
limited use of Q1. The other texts of *Romeo and Juliet*
have no claim to authority. The Second Quarto provided
the basis for a Third Quarto (1609), which in turn served
as copy for an undated Fourth Quarto and for the text in
the Folio of 1623. A Fifth Quarto, based on the Fourth,
appeared in 1637.

None of these texts—including the Second Quarto,
upon which the present edition is based—makes any real
division of the play into acts and scenes. (The last third of
Q1 does have a rough indication of scene division in the
form of strips of ornamental border across the page, and
the Folio has at the beginning *Actus Primus. Scena Prima,*
but nothing further.) The division used here, like that in
most modern texts, derives from the Globe edition, as do
the *Dramatis Personae* and the various indications of
place. Spelling and punctuation have been modernized, a
number of stage directions have been added (in square
brackets), and speech prefixes have been regularized. This
last change will be regretted by those who feel, perhaps
rightly, that at least some of the speech prefixes of Q2
show how Shakespeare thought of the character at each
moment of the dialogue. Lady Capulet, for example, is
variously designated in the speech prefixes of Q2 as *Wife,*
*Lady,* and sometimes *Mother*; Capulet is occasionally
referred to as *Father,* and Balthasar as *Peter*; the First
Musician of our text (4.5) is once called *Fidler* in Q2 and
several times *Minstrel* or *Minstrels.* Other deviations
(apart from obvious typographical errors) from Q2 are
listed in the textual notes. There the adopted reading is
given first, in italics, followed by a note in square
brackets if the source of the reading is Q1; this is followed by the rejected reading in roman. Absence of a note
in square brackets indicates that the adopted reading has
been taken from some other source and represents guess-

work at best. Apparently the editors of F as well as of Q3 and Q4 had no access to any authentic document.

In dealing with the troublesome stage direction at the end of 1.4, I have followed the solution adopted by H. R. Hoppe in his Crofts Classics edition (1947); and I have adopted the reading of "eyes' shot" for the customary "eyes shut" at 3.2.49 from the Pelican edition of John E. Hankins (Penguin, 1960), which presents a good argument for retaining the reading of Q2 with the addition of an apostrophe.

1.1.29 *in sense* [Q1] sense   34 *comes two* [Q1] comes   65 *swashing* washing
123 *drave* driue   150 *his* is   156 *sun* same   182 *well-seeming* [Q1] welseeing
205 *Bid a sick* [Q1] A sicke   205 *make* [Q1] makes   206 *Ah* [Q1] A

1.2.32 *on* one   65–73 *Signior . . . Helena* [prose in Q1 and F]   92 *fires* fier

1.3.2–76 [Q2 prints Nurse's speeches in prose]   66, 67 *honor* [Q1] houre
99 *make it* [Q1] make

1.4.7–8 *Nor . . . entrance* [added from Q1]   23 *Mercutio* Horatio   39 *done*
[Q1] dum   42 *of this sir-reverence* [Q1] or saue you reuerence   45 *like*
lights   47 *five* fine   53–91 *O . . . bodes* [verse from Q1; Q2 has prose]   57
*atomies* ottamie   63 *film* Philome   66 *maid* [Q1] man   113 *sail* [Q1] sute
114 s.d. *They . . . and* [Q2 combines with s.d. used here at beginning of 1.5]

1.5. s.d. [Q2 adds "Enter Romeo"]   1, 4, 7, 12 *First Servingman . . . Second
Servingman . . . First Servingman . . . First Servingman* [Q2 has "Ser." "I.,"
"Ser.," and "Ser."]   97 *ready* [Q1] did readie   144 *What's this? What's
this?* Whats tis? whats tis

2.1.9 *one* [Q1] on   10 *pronounce* [Q1] prouaunt   10 *dove* [Q1] day   12
*heir* [Q1] her   38 *et cetera* [Q1] or

2.2.16 *do* to   20 *eyes* eye   45 *were* wene   83 *washed* washeth   99 *havior*
[Q1] behauior   101 *more cunning* [Q1] coying   162 *than mine* then   167
*sweet* Neece   186 *Romeo* [Q1] Iu.   187–88 [between these lines Q2 has
"The grey eyde morne smiles on the frowning night, / Checkring the Easterne
Clouds with streaks of light, / And darknesse fleckted like a drunkard reeles, /
From forth daies pathway, made by *Tytans* wheeles," lines nearly identical
with those given to the Friar at 2.3.1–4; presumably Shakespeare first wrote
the lines for Romeo, then decided to use them in Friar Lawrence's next
speech, but neglected to delete the first version, and the printer mistakenly
printed it]

2.3.2 *Check'ring* Checking   3 *fleckèd* [Q1] fleckeld   74 *ring yet* [Q1] yet
ringing

2.4.18 *Benvolio* [Q1] Ro.   30 *fantasticoes* [Q1] phantacies   215 *Ah* A

2.5.11 *three* there

2.6.27 *music's* musicke

3.1.2 *are* [Q1; Q2 omits]  91 s.d. *Tybalt . . . flies* [Q1; Q2 has "Away Tybalt"]  110 *soundly too. Your* soundly, to your  124 *Alive* [Q1] He gan  126 *eyed* [Q1] end  168 *agile* [Q1] aged  190 *hate's* [Q1] hearts  194 *I* It

3.2.51 *determine of* determine  60 *one* on  72–73 [Q2 gives line 72 to Juliet, line 73 to Nurse]  76 *Dove-feathered* Rauenous doue-featherd  79 *damnèd* dimme

3.3. s.d. *Enter Friar* [Q1] Enter Frier and Romeo  40 *But . . . banishèd* [in Q2 this line is preceded by one line, "This may flyes do, when I from this must flie," which is substantially the same as line 41, and by line 43, which is probably misplaced]  52 *Thou* [Q1] Then  61 *madmen* [Q1] mad man  73 s.d. *Knock* They knocke  75 s.d. *Knock* Slud knock  108 s.d. *He . . . away* [Q1; Q2 omits]  117 *lives* lies  143 *misbehaved* mishaued  162 s.d. *Nurse . . . again* [Q1; Q2 omits]  168 *disguised* disguise

3.5.13 *exhales* [Q1] exhale  36 s.d. *Enter Nurse* [Q1] Enter Madame and Nurse  42 s.d. *He goeth down* [Q1; Q2 omits]  54 *Juliet* Ro.  83 *pardon him* padon  140 *gives* giue  182 *trained* [Q1] liand

4.1.7 *talked* talke  72 *slay* [Q1] stay  83 *chapless* chapels  85 *his shroud* his  98 *breath* [Q1] breast  100 *wanny* many  110 *In* Is  110 [after this line Q2 has "Be borne to buriall in thy kindreds graue"; presumably as soon as Shakespeare wrote these words he decided he could do better, and expressed the gist of the idea in the next two lines, but the canceled line was erroneously printed]  111 *shalt* shall  116 *waking* walking

4.3.49 *wake* walke  58 *Romeo, I drink* [after "Romeo" Q2 has "heeres drinke," which is probably a stage direction printed in error]  58 s.d. *She . . . curtains* [Q1; Q2 omits]

4.4.21 *faith* [Q1] father

4.5.65 *cure* care  82 *fond* some  95 s.d. *casting . . . curtains* [Q1; Q2 omits]  101 *by* [Q1] my  101 *amended* amended. Exit omnes  101 s.d. *Peter* [Q2 has "Will Kemp," the name of the actor playing the role]  128 *grief* [Q1] griefes  129 *And . . . oppress* [Q1; Q2 omits]  135, 138 *Pretty* [Q1] Prates

5.1.11 s.d. *booted* [detail from Q1]  15 *fares my* [Q1] doth my Lady  24 *e'en* [Q1 "euen"] in  24 *defy* [Q1] denie  50 *And* An  76 *pay* [Q1] pray

5.3. s.d. *with . . . water* [Q1; Q2 omits]  3 *yew* [Q1] young  21 s.d. *and Balthasar . . . iron* [Q1; Q2 has "Enter Romeo and Peter," and gives lines 40 and 43 to Peter instead of to Balthasar]  48 s.d. *Romeo . . . tomb* [Q1; Q2 omits]  68 *conjurations* [Q1] commiration  71 *Page* [Q2 omits this speech prefix]  102 *fair* [Q2 follows with "I will beleeue," presumably words that Shakespeare wrote, then rewrote in the next line, but neglected to delete]  108 *again. Here* [between these words Q2 has the following material, which

Shakespeare apparently neglected to delete: "come lye thou in my arme, /
Heer's to thy health, where ere thou tumblest in. / O true Appothecarie / Thy
drugs are quicke. Thus with a kisse I die. / Depart againe"]    137 *yew* yong
187 *too* too too    189 s.d. *Enter ... wife* [Q2 places after line 201, with
"Enter Capels" at line 189]    190 *shrieked* [Q1] shrike    199 *slaughtered*
Slaughter    209 *more early* [Q1] now earling

# A Note on the Source of
## *Romeo and Juliet*

The story of Romeo and Juliet was popular in Elizabethan times, and Shakespeare could have got his working outline of it from a number of places. Belleforest's *Histoires Tragiques* had a version, as did William Painter's *Palace of Pleasure*; and there had apparently been a play on the subject. Arthur Brooke, in an address "To the Reader" prefaced to his long narrative poem *The Tragicall Historye of Romeus and Juliet*, mentioned seeing "the same argument lately set foorth on stage"; but there is no evidence that Shakespeare worked from an older play or even that he consulted Belleforest or Painter, though he undoubtedly knew their works. All the evidence indicates that he worked directly from Brooke's poem, which Richard Tottell had printed in 1562 and Robert Robinson had reissued in 1587, shortly before the time that Shakespeare must have begun writing for the London stage.

Actually the story was popular, on the Continent at least, well before Elizabeth's time. Leaving out of account such obvious but distant analogues as the stories of Hero and Leander, Aeneas and Dido, Pyramus and Thisbe, and Troilus and Cressida, the first version of the story was one that appeared in Masuccio Salernitano's *Il Novellino* in 1476. This version had the clandestine lovers, the accommodating friar, the killing that led to the young man's banishment, the rival suitor, sleeping potion, thwarted messenger, and unhappy conclusion, but no suicides. It might have passed into oblivion had it not been for Luigi da Porto's *Istoria novellamente ritrovata di due Nobili Amanti* (published *ca.* 1530), which laid the scene in Verona and identified the feuding families as Montecchi and Capelletti and the lovers as Romeo and

Giulietta. Da Porto's story also named the friar Lorenzo and the slain man Thebaldo Capelletti and introduced the ball, the balcony scene, and the double suicide at the tomb. It was da Porto, moreover, who first named a minor character Marcuccio and gave him the icy hands that subsequent tellers of the tale regularly mentioned until Shakespeare discarded the detail and replaced it with a distinctive personality. Da Porto is also remembered for having Giulietta commit suicide by holding her breath—a detail which fortunately no one bothered to perpetuate.

Da Porto's tale was widely imitated both in Italy and in France, but the version of most importance to readers of Shakespeare was that of Matteo Bandello, who put the story into his *Novelle* (1554). Of all the versions before Shakespeare's, Bandello's is generally considered the best. It is a plain, straightforward narrative, unmarred by the sentimentality and moralizing that characterized the work of some of his adapters. In Bandello's story the masking appears; Peter is there (but as Romeo's servant), the Nurse has a significant part in the plot, and the rope ladder comes into play. Almost as important is the version of Pierre Boaistuau (1559), adapted from Bandello, which was included in Belleforest's *Histoires Tragiques*. Boaistuau made Romeo go to the ball in the hope of seeing his indifferent lady (the Rosaline of Shakespeare's play), worked out the business of the Capulets' restraint at discovering Romeo's presence, and developed the dilemma that Juliet finds herself in when she first hears of Tybalt's death; he also developed the character of the apothecary. All these things went into Painter's version (1567), which was a translation of Boaistuau, and into Brooke's, which was based on Boaistuau. The line of transmission from Masuccio to Shakespeare thus includes da Porto, Bandello, Boaistuau, and Brooke, in that order, with Painter standing unconsulted to one side. Shakespeare, however, used only Brooke directly and thus derived from the tradition only as much as Brooke passed on to him; but he borrowed freely from the great wealth of detail that Brooke himself had added.

Anyone interested in consulting Brooke's version for himself will find it in the first volume of Geoffrey Bullough's *Narrative and Dramatic Sources of Shakespeare* (London: Routledge and Kegan Paul, 1957). In spite of the tedious poulter's measure (iambic couplets in which the first line has twelve syllables and the second, fourteen) the poem is not entirely dull; and no other single source gave Shakespeare so much that was immediately useful. Readers should recognize at once the character and function of Benvolio (though Brooke neglected to give him a name), the Capulet that stormed at what he took to be his daughter's willful disobedience and threatened her with incarceration and endless misery, the garrulous, amoral Nurse and her conversations with the young lovers, and the needy apothecary. They will even find the clue to Mercutio's character (which Brooke did not develop) in the lines: "Even as a Lyon would emong the lambes be bolde, / Such was emong the bashfull maydes, Mercutio to beholde." Numerous such hints, together with bits of business, suggestions for metaphors, and passages of dialogue, catch the eye as one scans Brooke's lines, not so much because they are arresting in themselves but because they call to mind the use Shakespeare has made of them. And if one gets safely past Brooke's "Address to the Reader," with its heavy-handed condemnation of lust, disobedience, and superstitious friars, one finds that Brooke too treated the lovers with sympathy and allowed his friar the best of intentions. In fact, Brooke, having discharged himself of his Protestant moralizing in the "Address," tended to make Fortune responsible for most things in the story; and Shakespeare, as we know, took Brooke's Fortune along with all the rest.

What Shakespeare did with Brooke's clean but relatively inert story was to add complication and focus, intensify it by drastic compression, and establish the intricate relationship of part to part in a texture of language that functions admirably as dialogue even as it creates the unity of a dramatic poem. In this transformation he made it possible for us to tolerate the Nurse, love Capulet, and pity the apothecary. He relieved the Friar of the tedium that Brooke had encumbered him with, and he changed Escalus into a man who genuinely suffers and commands sympathy. In bringing Tybalt to the ball and making him the discoverer of Romeo's presence there, he gave real point to the disastrous street fight in Act 3; he also enlarged Paris' part in the story and ennobled his character, and he created Mercutio. More important, he made all three of these serve as foils to a Romeo who develops and matures in response to the challenges they present and who, before the end, has ironically become responsible for the deaths of all three. Shakespeare's real miracle, however, was Juliet, transformed from an adolescent arrogantly eager to outdo her elders to an appealing child-woman, barely fourteen, who learns to mix courage with her innocence, yet falls victim to a world that only briefly and unintentionally but fatally treats her as a plaything.

# Commentaries

## SAMUEL JOHNSON

### *From* The Plays of William Shakespeare

This play is one of the most pleasing of our author's performances. The scenes are busy and various, the incidents numerous and important, the catastrophe irresistibly affecting, and the process of the action carried on with such probability, at least with such congruity to popular opinions, as tragedy requires.

Here is one of the few attempts of Shakespeare to exhibit the conversation of gentlemen, to represent the airy sprightliness of juvenile elegance. Mr. Dryden mentions a tradition, which might easily reach his time, of a declaration made by Shakespeare, that "he was obliged to kill Mercutio in the third act, lest he should have been killed by him." Yet he thinks him "no such formidable person, but that he might have lived through the play, and died in his bed," without danger to the poet. Dryden well knew, had he been in quest of truth, that, in a pointed sentence, more regard is commonly had to the words than the thought, and that it is very seldom to be rigorously understood. Mercutio's wit, gaiety, and courage, will always procure him friends that wish him a longer life; but his death is not precipitated, he has lived out the time allotted

From *The Works of Samuel Johnson, LL.D.* 9 vols. Oxford, 1825. This selection first appeared in *The Plays of William Shakespeare* (London, 1765).

him in the construction of the play; nor do I doubt the ability of Shakespeare to have continued his existence, though some of his sallies are, perhaps, out of the reach of Dryden; whose genius was not very fertile of merriment, nor ductile to humor, but acute, argumentative, comprehensive, and sublime.

The nurse is one of the characters in which the author delighted; he has, with great subtlety of distinction, drawn her at once loquacious and secret, obsequious and insolent, trusty and dishonest.

His comic scenes are happily wrought, but his pathetic strains are always polluted with some unexpected depravations. His persons, however distressed, have a conceit left them in their misery, a miserable conceit.

[1765]

# SAMUEL TAYLOR COLERIDGE

## *From* The Lectures of 1811–1812, Lecture VII

In a former lecture I endeavored to point out the union of the poet and the philosopher, or rather the warm embrace between them, in the *Venus and Adonis* and *Lucrece* of Shakespeare. From thence I passed on to *Love's Labor's Lost*, as the link between his character as a poet, and his art as a dramatist; and I showed that, although in that work the former was still predominant, yet that the germs of his subsequent dramatic power were easily discernible.

I will now, as I promised in my last, proceed to *Romeo and Juliet*, not because it is the earliest, or among the earliest of Shakespeare's works of that kind, but because in it are to be found specimens, in degree, of all the excellences which he afterwards displayed in his more perfect dramas, but differing from them in being less forcibly evidenced, and less happily combined: all the parts are more or less present, but they are not united with the same harmony.

There are, however, in *Romeo and Juliet* passages where the poet's whole excellence is evinced, so that nothing superior to them can be met with in the productions of his after years. The main distinction between this play and others is, as I said, that the parts are less happily combined, or to borrow a phrase from the painter, the whole work is less in keeping. Grand portions are pro-

From *Shakespearean Criticism* by Samuel Taylor Coleridge. 2nd ed., ed. Thomas Middleton Raysor. 2 vols. New York: E. P. Dutton and Company, Inc., 1960; London: J. M. Dent & Sons, Ltd., 1961. The exact text of Coleridge's lecture does not exist; what is given here is the transcript of a shorthand report taken by an auditor, J. P. Collier.

duced: we have limbs of giant growth; but the production, as a whole, in which each part gives delight for itself, and the whole, consisting of these delightful parts, communicates the highest intellectual pleasure and satisfaction, is the result of the application of judgment and taste. These are not to be attained but by painful study, and to the sacrifice of the stronger pleasures derived from the dazzling light which a man of genius throws over every circumstance, and where we are chiefly struck by vivid and distinct images. Taste is an attainment after a poet has been disciplined by experience and has added to genius that talent by which he knows what part of his genius he can make acceptable, and intelligible to the portion of mankind for which he writes.

In my mind it would be a hopeless symptom, as regards genius, if I found a young man with anything like perfect taste. In the earlier works of Shakespeare we have a profusion of double epithets, and sometimes even the coarsest terms are employed, if they convey a more vivid image; but by degrees the associations are connected with the image they are designed to impress, and the poet descends from the ideal into the real world so far as to conjoin both—to give a sphere of active operations to the ideal, and to elevate and refine the real.

In *Romeo and Juliet* the principal characters may be divided into two classes: in one class passion—the passion of love—is drawn and drawn truly, as well as beautifully; but the persons are not individualized farther than as the actor appears on the stage. It is a very just description and development of love, without giving, if I may so express myself, the philosophical history of it—without showing how the man became acted upon by that particular passion, but leading it through all the incidents of the drama and rendering it predominant.

Tybalt is, in himself, a commonplace personage. And here allow me to remark upon a great distinction between Shakespeare and all who have written in imitation of him. I know no character in his plays, (unless indeed Pistol be an exception) which can be called the mere portrait of an individual: while the reader feels all the satisfaction arising from individuality, yet that very individual is a sort of class character, and this circumstance renders Shakespeare the poet of all ages.

Tybalt is a man abandoned to his passions—with all the pride of family, only because he thought it belonged to him as a member of that family, and valuing himself highly, simply because he does not care for death. This indifference to death is perhaps more common than any other feeling: men are apt to flatter themselves extravagantly, merely because they possess a quality which it is a disgrace not to have, but which a wise man never puts forward, but when it is necessary.

Jeremy Taylor in one part of his voluminous works, speaking of a great man, says that he was naturally a coward, as indeed most men are, knowing the value of life, but the power of his reason enabled him, when required, to conduct himself with uniform courage and hardihood. The good bishop, perhaps, had in his mind a story, told by one of the ancients, of a Philosopher and a Coxcomb, on board the same ship during a storm: the Coxcomb reviled the Philosopher for betraying marks of fear: "Why are you so frightened? I am not afraid of being drowned: I do not care a farthing for my life."—"You are perfectly right," said the Philosopher, "for your life is not worth a farthing."

Shakespeare never takes pains to make his characters win your esteem, but leaves it to the general command of the passions and to poetic justice. It is most beautiful to observe, in *Romeo and Juliet*, that the characters principally engaged in the incidents are preserved innocent from all that could lower them in our opinion, while the rest of the personages, deserving little interest in themselves, derive it from being instrumental in those situations in which the more important personages develop their thoughts and passions.

Look at Capulet—a worthy, noble-minded old man of high rank, with all the impatience that is likely to accompany it. It is delightful to see all the sensibilities of our nature so exquisitely called forth; as if the poet had the hundred arms of the polypus, and had thrown them out in all directions to catch the predominant feeling. We may see in Capulet the manner in which anger seizes hold of everything that comes in its way, in order to express itself, as in the lines where he reproves Tybalt for his fierceness of behavior, which led him to wish to insult a Montague, and disturb the merriment.

> Go to, go to;
> You are a saucy boy. Is't so, indeed?
> This trick may chance to scath you;—I know what.
> You must contrary me! marry, 'tis time.—
> Well said, my hearts!—You are a princox: go:
> Be quiet or—More light, more light!—For shame!
> I'll make you quiet.—What! cheerly, my hearts!
>
> (1.5.84–90)

The line

> This trick may chance to scath you;—I know what,

was an allusion to the legacy Tybalt might expect; and then, seeing the lights burn dimly, Capulet turns his anger against the servants. Thus we see that no one passion is so predominant, but that it includes all the parts of the character, and the reader never has a mere abstract of a passion, as of wrath or ambition, but the whole man is presented to him—the one predominant passion acting, if I may so say, as the leader of the band to the rest.

It could not be expected that the poet should introduce such a character as Hamlet into every play; but even in those personages, which are subordinate to a hero so eminently philosophical, the passion is at least rendered instructive, and induces the reader to look with a keener eye and a finer judgment into human nature.

Shakespeare has this advantage over all other dramatists—that he has availed himself of his psychological genius to develop all the minutiae of the human heart:

showing us the thing that, to common observers, he seems solely intent upon, he makes visible what we should not otherwise have seen: just as, after looking at distant objects through a telescope, when we behold them subsequently with the naked eye, we see them with greater distinctness, and in more detail, than we should otherwise have done.

Mercutio is one of our poet's truly Shakespearean characters; for throughout his plays, but especially in those of the highest order, it is plain that the personages were drawn rather from meditation than from observation, or to speak correctly, more from observation, the child of meditation. It is comparatively easy for a man to go about the world, as if with a pocketbook in his hand, carefully noting down what he sees and hears: by practice he acquires considerable facility in representing what he has observed, himself frequently unconscious of its worth or its bearings. This is entirely different from the observation of a mind, which, having formed a theory and a system upon its own nature, remarks all things that are examples of its truth, confirming it in that truth and, above all, enabling it to convey the truths of philosophy, as mere effects derived from, what we may call, the outward watchings of life.

Hence it is that Shakespeare's favorite characters are full of such lively intellect. Mercutio is a man possessing all the elements of a poet: the whole world was, as it were, subject to his law of association. Whenever he wishes to impress anything, all things become his servants for the purpose: all things tell the same tale, and sound in unison. This faculty, moreover, is combined with the manners and feelings of a perfect gentleman, himself utterly unconscious of his powers. By his loss it was contrived that the whole catastrophe of the tragedy should be brought about: it endears him to Romeo and gives to the death of Mercutio an importance which it could not otherwise have acquired.

I say this in answer to an observation, I think by Dryden (to which indeed Dr. Johnson has fully replied), that

Shakespeare having carried the part of Mercutio as far as he could, till his genius was exhausted, had killed him in the third act, to get him out of the way. What shallow nonsense! As I have remarked, upon the death of Mercutio the whole catastrophe depends; it is produced by it. The scene in which it occurs serves to show how indifference to any subject but one, and aversion to activity on the part of Romeo, may be overcome and roused to the most resolute and determined conduct. Had not Mercutio been rendered so amiable and so interesting, we could not have felt so strongly the necessity for Romeo's interference, connecting it immediately, and passionately, with the future fortunes of the lover and his mistress.

But what am I to say of the Nurse? We have been told that her character is the mere fruit of observation—that it is like Swift's "Polite Conversation," certainly the most stupendous work of human memory, and of unceasingly active attention to what passes around us, upon record. The Nurse in *Romeo and Juliet* has sometimes been compared to a portrait by Gerard Dow, in which every hair was so exquisitely painted, that it would bear the test of the microscope. Now, I appeal confidently to my hearers whether the closest observation of the manners of one or two old nurses would have enabled Shakespeare to draw this character of admirable generalization? Surely not. Let any man conjure up in his mind all the qualities and peculiarities that can possibly belong to a nurse, and he will find them in Shakespeare's picture of the old woman: nothing is omitted. This effect is not produced by mere observation. The great prerogative of genius (and Shakespeare felt and availed himself of it) is now to swell itself to the dignity of a god, and now to subdue and keep dormant some part of that lofty nature, and to descend even to the lowest character—to become everything, in fact, but the vicious.

Thus, in the Nurse you have all the garrulity of old age, and all its fondness; for the affection of old age is one of the greatest consolations of humanity. I have often thought what a melancholy world this would be without children, and what an inhuman world without the aged.

You have also in the Nurse the arrogance of ignorance, with the pride of meanness at being connected with a great family. You have the grossness, too, which that situation never removes, though it sometimes suspends it; and, arising from that grossness, the little low vices attendant upon it, which, indeed, in such minds are scarcely vices.—Romeo at one time was the most delightful and excellent young man, and the Nurse all willingness to assist him; but her disposition soon turns in favor of Paris, for whom she professes precisely the same admiration. How wonderfully are these low peculiarities contrasted with a young and pure mind, educated under different circumstances!

Another point ought to be mentioned as characteristic of the ignorance of the Nurse: it is, that in all her recollections, she assists herself by the remembrance of visual circumstances. The great difference, in this respect, between the cultivated and the uncultivated mind is this—that the cultivated mind will be found to recall the past by certain regular trains of cause and effect; whereas, with the uncultivated mind, the past is recalled wholly by coincident images or facts which happened at the same time. This position is fully exemplified in the following passages put into the mouth of the Nurse:

> Even or odd, of all days in the year,
> Come Lammas eve at night shall she be fourteen.
> Susan and she—God rest all Christian souls!—
> Were of an age.—Well, Susan is with God;
> She was too good for me. But, as I said,
> On Lammas eve at night shall she be fourteen;
> That shall she, marry: I remember it well.
> 'Tis since the earthquake now eleven years;
> And she was wean'd,—I never shall forget it,—
> Of all the days of the year, upon that day;
> For I had then laid wormwood to my dug,
> Sitting in the sun under the dove-house wall:
> My lord and you were then at Mantua.—
> Nay, I do bear a brain:—but, as I said,

> When it did taste the wormwood on the nipple
> Of my dug, and felt it bitter, pretty fool,
> To see it tetchy, and fall out with the dug!
> Shake, quoth the dove-house: 'twas no need, I trow,
> To bid me trudge.
> And since that time it is eleven years;
> For then she could stand alone.

(1.3.16–36)

She afterwards goes on with similar visual impressions, so true to the character. More is here brought into one portrait than could have been ascertained by one man's mere observation, and without the introduction of a single incongruous point. . . .

Another remark I may make upon *Romeo and Juliet* is, that in this tragedy the poet is not, as I have hinted, entirely blended with the dramatist—at least, not in the degree to be afterwards noticed in *Lear*, *Hamlet*, *Othello*, or *Macbeth*. Capulet and Montague not unfrequently talk a language only belonging to the poet, and not so characteristic of, and peculiar to, the passions of persons in the situations in which they are placed—a mistake, or rather an indistinctness, which many of our later dramatists have carried through the whole of their productions.

When I read the song of Deborah, I never think that she is a poet, although I think the song itself a sublime poem: it is as simple a dithyrambic production as exists in any language; but it is the proper and characteristic effusion of a woman highly elevated by triumph, by the natural hatred of oppressors, and resulting from a bitter sense of wrong: it is a song of exultation on deliverance from these evils, a deliverance accomplished by herself. When she exclaims, "The inhabitants of the villages ceased, they ceased in Israel, until that I, Deborah, arose, that I arose a mother in Israel," it is poetry in the highest sense: we have no reason, however, to suppose that if she had not been agitated by passion, and animated by victory, she would have been able so to express herself; or that if she had been placed in different circumstances, she would have used such language of truth and passion. We are to remember that Shakespeare, not placed under circumstances of excitement, and only wrought upon by his own vivid and vigorous imagination, writes a language that invariably, and intuitively becomes the condition and position of each character.

On the other hand, there is a language not descriptive of passion, not uttered under the influence of it, which is at the same time poetic, and shows a high and active fancy, as when Capulet says to Paris,

> Such comfort as do lusty young men feel,
> When well-apparell'd April on the heel
> Of limping winter treads, even such delight
> Among fresh female buds, shall you this night
> Inherit at my house.
>
> (1.2.26–30)

Here the poet may be said to speak, rather than the dramatist; and it would be easy to adduce other passages from this play, where Shakespeare, for a moment forgetting the character, utters his own words in his own person.

In my mind, what have often been censured as Shakespeare's conceits are completely justifiable, as belonging to the state, age, or feeling of the individual. Sometimes, when they cannot be vindicated on these grounds, they may well be excused by the taste of his own and of the preceding age; as for instance, in Romeo's speech,

> Here's much to do with hate, but more with love:—
> Why then, O brawling love! O loving hate!
> O anything, of nothing first created!
> O heavy lightness! serious vanity!
> Misshapen chaos of well-seeming forms!
> Feather of lead, bright smoke, cold fire, sick health!
> Still-waking sleep, that is not what it is!
>
> (1.1.178–84)

I dare not pronounce such passages as these to be absolutely unnatural, not merely because I consider the author a much better judge than I can be, but because I can understand and allow for an effort of the mind, when it would describe what it cannot satisfy itself with the description of, to reconcile opposites and qualify contradictions, leaving a middle state of mind more strictly appropriate to the imagination than any other, when it is, as it were, hovering between images. As soon as it is fixed on one image, it becomes understanding; but while it is unfixed and wavering between them, attaching itself permanently to none, it is imagination. . . .

It remains for me to speak of the hero and heroine, of Romeo and Juliet themselves; and I shall do so with unaffected diffidence, not merely on account of the delicacy, but of the great importance of the subject. I feel that it is impossible to defend Shakespeare from the most cruel of all charges—that he is an immoral writer—without entering fully into his mode of portraying female characters, and of displaying the passion of love. It seems to me that he has done both with greater perfection than any other writer of the known world, perhaps with the single exception of Milton in his delineation of Eve. . . .

Shakespeare has described this passion in various states and stages, beginning, as was most natural, with love in the young. Does he open his play by making Romeo and Juliet in love at first sight—at the first glimpse, as any ordinary thinker would do? Certainly not: he knew what he was about, and how he was to accomplish what he was about: he was to develop the whole passion, and he commences with the first elements—that sense of imperfection, that yearning to combine itself with something lovely. Romeo became enamored of the idea he had formed in his own mind, and then, as it were, christened the first real being of the contrary sex as endowed with the perfections he desired. He appears to be in love with Rosaline; but, in truth, he is in love only with his own idea. He felt that necessity of being beloved which no noble mind can be without. Then our poet, or poet who so well knew human nature, introduces Romeo to Juliet, and makes it not only a violent, but a permanent love—a point for which Shakespeare has been ridiculed by the ignorant and unthinking. Romeo is first represented in a state most susceptible of love, and then, seeing Juliet, he took and retained the infection.

This brings me to observe upon a characteristic of Shakespeare, which belongs to a man of profound thought and high genius. It has been too much the custom, when anything that happened in his dramas could not easily be explained by the few words the poet has employed, to pass it idly over, and to say that it is beyond our reach, and beyond the power of philosophy—a sort of terra incognita for discoverers—a great ocean to be hereafter explored. Others have treated such passages as hints and glimpses of something now nonexistent, as the sacred fragments of an ancient and ruined temple, all the portions of which are beautiful, although their particular relation to each other is unknown. Shakespeare knew the human mind, and its most minute and intimate workings, and he never introduces a word, or a thought, in vain or out of place: if we do not understand him, it is our own fault or the fault of copyists and typographers; but study, and the possession of some small stock of the knowledge by which he worked, will enable us often to detect and explain his meaning. He never wrote at random, or hit upon points of character and conduct by chance; and the smallest fragment of his mind not unfrequently gives a clue to a most perfect, regular, and consistent whole.

As I may not have another opportunity, the introduction of Friar Lawrence into this tragedy enables me to remark upon the different manner in which Shakespeare has treated the priestly character, as compared with other writers. In Beaumont and Fletcher priests are represented as a vulgar mockery; and, as in others of their dramatic personages, the errors of a few are mistaken for the demeanor of the many: but in Shakespeare they always carry with them our love and respect. He made no injurious abstracts: he took no copies from the worst parts of our nature; and, like the rest, his characters of priests are truly drawn from the general body.

# H. B. CHARLTON

# *From* Shakespearian Tragedy

In their general structure and idea, the three tragedies so far reviewed were in the current dramatic tradition of their day. But *Romeo and Juliet* is a departure, a comprehensive experiment. It links the English stage to the Renaissance tragedy which by precept and by practice Cinthio[1] in the middle of the sixteenth century had established in Italy.

Cinthio's principles were in the main an adaptation of Seneca's, or rather of what he took to be Seneca's purposes, to the immediate needs of Cinthio's contemporary theatre. His own object he declared to be *"servire l'età, a gli spettatori."* Tragedy must grip its audience. It must therefore reflect a range of experience and base itself on a system of values which are felt by its audience to be real. Many of his proposals are the direct outcome of this general principle, and one or two of them are especially pertinent to our argument. For instance, tragedy must no longer rely mainly for its material on ancient mythology nor on accredited history; for these depict a world which may have lost urgent contact with a modern audience's sense of life. The best plots for modern tragedy will be found in modern fiction. For modern fiction is the mythology of today. It is the corpus of story through which the world appears as it seems to be to living men;

From *Shakespearian Tragedy* by H. B. Charlton. London and New York: Cambridge University Press, 1948. Reprinted by permission of Cambridge University Press.

[1]See H. B. Charlton, *Senecan Tradition in Renaissance Tragedy*, first published in 1921 as an introduction to *The Poetical Works of Sir William Alexander* (Manchester University Press and Scottish Texts Society) and reissued separately by the Manchester University Press in 1946.

it mirrors accepted codes of conduct, displays the particular manner of contemporary consciousness, and adopts the current assumptions of human values. Let the dramatist, therefore, draw his plots from the novelists. An inevitable consequence followed from this. There is nothing in which the outlook on life adopted˙ by the modern world is more different from that of the ancient classical world than in its apprehension of the human and spiritual significance of the love of man for woman. Love has become for the modern world its most engrossing interest and often its supreme experience. Modern fiction turns almost exclusively on love. So when dramatists took their tales from the novelists, they took love over as the main theme of their plays. Seven of Cinthio's nine plays borrow their plots from novels (most of them from his own series, the *Hecatommithi*); the other two are "classical," but are two of the great classical love stories, *Dido* and *Cleopatra*. Jason de Nores, a much more conservatively Aristotelian expositor than his contemporary Cinthio, to exemplify the form which the most perfect tragedy could take, constructs the plot for it from one of Boccaccio's tales.

Whether by direct influence or by mere force of circumstance, Cinthio's practice prevailed. Sixteenth-century tragedy found rich material in the novels. But the traditionalists were perpetually reminding the innovators that tragedy always had had and always must have an historical hero. *"In tragoedia reges, principes, ex urbibus, arcibus, castris,"* Scaliger, the Parnassian legislator, announced. No one would accept a hero as great unless his memory were preserved in the historian's pages. *"C'est l'histoire qui persuade avec empire,"* as Corneille put it. Shakespeare, an eager and humble apprentice, naturally followed traditional custom. *Titus Andronicus*, *Richard III*, and *Richard II* belong in the main to the conventional pattern. They deal with historical material. Their heroes are of high rank and potent in determining the destiny of nations. The plot is never mainly a lovers' story, though a love intrigue intrudes sporadically here

and there within the major theme. But somehow the pre-
scriptions had not produced the expected result. There
was something unsatisfying in these plays as divinations
of man's tragic lot. And so the conventions were jetti-
soned in *Romeo and Juliet*.

Shakespeare was casting in fresh directions to find
the universality, the momentousness, and above all the
inevitability of all-compelling tragedy. In particular, he
was experimenting with a new propelling force, a new
final sanction as the determinant energy, the *ultima ratio*
of tragedy's inner world; and though *Romeo and Juliet* is
set in a modern Christian country, with church and priest
and full ecclesiastical institution, the whole universe of
God's justice, vengeance, and providence is discarded and
rejected from the directing forces of the play's dramatic
movement. In its place, there is a theatrical resuscita-
tion of the half-barbarian, half-Roman deities of Fate and
Fortune.

The plot of *Romeo and Juliet* is pure fiction. Shakespeare took it from Arthur Broke's poem, *The Tragicall
Historie of Romeus and Juliet* (1562). Shakespeare knew
from Broke's title page that the tale was taken from an
Italian novelist, "written first in Italian by Bandell." He
knew, too, what sort of novels Bandello wrote, for Painter
had retold them in his *Palace of Pleasure* (1567). They
were clear fictions. Moreover the hero and the heroine,
Romeo and Juliet, had none of the pomp of historic circumstance about them; they were socially of the minor
aristocracy who were to stock Shakespeare's comedies,
and their only political significance was an adventitious
role in the civic disturbance of a small city-state. Romeo
and Juliet were in effect just a boy and a girl in a novel;
and as such they had no claim to the world's attention
except through their passion and their fate.

To choose such folk as these for tragic heroes was aes-
thetically well-nigh an anarchist's gesture; and the dramatist provided a sort of program-prologue to prompt the
audience to see the play from the right point of view. In
this playbill the dramatist draws special attention to two

features of his story. First, Verona was being torn by a terrible, bloodthirsty feud which no human endeavor had been able to settle; this was the direct cause of the death of the lovers, and but for those deaths it never would have been healed. Second, the course of the young lovers' lives is from the outset governed by a malignant destiny; fatal, star-crossed, death-marked, they are doomed to piteous destruction.

The intent of this emphasis is clear. The tale will end with the death of two ravishingly attractive young folk; and the dramatist must exonerate himself from all complicity in their murder, lest he be found guilty of pandering to a liking for a human shambles. He disowns responsibility and throws it on Destiny, Fate. The device is well warranted in the tragic tradition, and especially in its Senecan models. But whether, in fact, it succeeds is a matter for further consideration. The invocation of Fate is strengthened by the second feature scored heavily in the prologue, the feud. The feud is, so to speak, the means by which Fate acts. The feud is to provide the sense of immediate, and Fate that of ultimate, inevitability. For it may happen that, however the dramatist deploys his imaginative suggestions, he may fail to summon up a Fate sufficiently compelling to force itself upon the audience as unquestioned shaper of the tragic end. In such circumstance Romeo's and Juliet's death would be by mere chance, a gratuitous intervention by a dramatist exercising his homicidal proclivities for the joy of his audience. Hence the feud has a further function. It will be the dramatist's last plea for exculpation or for mercy; and it will allow his audience to absolve him or to forgive him without loss of its own "philanthropy"; for through death came the healing of the feud, and with it, the removal of the threat to so many other lives.

It becomes, therefore, of critical importance to watch Shakespeare's handling of these two motives, Fate and Feud, to see how he fits them to fulfill their function, and to ask how far in fact they are adequate to the role they must perforce play. Both Fate and Feud, although absent as motives from the earliest European form of the Romeo and Juliet story, had grown variously in the successive tellings of the tale before it came to Broke.[2] The general trend had been to magnify the virulence of the feud, and, even more notably, to swell the sententious apostrophizing of Fate's malignity. Broke, for instance, misses no opportunity for such sententiousness. Longer or shorter, there are at least fifteen passages in his poem where the malignity of Fate is his conventionally poetic theme. "Froward fortune," "fortune's cruel will," "wavering fortune," "tickel fortune," "when fortune list to strike," "false fortune cast for her, poore wretch, a myschiefe newe to brewe," "dame fortune did assent," "with piteous plaint, fierce fortune doth he blame," "till Attropos shall cut my fatall thread of lyfe," "though cruel fortune be so much my dedly foe," "the blyndfyld goddesse that with frowning face doth fraye, and from theyr seate the mighty kinges throwes downe with hedlong sway," "He cryed out, with open mouth, against the starres above, The fatall sisters three, he said, had done him wrong"—so, again and again, does Broke bring in

> The diversenes, and eke the accidents so straunge,
> Of frayle unconstant Fortune, that delyteth still in chaunge.[3]

Romeo cries aloud

> Against the restles starres, in rolling skyes that raunge,
> Against the fatall sisters three, and Fortune full of chaunge.[4]

There are more elaborate set speeches on the same theme:

[2]For differences between the many pre-Shakespearian versions, see H. B. Charlton, *Romeo and Juliet as an Experimental Tragedy* (British Academy Shakespeare Lecture, 1939) and "France as Chaperone of Romeo and Juliet" in *Studies in French presented to M. K. Pope*, Manchester University Press (1939).
[3]Broke, *Romeus and Juliet* (Hazlitt's *Shakespeare's Library*, Vol. I, 1875), p. 142.
[4]*Ibid.*, p. 151.

For Fortune chaungeth more, than fickel fantasie;
In nothing Fortune constant is, save in unconstancie.
Her hasty ronning wheele, is of a restles coorse,
That turnes the clymers hedlong downe, from better to the
    woorse,
and those that are beneth, she heaveth up agayne.[5]

So when Shakespeare took up the story, Broke had already sought to drench it in fatality. But since Shakespeare was a dramatist, he could not handle Fate and Feud as could a narrative poet. His feud will enter, not descriptively, but as action; and for fate he must depend on the sentiments of his characters and on an atmosphere generated by the sweep of the action. The feud may be deferred for a moment to watch Shakespeare's handling of Fate.

His most frequent device is to adapt what Broke's practice had been; instead of letting his persons declaim formally, as Broke's do, against the inconstancy of Fortune, he endows them with dramatic premonitions. Setting out for Capulet's ball, Romeo is suddenly sad:

> my mind misgives
> Some consequence, yet hanging in the stars,
> Shall bitterly begin his fearful date
> With this night's revels; and expire the term
> Of a despised life, clos'd in my breast,
> By some vile forfeit of untimely death:
> But he that hath the steerage of my course
> Direct my sail!

(1.4.106–13)

As the lovers first declare their passion, Juliet begs Romeo not to swear, as if an oath might be an evil omen:

> I have no joy of this contract tonight:
> It is too rash, too unadvised, too sudden;

[5]*Ibid.*, p. 147. See also pp. 97, 115.

> Too like the lightning, which doth cease to be
> Ere one can say "It lightens."
>
> (2.2.117–20)

Romeo, involved in the fatal fight, cries "O, I am fortune's fool!" (3.1.138). Looking down from her window at Romeo as he goes into exile, Juliet murmurs

> O God, I have an ill-divining soul!
> Methinks I see thee, now thou art below,
> As one dead in the bottom of a tomb.
>
> (3.5.54–56)

With dramatic irony Juliet implores her parents to defer her marriage with Paris:

> Or, if you do not, make the bridal bed
> In that dim monument where Tybalt lies.
>
> (202–03)

Besides these promptings of impending doom there are premonitions of a less direct kind. The friar fears the violence of the lover's passion:

> These violent delights have violent ends
> And in their triumph die, like fire and powder,
> Which as they kiss consume.
>
> (2.6.9–11)

Another source of omen in the play is the presaging of dreams; for from the beginning of time, "the world of sleep, the realm of wild reality" has brought dreams which look like heralds of eternity and speak like Sybils of the future. There is much dreaming in *Romeo and Juliet*. Mercutio may mock at dreams as children of an idle brain, begot of nothing but vain fantasy. But when Romeo says he "dream'd a dream tonight," Mercutio's famous flight of fancy recalls the universal belief in dreams as foreshadowings of the future. Again Romeo dreams; this time, "I dreamt my lady came and found me dead" (5.1.6). As his man Balthasar waits outside Juliet's tomb, he dreams that his master and another are fighting and the audience knows how accurately the dream mirrors the true facts.

But Shakespeare not only hangs omens thickly round his play. He gives to the action itself a quality apt to conjure the sense of relentless doom. It springs mainly from his compression of the time over which the story stretches. In all earlier versions there is a much longer lapse. Romeo's wooing is prolonged over weeks before the secret wedding; then, after the wedding, there is an interval of three or four months before the slaying of Tybalt; and Romeo's exile lasts from Easter until a short time before mid-September when the marriage with Paris was at first planned to take place. But in Shakespeare all this is pressed into three or four days. The world seems for a moment to be caught up in the fierce play of furies reveling in some mad supernatural game.

But before asking whether the sense of an all-controlling Fate is made strong enough to fulfill its tragic purpose let us turn to the feud. Here Shakespeare's difficulties are even greater. Italian novelists of the quattro- or cinquecento, throwing their story back through two or three generations, might expect their readers easily to accept a fierce vendetta. But the Verona which Shakespeare depicts is a highly civilized world, with an intellectual and artistic culture and an implied social attainment altogether alien from the sort of society in which a feud is a more or less natural manifestation of enmity. The border country of civilization is the home of feuds, a region where social organization is still of the clan, where the head of the family-clan is a strong despot, and where law has not progressed beyond the sort of wild justice of which one instrument is the feud.

> For ere I cross the border fells,
> The tane of us shall die

It was well-nigh impossible for Shakespeare to fit the blood lust of a border feud into the social setting of his Verona. The heads of the rival houses are not at all the fierce chieftains who rule with ruthless despotism. When old Capulet, in fireside gown, bustles to the scene of the fray and calls for his sword, his wife tells him bluntly that it is a crutch which an old man such as he should want, and not a weapon. Montague, too, spits a little verbal fire, but his wife plucks him by the arm and tells him to calm down: "thou shalt not stir one foot to seek a foe." Indeed, these old men are almost comic figures, and especially Capulet. His querulous fussiness, his casual bonhomie, his almost senile humor, and his childish irascibility hardly make him the pattern of a clan chieftain. Even his domestics put him in his place:

> Go, you cotquean, go,
> Get you to bed; faith, you'll be sick tomorrow
> For this night's watching,
>
> (4.4.6–8)

the Nurse tells him; and the picture is filled in by his wife's reminder that she has put a stop to his "mouse-hunting." There is of course the prince's word that

> Three civil brawls, bred of an airy word,
> By thee, old Capulet, and Montague,
> Have thrice disturb'd the quiet of our streets.
>
> (1.1.92–94)

But these brawls bred of an airy word are no manifestations of a really ungovernable feud. When Montague and Capulet are bound by the prince to keep the peace, old Capulet himself says

> 'tis not hard, I think,
> For men so old as we to keep the peace.
>
> (1.2.2–3)

and there is a general feeling that the old quarrel has run its course. Paris, suitor to Juliet, says it is a pity that the Capulets and the Montagues have lived at odds so long. And Benvolio, a relative of the Montagues, is a consistent peacemaker. He tries to suppress a brawl amongst the rival retainers and invites Tybalt, a Capulet, to assist him in the work. Later he begs his friends to avoid trouble by keeping out of the way of the Capulets, for it is the season of hot blood:

> I pray thee, good Mercutio, let's retire:
> The day is hot, the Capulets abroad,
> And if we meet, we shall not scape a brawl;
> For now, these hot days, is the mad blood stirring.
>
> (3.1.1–4)

When the hot-blooded Mercutio does incite Tybalt to a quarrel it is again Benvolio who tries to preserve the peace:

> We talk here in the public haunt of men:
> Either withdraw unto some private place,
> And reason coldly of your grievances,
> Or else depart.
>
> (51–54)

Hence the jest of Mercutio's famous description of Benvolio as an inveterate quarreler, thirsting for the slightest excuse to draw sword.

Moreover, the rival houses have mutual friends. Mercutio, Montague Romeo's close acquaintance, is an invited guest at the Capulets' ball. Stranger still, so is Romeo's cruel lady, Rosaline, who in the invitation is addressed as Capulet's cousin. It is odd that Romeo's love for her, since she was a Capulet, had given him no qualms on the score of the feud. When Romeo is persuaded to go gate-crashing to the ball because Rosaline will be there, there is no talk at all of its being a hazardous undertaking. Safety will require, if even so much,

no more than a mask.[6] On the way to the ball, as talk is
running gaily, there is still no mention of danger
involved. Indeed, the feud is almost a dead letter so far.
The son of the Montague does not know what the
Capulet daughter looks like, nor she what he is like. The
traditional hatred survives only in one or two high-
spirited, hot-blooded scions on either side, and in the
kitchen folk. Tybalt alone resents Romeo's presence at
the ball, yet it is easy for all to recognize him; and
because Tybalt feels Romeo's coming to be an insult, he
seeks him out next day to challenge him, so providing the
immediate occasion of the new outburst. Naturally, once
blood is roused again, and murder done, the ancient
rancor springs up with new life. Even Lady Capulet
has comically Machiavellian plans for having Romeo
poisoned in Mantua. But prior to this the evidences of
the feud are so unsubstantial that the forebodings of
Romeo and Juliet, discovering each other's name, seem
prompted more by fate than feud. There will, of course,
be family difficulties; but the friar marries them without
a hesitating qualm, feeling that such a union is bound to
be accepted eventually by the parents, who will thus be
brought to amity.

The most remarkable episode, however, is still to be
named. When Tybalt discovers Romeo at the ball, infuri-
ated he rushes to Capulet with the news. But Capulet, in
his festive mood, is pleasantly interested, saying that
Romeo is reputed to be good-looking and quite a pleasant
boy. He tells Tybalt to calm himself, to remember his
manners, and to treat Romeo properly:

> Content thee, gentle coz, let him alone:
> He bears him like a portly gentleman;

[6]In the earlier versions the mask is not a precaution for safety. Shakespeare,
taking it partly as such, has to realize how utterly ineffective it is. Romeo is
soon known:

> This, by his voice, should be a Montague!
> Fetch me my rapier, boy. What dares the slave
> Come hither, cover'd with an antic face,
> To fleer and scorn at our solemnity?            (1.5.56–59)

And, to say truth, Verona brags of him
To be a virtuous and well govern'd youth:
I would not for the wealth of all the town
Here in my house do him disparagement:
Therefore be patient, take no note of him:
It is my will, the which if thou respect,
Show a fair presence and put off these frowns,
An ill-beseeming semblance for a feast.

(1.5.67–76)

When Tybalt is reluctant, old Capulet is annoyed and testily tells him to stop being a saucy youngster:

He shall be endured:
What, goodman boy! I say, he shall: go to.
And I the master here or you? Go to.
You'll not endure him! God shall mend my soul!
You'll make a mutiny among my guests
You will set cock-a-hoop. You'll be the man!
. . . Go to, go to;
You are a saucy boy: is't so indeed?
This trick may chance to scathe you, I know what:
You must contrary me! marry, tis' time.
Well said, my hearts! You are a princox; go. (78–88)

This is a scene which sticks in the memory; for here the dramatist, unencumbered by a story, is interpolating a lively scene in his own kind, a vignette of two very amusing people in an amusing situation. But it is unfortunate for the feud that this episode takes so well. For clearly old Capulet is unwilling to let the feud interrupt a dance; and a quarrel which is of less moment than a galliard is being appeased at an extravagant price, if the price is the death of two such delightful creatures as Romeo and Juliet;

their parents' rage,
Which, but their children's end, naught could remove,

(Prologue, 10–11)

loses all its plausibility. A feud like this will not serve as the bribe it was meant to be; it is no atonement for the death of lovers. Nor, indeed, is it coherent and impressive enough as part of the plot to propel the sweep of necessity in the sequence of events. If the tragedy is to march relentlessly to its end, leaving no flaw in the sense of inevitability which it seeks to prompt, it clearly must depend for that indispensable tragic impression not on its feud, but on its scattered suggestions of doom and of malignant fate. And, as has been seen, Shakespeare harps frequently on this theme.

But how far can a Roman sense of Fate be made real for a modern audience? It is no mere matter of exciting thought to "wander through eternity" in the wake of the mystery which surrounds the human lot. Mystery must take on positive shape, and half-lose itself in dread figures controlling human life in their malice. The forms and the phrases by which these powers had been invoked were a traditional part in the inheritance of the Senecan drama which came to sixteenth-century Europe. Fortuna, Fatum, Fata, Parcae: all were firmly established in its *dramatis personae*. Moreover their role in Virgilian theocracy was familiar to all with but a little Latin:

> Qua visa est fortuna pati Parcaeque sinebant
> Cedere res Latio, Turnum et tua moenia texi;
> Nunc iuvenem imparibus video concurrere fatis,
> Parcarumque dies et vis inimica propinquat.[7]

For Roman here indeed were the shapers of destiny, the ultimate ἀνάγκη which compels human fate, whether as the μοῖρα of individual lot, or the εἱμαρμένη of a world order. Horace himself linked Fortuna in closest companionship with Necessitas: *"te semper anteit serva Necessitas,"* he writes in his prayer to Fortuna.[8] It was a note which reverberated through Senecan stoicism.

[7] *Aeneid* XII. 147.
[8] *Odes* I.xxxv.

But with what conviction could a sixteenth-century spectator take over these ancient figures? Even the human beings of an old mythology may lose their compelling power; "what's Hecuba to him, or he to Hecuba?" But the gods are in a much worse case; pagan, they had faded before the God of the Christians: *Vicisti, Galilæe!* Fate was no longer a deity strong enough to carry the responsibility of a tragic universe; at most, it could intervene casually as pure luck, and bad luck as a motive turns tragedy to mere chance. It lacks entirely the ultimate tragic ἀνάγκη. It fails to provide the indispensable inevitability.

Is then Shakespeare's *Romeo and Juliet* an unsuccessful experiment? To say so may seem not only profane but foolish. In its own day, as the dog's-eared Bodley Folio shows, and ever since, it has been one of Shakespeare's most preferred plays. It is indeed rich in spells of its own. But as a pattern of the idea of tragedy, it is a failure. Even Shakespeare appears to have felt that, as an experiment, it had disappointed him. At all events, he abandoned tragedy for the next few years and gave himself to history and to comedy; and even afterwards, he fought shy of the simple theme of love, and of the love of anybody less than a great political figure as the main matter for his tragedies.

Nevertheless it is obvious that neither sadism nor masochism is remotely conscious in our appreciation of *Romeo and Juliet*, nor is our "philanthropy" offended by it. But the achievement is due to the magic of Shakespeare's poetic genius and to the intermittent force of his dramatic power rather than to his grasp of the foundations of tragedy.

There is no need here to follow the meetings of Romeo and Juliet through the play, and to recall the spell of Shakespeare's poetry as it transports us along the rushing stream of the lovers' passion, from its sudden outbreak to its consummation in death. Romeo seals his "dateless bargain to engrossing death," choosing shipwreck on the dashing rocks to secure peace for his "sea-sick weary bark." Juliet has but a word: "I'll be brief. O happy dagger!" There is need for nothing beyond this. Shakespeare, divining their naked passion, lifts them above the world and out of life by the mere force of it. It is the sheer might of poetry. Dramatically, however, he has subsidiary resources. He has Mercutio and the Nurse.

Shakespeare's Mercutio has the gay poise and the rippling wit of the man of the world. By temperament he is irrepressible and merry; his charm is infectious. His speech runs freely between fancies of exquisite delicacy and the coarser fringe of worldly humor; and he has the sensitiveness of sympathetic fellowship. Such a man, if any at all, might have understood the depth of Romeo's love for Juliet. But the camaraderie and the worldly *savoir-faire* of Mercutio give him no inkling of the nature of Romeo's passion. The love of Romeo and Juliet is beyond the ken of their friends; it belongs to a world which is not their world; and so the passing of Romeo and Juliet is not as other deaths are in their impact on our sentiments.

Similarly, too, the Nurse. She is Shakespeare's greatest debt to Broke, in whose poem she plays a curiously unexpected and yet incongruously entertaining part. She is the one great addition which Broke made to the saga. She is garrulous, worldly, coarse, vulgar, and babblingly given to reminiscence stuffed with native animal humor and self-assurance. Shakespeare gladly borrowed her, and so gave his Juliet for her most intimate domestic companion a gross worldly creature who talks much of love and never means anything beyond sensuality. Like Romeo's, Juliet's love is completely unintelligible to the people in her familiar circle. To her nurse, love is animal lust. To her father, who has been a "mouse-hunter" in his time, and to her mother, it is merely a social institution, a worldly arrangement in a very worldly world. This earth, it would seem, has no place for passion like Romeo's and Juliet's. And so, stirred to sympathy by Shakespeare's poetic power, we tolerate, perhaps even approve, their death. At least for the moment.

But tragedy lives not only for its own moment, nor by long "suspensions of disbelief." There is the inevitable afterthought and all its "obstinate questionings." Our sentiments were but momentarily gratified. And finally our deeper consciousness protests. Shakespeare has but conquered us by a trick: the experiment carries him no nearer to the heart of tragedy.

MICHAEL GOLDMAN

# *Romeo and Juliet*:
# The Meaning of a
# Theatrical Experience

Everything in *Romeo and Juliet* is intense, impatient, threatening, explosive. We are caught up in speed, heat, desire, riots, running, jumping, rapid-fire puns, dirty jokes, extravagance, compressed and urgent passion, the pressure of secrets, fire, blood, death. Visually, the play remains memorable for a number of repeated images—street brawls, swords flashing to the hand, torches rushing on and off, crowds rapidly gathering. The upper stage is used frequently, with many opportunities for leaping or scrambling or stretching up and down and much play between upper and lower areas. The dominant bodily feelings we get as an audience are oppressive heat, sexual desire, a frequent whiz-bang exhilarating kinesthesia of speed and clash, and above all a feeling of the keeping-down and separation of highly charged bodies, whose pressure toward release and whose sudden discharge determine the rhythm of the play.

The thematic appropriateness of these sensations to Shakespeare's first great tragedy of the unsounded self is obvious enough, perhaps too obvious. Shakespeare's tragic heroes usually pass from isolation to isolation. Romeo cannot be one of the boys or Hamlet one of his northern world's competent, adaptable young men. At the beginning the isolation is that of the unsounded self, some form of self-sufficiency, remoteness, or withdrawal. The

From Michael Goldman, *Shakespeare and the Energies of Drama* (Princeton, N.J.: Princeton University Press, 1972), pp. 33–44.

hero strikes us as a kind of closed structure. He very clearly carries a packaged energy; on first meeting him we recognize the container and the seal. (Think of Romeo or Hamlet for swift opening indications of these.) The ultimate isolation comes in the rupture of the package, the energy's discharge. The drama marks the change. Romeo and Juliet are isolated by the sudden demands of love returned, and the world of their play reflects the violence of the transformation.

The type of outline just given is useful but treacherous. It is useful because it sharpens our sense of the Shakespearean dramatic situation and gives us a reasonably pertinent norm by which to measure individual developments. But to follow it out in detail, to translate each tragedy back into the outline, to tell it like a story for any of the plays would be to lose exactly what makes the idea of the unsounded self important—that it is basic to drama, something far different from story or subject or theme. This is what is wrong with thinking about theatrical impressions in terms of thematic appropriateness, as a kind of varnish over the poetry and plot.

What ideally has to be done and is perhaps more easily attempted for *Romeo and Juliet* than for later plays is to talk about what the experience of the whole amounts to. The impression is strong and distinctive; why do we mark it as we do? The problem is to take all the elements that affect us in the theater and examine them as they arrange themselves in our response, asking what relevance this configuration bears to our lives.

If we try to see what the deep effect of the combination of these elements is, the crucial question is that of the relation that connects the plot, the visual spectacle, and the wordplay. Clearly they share a common busyness, suddenness, and violence. "These violent delights have violent ends" is enough to explain their congruence at least superficially. But it does not account for the richness of our response to the elaborate detail of the drama. Nor does it account for the peculiar aptness we sense in certain kinds of detail. Why are there so many puns and such obscene ones? Why should Mercutio and the Nurse be given long, digressive bravura speeches? Why is the balcony stressed, and the athleticism it entails? Why should certain lines like "Wherefore art thou Romeo?" or "What's in a name?" or "A feasting presence full of light" stick in the memory? The last may be explained by its "beauty out of context"—always a doubtful procedure—but the other lines resist even that easy question-begging method, and consequently give us a good place to begin.

> "Wherefore art thou Romeo?"                    (2.2.33)

Romeo's name presents a problem to others besides Juliet but she characteristically sees more deeply into the difficulty. For it is not enough to decide whether Romeo should be called humors, madman, passion, lunatic, villain, coward, boy, Capulet, Montague, or even Romeo. The question is really why he must have a name at all. *Romeo and Juliet* is a tragedy of naming, a tragedy in which at times Romeo's name seems to be the villain:

> As if that name,
> Shot from the deadly level of a gun,
> Did murder her, as that name's cursed hand
> Murder'd her kinsman. O, tell me, friar, tell me,
> In what vile part of this anatomy
> Doth my name lodge? Tell me, that I may sack
> The hateful mansion.                          (3.3.102–8)

But though this echoes Juliet's other famous question and her insistence that a name is after all "nor hand, nor foot, / Nor arm, nor face," it is far different from "What's in a name?" in even its immediate implications. The trouble with Romeo's name here is not that it is a trivial attribute that raises accidental difficulties, but that "Romeo" now has a history, an inescapable reality of its own. It is the name of the man who has killed Tybalt; it is attached to a past and Romeo is responsible for it.

It is Romeo who is banished for what Romeo has done. His anguish, though emotionally an intensification of Juliet's in the balcony scene, is logically an answer to her question. This, among other things, is what's in a name.

Not only do names have a peculiar substantiality in the play (they can murder, die, be torn; every tongue that speaks "But Romeo's name speaks heavenly eloquence") but words themselves take on a namelike intensity. That is, they take on, usually by repetition, the importance and attributes of persons:

> Say thou but "I"
> And that bare vowel "I" shall poison more
> Than the death-darting eye of cockatrice.
> I am not I, if there be such an I;
> Or those eyes shut, that makes thee answer "I."[1]

> ". . . banished."
> That "banished," that one word "banished,"
> Hath slain ten thousand Tybalts.    (3.2.45–49, 112–14)

Here, as with "day" in 4.5,[2] the effect in the theater is not to deepen the meaning of the word but at once to strip the meaning away through endless repetition and to give it a namelike life of its own.

As these examples suggest, naming is characteristically associated with separation in the play. It is no accident that at the time of painful separation on the morning after their marriage the lovers' aubade turns on the name of a bird:

[1]Restoring the Q2 reading of "I" for "ay" in ll.45, 48, and 49.

[2]    Most lamentable day, most woeful day,
    That ever, ever, I did yet behold!
    O day, O day! O day! O hateful day!
    Never was seen so black a day as this.
    O woeful day, O woeful day! (50–54)

It was the nightingale, and not the lark . . .

It was the lark, the herald of the morn,
No nightingale.

(3.5.2–7)

They are passing from a night of sensual union to a day of
exile. Night, as Mercutio has observed, is a time of free
association, of fantastic invention, but day makes stricter
demands upon our consciousness. When Romeo agrees to
call the bird by some other name, Juliet must quickly
admit that it is indeed the lark. The lovers relinquish the
right to rename the world as they please; they must know
the world's names for things if they wish to stay alive
in it.

The play's everpresent thrust toward punning heightens
our sense of the accepted meaning of words and of the
rampant psychic energy that rises to break the meanings
down. The wordplay makes its contribution as much by
its quantity and irrepressibility as by its content. The puns
are rapid and raw, emphasizing the suddenness and violence that is part of all punning, while the very process of
punning raises issues that are central to the play. A pun is
a sudden exchange of names, uniting objects we are not
ordinarily allowed to unite, with a consequent release of
energy, often violent and satisfying, and always satisfying
to the extent that it is violent. It is something both terrible
and lovely; we say "That's awful," when we mean
"That's good." Romeo and Juliet themselves are like the
components of a particularly good pun—natural mates
whom authority strives to keep apart and whose union is
not only violent but illuminating, since it transforms and
improves the order it violates, though it is necessarily
impermanent.

The fury of the pun is the fury of our submerged innocence; we play with words as Romeo and Juliet play with
the lark and nightingale. Punning restores to us—under
certain very narrow conditions, and for a brief interval—
our freedom to change names and to make connections

we have been taught to suppress, to invent language, to reconstitute the world as we please. *Romeo and Juliet* begins with a series of puns leading to a street brawl culminating in a dangerous mistake (Benvolio, intending to restore order, draws his sword) that spreads the conflict to include nearly the entire company. The sequence is significant, for the energy of the pun, fully released in an organized society where names and rules are important, tends to be disastrous. Capulet and Montague lackeys lurk around the stage like forbidden meanings looking for an opportunity to discharge themselves. And at the level of responsible authority, the equivalent of the lackeys' idle brawling (or the overwhelming passion of the young lovers) is the capacity for instant and mistaken decision. From Benvolio's intervention in the opening street brawl to Romeo's suicide in the tomb, the play is a tissue of precipitous mistakes. Capulet hands a guest list to a servant who cannot read and the tragedy is initiated (significantly it is a list of names—all of which are read out—that is the villain). Mercutio's death is a mistake; and Romeo's error, like Capulet's and Benvolio's, enacts itself as a backfiring gesture, an action that—like a pun—subverts its manifest intention. Romeo's pathetic "I thought all for the best," rings in our ears when we see Lawrence and Capulet stricken by the lovers' death.

Counter to all the hasty and disastrous action of the play, there runs a surge of simple authoritative confidence, voiced at different times by almost every major character. The first scene ends with Romeo's assertion that he will always love Rosaline. As Romeo goes off, Capulet enters insisting that it will be easy to keep the peace. The juxtaposition of these two errors goes beyond simple irony; the encounter between confident assumption and the sudden event is one of the play's important motifs, just as the disparity between principle and practice is one of its recurrent themes. The Friar's first speech, for example, is often seen as a moralization of the action of *Romeo and Juliet*, and indeed there is a clear and effective dramatic connection between his homily and the action that surrounds it. The contrast between the night-time intensity of the scene immediately preceding, and the complacent tranquility of Lawrence's reflections is obviously intended, and to further enforce the connection, he begins by moralizing the contrast:

> The grey-ey'd morn smiles on the frowning night . . .
> And flecked darkness like a drunkard reels
> From forth day's path                              (2.3.1–4)

As he goes on, he seems to anticipate events that are to follow, but on closer inspection, his remarks are not precisely appropriate:

> Virtue itself turns vice, being misapplied;
> And vice sometime's by action dignified.          (21–22)

The first of these lines fits the lovers and much else in the play, but the second, though on the surface equally fitting, turns out to be harder to apply. Romeo is apparently acting in accordance with its teaching when he buys forbidden poison to use on himself, as is Capulet when he decides that a hasty marriage (which he has earlier roundly denounced) will rouse Juliet from her sorrows, or as the Nurse is when she advises Juliet to marry Paris. And Friar Lawrence certainly imagines he is taking a virtuous course when he offers poison to Juliet. By the play's end, of course, Lawrence's intervention has proved an example of virtue misapplied. The very confidence of his assertions becomes a source of disaster when he acts, and the very ease of his rhetoric is part of the texture of his actions. Friar Lawrence makes a strong bid to be the moral center of the play, but it is his bid that finally interests us more than his vision. Just as he shares a penchant for confidently interpreting events with Capulet, the Nurse, and Romeo, among others, like them he has a disturbing capacity for guessing wrong.

At the end of the play Lawrence is pardoned. "We still have known thee for a holy man." The Friar deserves his reputation, and it is as necessary to society that he have his name for holiness as that he utter his sound and inappropriate *sententiae*. If he were not capable of making terrible mistakes, there would be no need of him. We must have friars and fathers, and all the system of responsibility that goes with naming, for the very reason that these figures fail in their responsibility: there is an energy in life that changes names, that breaks down the rules of language, of law, and even of luck.[3]

Romeo and Juliet bear the brunt of discovering this energy, and, like all tragic victims, they are isolated— even from each other—before they are destroyed. Characteristically, we remember them as separated: the drug comes between them in the final scene, earlier the balcony divides them; in the nightingale-lark scene they are together only at the moment of leave-taking. On all three occasions, the probable use of the stage serves to underline the strain that the effort toward contact demands of them—in Romeo's yearning upward toward the balcony, the perilous rope-ladder descent, the torches and crowbars breaking into the tomb. And of course there are always insistent voices—Mercutio and his friends, the Nurse, Paris, the watch—calling them away, repeating their names, threatening to interrupt them.

It is not fanciful to see their last scene in the tomb as suggestive of sexual union and of the sexual act. A battle takes place at the door, it is torn open—and on stage the barrier is finally only a curtain that gives easily enough after some bloodshed. It is also almost certainly the same inner stage or pavilion where Juliet has gone to bed on the eve of her wedding to Paris, and so it must remind the audience of that innocent chamber. (The curtains close as

[3]The play is famous for its long arias, of which there are two kinds. The speeches of the lovers are expressions of their isolation and desire; separated from each other, they speak at length. The Nurse, Mercutio, and Capulet, however, are given great bursts of speech in company; and the reaction of those around them is important. Their set-pieces are met with outcry; but they are carried away and will not stop. Each is a force in nature breaking into the expected or permissible flow of things; each imitates the impulsive action of the play, "of nothing first create"; each adds to the prevailing sense of impatience and irrepressible energy.

she falls on the bed, are opened in 4.5 to show her apparently dead, and only open again, revealing her still prostrate, as Romeo breaks into the tomb.) The identification is given force by the new stream of wordplay that has entered since Tybalt's death, reversing the dominant pun of the play. Up to that point the language of combat has been transformed by punning into suggestions of sexual encounter ("Draw thy tool"); but in the concluding scenes, violent death is repeatedly described in terms of sex and the marriage festival. Romeo vows, "Well, Juliet, I will lie with thee tonight," meaning he will die; the lovers toast each other with poison ("Here's to my love," "This do I drink to thee"); and, in one of the great condensing images of the play, Juliet's beauty makes the "vault a feasting presence full of light." This last phrase catches up the play's repeated impressions of light and fire illuminating the night and suffuses the death of the lovers with a suggestion of their long-denied marriage banquet.

*Romeo and Juliet*, with its emphasis on language, young love, and the affectations and confusions of both, has clear affinities with the Shakespearean comedies of its period. Except for its fatalities, it follows the standard form of New Comedy. The two lovers are kept apart by a powerful external authority (some form of parental opposition is of course typical), and much of the action concerns their efforts to get around the obstacles placed in their path. Their ultimate union—in a marriage feast—results in a transformation of the society that has opposed them.

Like Romeo, Juliet, as she moves toward tragedy, is sometimes treated in a manner familiar from the early comedies: a sense of the "real" is produced by contrasting serious and superficial versions of the same situation or event. As Romeo progresses in seriousness from Rosaline to Juliet, so Juliet advances through at least three stages to her waking in the tomb. Lawrence sends her on her way with his usual cheery assurance, and even Romeo approaches his descent into the grave with a kind of boyish eagerness, but Juliet goes beyond them. Originally she shares their confident reading of the scene:

> . . . bid me go into a new-made grave
> And hide me with a dead man in his shroud,—
> Things that, to hear them told, have made me tremble;
> And I will do it without fear or doubt.      (4.1.84–87)

But her anticipatory vision of the tomb in 4.3 powerfully forecasts her actual fate:

> What if it be a poison, which the friar
> Subtly hath minist'red to have me dead . . .
> How if, when I am laid into the tomb,
> I wake before the time that Romeo
> Come to redeem me? . . .
> The horrible conceit of death and night,
> Together with the terror of the place,—
> As in a vault, an ancient receptacle,
> Where, for this many hundred years, the bones
> Of all my buried ancestors are pack'd;
> Where bloody Tybalt, yet but green in earth,
> Lies fest'ring in his shroud.      (24–43)

"Fear and doubt" do afflict her, but it is even more notable that Juliet is the only one in the play who begins to guess what the final scene will be like.

In the tomb itself, Juliet continues to display her distinctive isolation and awareness. Her fate is given a final impressiveness by a gesture that carries on the special violence of the play. Shakespeare follows his source, Brooke's *The Tragical History of Romeus and Juliet*, in having Juliet commit suicide with Romeo's knife. But his Juliet, unlike Brooke's, first canvasses other ways to die—the poisoned cup, a kiss. These deaths, like Romeo's, are elegant, leave no mark upon the body, and have the comforting theatrical import of an easy transcendence of death—but they are not available to her; the impulsive pace of the action will not allow it. The watch is heard. She reaches for the dagger instead:

This is thy sheath; there rust, and let me die.     (5.3.170)

The death is messy, violent, sexual. It is interesting that Romeo's is the more virginal, and that Juliet's is the first in the play that has not been immediately caused by a misunderstanding.

Against the play's general background, its rapidly assembling crowds, its fevered busyness, its continual note of impatience and the quick violence of its encounters, the image that remains most strongly in our minds is not of the lovers as a couple, but of each as a separate individual grappling with internal energies that both threaten and express the self, energies for which language is inadequate but that lie at the root of language, that both overturn and enrich society. Touched by adult desire, the unsounded self bursts out with the explosive, subversive, dangerous energy of the sword, gunpowder, the plague; and every aspect of our experience of *Romeo and Juliet* in the theater engages us in this phenomenon—from the crude rush of the brawling lackeys to the subliminal violence of the puns. We undergo, in a terrible condensation like the lightning-flash, the self-defining, self-immolating surge with which adolescence is left behind. As Juliet swiftly outgrows the comforts of the family circle, so Romeo moves far from the youthful packs that roam the streets of Verona, so many Adonises hunting and scorning. The lovers remain in the audience's minds in a typical pose and atmosphere, lights burning in the darkness, their names called, their farewells taken, each isolated in a moment of violent and enlightening desire.

SUSAN SNYDER

# Beyond Comedy:
## *Romeo and Juliet*

Both *Romeo and Juliet* and *Othello* use the world of
romantic comedy as a point of departure, though in different
ways. In the early play a well-developed comic movement is
diverted into tragedy by mischance. The change of direction
is more or less imposed on the young lovers, who therefore
impress us primarily as victims. Othello and Desdemona are
victims too, in one sense, but in their tragedy destruction
comes from within as well, and comedy is one means by
which Shakespeare probes more deeply into his characters
and their love. He gives us in the early scenes a brief but
complete comic structure and then develops his tragedy of
love by exploiting the points of strain and paradox within the
system of comic assumptions that informs that structure.

That these two plays are Shakespeare's only ventures
into the Italianate tragedy of love and intrigue is no co-
incidence. The very features that distinguish this subgenre
from the more dominant fall-of-the-mighty strain move it
closer to comedy: its sources are typically novelle rather
than well-known histories, its heroes are of lesser rank, its
situations are private rather than public, its main motive
force is love. Madeleine Doran, whose designation and
description I follow for this kind of tragedy, has pointed
out its affinity with comedy: "We are in the region where

From Susan Snyder, *The Comic Matrix of Shakespeare's Tragedies*
(Princeton, N.J.: Princeton University Press, 1979), pp. 56–70.

tragedy and comedy are cut out of the same cloth."[1]
The source tales of *Romeo* and *Othello*[2] would, I think,
suggest quite readily to Shakespeare the possibility of
using comic convention as a springboard for tragedy.

The movement of *Romeo and Juliet* is unlike that of any
other Shakespearean tragedy. It becomes, rather than is,
tragic. Other tragedies have reversals, but here the
reversal is so complete as to constitute a change of genre.
Action and characters begin in the familiar comic mold
and are then transformed, or discarded, to compose the
shape of tragedy.[3] In this discussion I shall have to disre-

---

[1]*Endeavors of Art,* p. 137; Italianate intrigue tragedy is discussed on pp.
128–142. Doran includes under this heading the revenge tragedies *Titus
Andronicus* and *Hamlet*; but these touch only peripherally on sexual love, and
as she notes, they also "cross the lines of the other big class, the tragedy of
power" (p. 131). On the other side, Leo Salingar distinguishes the four *comedies* based on novelle—*Merchant of Venice, Much Ado, All's Well,* and *Measure for Measure*—as verging on the tragic in somberness of mood and
seriousness of issue, though not in structure; see *Shakespeare and the Traditions of Comedy* (Cambridge, 1974), pp. 301–305.

[2]Arthur Brooke's *Tragical History of Romeus and Juliet* (1562) recounts a
story that appears also in the novella collections of Bandello and Painter;
another such collection, Giraldi Cinthio's *Hecatommithi* (1565), provided the
source for *Othello.*

[3]Various critics have commented on the comic thrust of the early acts of
*Romeo,* with interpretations ranging from H. A. Mason's somewhat lame and
impotent conclusion, "Shakespeare decided that in a general way the play
needed as much comedy as he could get in" (*Shakespeare's Tragedies of
Love* [London, 1970], p. 29), to Harry Levin's well-argued contention that the
play invokes the artifices of romantic comedy in order to transcend them
("Form and Formality in *Romeo and Juliet,*" *Shakespeare Quarterly* 11
[1960]: 3–11). Levin's essay is illuminating on the play's style; he does not
speculate on what the transcendence-of-artifice theme (admittedly already
used by Shakespeare in a comedy, *Love's Labour's Lost*) has to do with
tragic structure. Franklin Dickey deals at some length with *Romeo* as
"comical tragedy" in *Not Wisely But Too Well,* pp. 63–88. But Dickey's treatment of comedy is nonorganic, dwelling on such features as the witty
heroine, the motif of lovers' absurdity, the debate on love's nature, the elaborate patterning of language, and the *commedia dell'arte* type-characters. He
does not deal with why Shakespeare would want to present a tragic story this
way or how the large comic element shapes the play as a whole. To explain
the presence of that element, Dickey invokes the conventional association of
love with comedy. J. M. Nosworthy thinks the comic admixture a mistake
and blames it on Shakespeare's immaturity, as well as on the influence of
Porter's *Two Angry Women of Abington.* "The Two Angry Families of
Verona," *Shakespeare Quarterly* 3 (1952): 219–226.

gard much of the play's richness, especially of language and characterization, in order to isolate that shaping movement. But isolating it can reveal a good deal about *Romeo*, and may suggest why this early experimental tragedy has seemed to many to fall short of full tragic effect.

It was H. B. Charlton, concurring in this judgment, who classed the play as "experimental." According to Charlton, Shakespeare in his early history-based tragic plays failed to find a pattern of event and character that would make the dramatic outcome feel inevitable; in *Romeo* he took a whole new direction, that of the modern fiction-based tragedy advocated by the Italian critic Giraldi Cinthio.[4] Certainly dramatic thrust and necessity are unsolved problems in *Titus Andronicus* and *Richard III*, and perhaps in *Richard II* too. But one need not turn to Italian critical theory to explain the new direction of *Romeo*. Given the novella-source, full of marriageable young people and domestic concerns, it seems natural enough that Shakespeare would think of turning his own successful work in romantic comedy to account in his apprenticeship as a tragedian.

We have seen that comedy is based on a principle of "evitability." It endorses opportunistic shifts and realistic accommodations as means to new social health. It renders impotent the imperatives of time and law, either stretching them to suit the favored characters' needs or simply brushing them aside. In the tragic world, which is governed by inevitability and which finds its highest value in personal integrity, these imperatives have full force. Unlike the extrinsic, alterable laws of comedy, law in tragedy is inherent—in the protagonist's own nature and in the larger patterns, divine, natural, and social, with which that personal nature brings him into conflict. Tragic law cannot be altered, and tragic time cannot be suspended. The events of tragedy acquire urgency in their uniqueness and irrevocability: they will never happen again, and one by one they move the hero closer to the end of his own personal time.

[4]Charlton, *"Romeo and Juliet" as an Experimental Tragedy*, British Academy Shakespeare Lecture, 1939 (London, 1940), pp. 8–12.

Comedy is organized like a game. The ascendancy goes to the clever ones who can take advantage of sudden openings, contrive strategies, and adapt flexibly to an unexpected move from the other side. But luck and instinct win games as well as skill, and I have discussed in the preceding chapter the natural law of comedy that crowns lovers, whether clever or not, with final success. Romeo and Juliet, young and in love and defiant of obstacles, are attuned to the basic movement of the comic game toward marriage and social regeneration. But they do not win: the game turns into a sacrifice, and the favored lovers become victims of time and law. We can better understand this shift by looking at the two distinct worlds of the play and at some secondary characters who help to define them.

If we divide the play at Mercutio's death, the death that generates all those that follow, it becomes apparent that the play's movement up to this point is essentially comic. With the usual intrigues and go-betweens, the lovers overcome obstacles and unite in marriage. Their personal action is set in a broader social context, so that the marriage promises not only private satisfaction but renewed social unity:

> For this alliance may so happy prove
> To turn your households' rancour to pure love.
>
> (2.3.91–92)

The household's rancor is set out in the play's first scene. This Verona of the Montague-Capulet feud is exactly the typical starting point of a comedy described by Frye—"a society controlled by habit, ritual bondage, arbitrary law and the older characters."[5] The scene's formal balletic structure, a series of matched representatives of the warring families entering neatly on cue, conveys the inflexibility of this society, the arbitrary barriers that limit freedom of action.

---

[5] *Anatomy*, p. 169. Although the younger generation participate in the feud, they have not created it; it is a habit bequeathed to them by their elders.

The feud itself seems more a matter of mechanical reflex than of deeply felt hatred. Charlton noted the comic tone of its presentation in this part of the play.[6] The "parents' rage" that sounded so ominous in the prologue becomes in representation an irascible humour: two old men claw at each other, only to be dragged back by their wives and scolded by their prince. Charlton found the play flawed by this failure to plant the seeds of tragedy; but the treatment of the feud makes good sense if Shakespeare is playing on *comic* expectations. At this point, the feud functions in *Romeo* very much as the various legal restraints do in Shakespearean comedy. Imposed from outside on the youthful lovers, who feel themselves no part of it, the feud is a barrier placed arbitrarily between them, like the Athenian law giving fathers the disposition of their daughters which stands between Lysander and Hermia in *A Midsummer Night's Dream*—something set up in order to be broken down.

Other aspects of this initial world of *Romeo* suggest comedy as well. Its characters are the gentry and servants familiar in romantic comedies, and they are preoccupied, not with wars and the fate of kingdoms, but with arranging marriages and managing the kitchen. More important, it is a world of possibilities, with Capulet's feast represented to more than one young man as a field of choice. "Hear all, all see," says Capulet to Paris, "And like her most whose merit most shall be" (1.2.30–31). "Go thither," Benvolio tells Romeo, who is disconsolate over Rosaline, "and with unattainted eye / Compare her face with some that I shall show" (88–89) and she will be forgotten for some more approachable lady. Romeo rejects the words, of course, but in action he soon displays a classic comic adaptability, switching from the impossible love to the possible.

Violence and disaster are not totally absent from this milieu, but they are unrealized threats. The feast again provides a kind of comic emblem, when Tybalt's proposed

<hr />

[6]*Experimental Tragedy*, pp. 36–40.

violence is rendered harmless by Capulet's festive
accommodation.

> Therefore be patient, take no note of him;
> It is my will; the which if thou respect,
> Show a fair presence and put off these frowns,
> An ill-beseeming semblance for a feast.     (1.5.73–76)

This overruling of Tybalt is significant because Tybalt in
his inflexibility is a potentially tragic character, indeed the
only one in the first part of the play. If we recognize in
him an irascible humour type, an *alazon*, we should also
recognize that the tragic hero is an *alazon* transposed.[7]
Tybalt alone takes the feud really seriously. It is his *inner*
law, the propeller of his fiery nature. His natural frame of
reference is the heroic one of honor and death:

> What, dares the slave
> Come hither, cover'd with an antic face,
> To fleer and scorn at our solemnity?
> Now, by the stock and honour of my kin,
> To strike him dead I hold it not a sin.     (57–61)

Tybalt's single set of absolutes cuts him off from a whole
range of speech and action available to the other young
men of the play: lyric love, witty fooling, friendly conversation. Ironically, his imperatives come to dominate the
play's world only when he himself departs from it. While
he is alive, Tybalt is an alien.

In a similar way, the passing fears of calamity voiced
at times by Romeo, Juliet, and Friar Laurence are not
allowed to dominate the atmosphere of the early acts. The
love of Romeo and Juliet is already imaged as a flash of
light swallowed by darkness, an image invoking inexorable natural law; but it is also expressed as a sea venture,
which suggests luck and skill set against natural hazards

---

[7]Maynard Mack, "Engagement and Detachment in Shakespeare's Plays," in
*Essays on Shakespeare and Elizabethan Drama in Honor of Hardin Craig*,
ed. Richard Hosley (Columbia, Mo., 1962), pp. 287–291.

and chance seized joyously as an opportunity for action. "Direct my sail," says Romeo to his captain Fortune. Soon he feels himself in command:

> I am no pilot; yet, wert thou as far
> As that vast shore wash'd with the farthest sea,
> I should adventure for such merchandise.[8]

The spirit is Bassanio's as he adventures for Portia, a Jason voyaging in quest of the Golden Fleece (*MV* 1.1.167–72). Romeo is ready for difficulties with a traditional lovers' stratagem, one which Shakespeare had used before in *Two Gentlemen*: A rope ladder, "cords made like a tackled stair; / Which to the high top-gallant of my joy / Must be my convoy in the secret night" (2.4.183–85).

But before Romeo can mount his tackled stair, Mercutio's death intervenes to cut off this world of exhilarating venture. Shakespeare developed this character, who in the source is little more than a name and a cold hand, into the very incarnation of comic atmosphere. Mercutio is the clown of romantic comedy, recast in more elegant mold but equally ready to take off from the plot in verbal play and to challenge idealistic love with his own brand of comic earthiness.

> Nay, I'll conjure too.
> Romeo! humours! madman! passion! lover!
> Appear thou in the likeness of a sigh;
> Speak but one rhyme and I am satisfied;
> Cry but 'Aye me!' pronounce but 'love' and 'dove';
> . . . . . . . . . . . . . .
> I conjure thee by Rosaline's bright eyes,
> By her high forehead and her scarlet lip,
> By her fine foot, straight leg, and quivering thigh,
> And the demesnes that there adjacent lie. (2.1.6–20)

He is the best of game-players, endlessly inventive and full of quick moves and countermoves. Speech for him is a constant exercise in multiple possibilities: puns abound,

---

[8] 1.4.113; 2.2.82–84. Later Mercutio hails the lovers' go-between, the Nurse, with "A sail, a sail!" (2.4.108).

roles are taken up at whim (that of conjuror, for instance, in the passage just quoted), and his Queen Mab brings dreams not only to lovers like Romeo but to courtiers, lawyers, parsons, soldiers, maids. These have nothing to do with the case at hand, which is Romeo's premonition of trouble, but Mercutio is not bound by events. They serve him merely as convenient launching pads for his flights of wit. When all this vitality, which has till now ignored all urgencies, is cut off abruptly by Tybalt's sword, it must come as a shock to a spectator unfamiliar with the play. In Mercutio's sudden, violent end, Shakespeare makes the birth of tragedy coincide exactly with the symbolic death of comedy. The alternative view, the element of freedom and play, dies with Mercutio. Where many courses were open before, now there seems only one. Romeo sees at once that an irreversible process has begun:

> This day's black fate on more days doth depend [hang over];
> This but begins the woe others must end.          (3.1.121–22)

It is the first sign in the play's dialogue pointing unambiguously to tragic necessity. Romeo's future is now determined: he *must* kill Tybalt, he *must* run away, he is Fortune's fool.

This helplessness is the most striking feature of the second, tragic world of *Romeo*. The temper of this new world is largely a function of onrushing events. Under pressure of events, the feud turns from farce to fate; tit for tat becomes blood for blood. Lawless as it seems to Prince Escalus, the feud is dramatically "the law" in *Romeo*. Before, it was external and avoidable. Now it moves inside Romeo to be his personal law. This is why he takes over Tybalt's rhetoric of honor and death:

> Alive in triumph and Mercutio slain!
> Away to heaven respective lenity,
> And fire-ey'd fury be my conduct now!
> Now, Tybalt, take the 'villain' back again
> That late thou gav'st me.                        (124–28)

Even outside the main chain of vengeance, the world is suddenly full of imperatives. Others besides Romeo feel helpless. Against his will Friar John is detained at the monastery; against his will the Apothecary sells poison to Romeo. Urgency becomes the norm. Nights run into mornings, and the characters seem never to sleep. The new world finds its emblem not in the aborted attack but in the aborted feast. As Tybalt's violence was out of tune with the Capulet festivities in Act 2, so in the changed world of Acts 3 and 4 the projected wedding of Juliet and Paris is made grotesque when Shakespeare insistently links it with death.[9] Preparations for the wedding feast parallel those made for the party in the play's first part, so as to make more wrenching the contrast when Capulet must order,

> All things that we ordained festival
> Turn from their office to black funeral:
> Our instruments to melancholy bells,
> Our wedding cheer to a sad burial feast,
> Our solemn hymns to sullen dirges change.     (4.5.84–88)

The play's last scene shows how completely the comic movement has been reversed. It is inherent in that movement, as we have seen, that the young get their way at the expense of the old. The final tableau of comedy features young couples joined in love; parents and authority figures are there, if at all, to ratify with more or less good grace what has been accomplished against their wills. But here, the stage is strikingly full of elders—the Friar, the Prince, Capulet, Lady Capulet, Montague. Their power is not passed on. Indeed, there are no young to take over. If Benvolio survives somewhere offstage, we have long since forgotten this adjunct character. Romeo, Juliet, Tybalt, Mercutio, and Paris are all dead. In effect, the entire younger generation has been wiped out.

I have been treating these two worlds as separate, consistent wholes in order to bring out their opposition, but I do

[9]3.4.23–28; 3.5.202–203; 4.1.6–8, 77–85, 107–108, 4.5.35–39.

not wish to deny dramatic unity to *Romeo and Juliet*. Shakespeare was writing one play, not two; and in spite of the clearly marked turning point we are aware of premonitions of disaster before the death of Mercutio, and hopes for avoiding it continue until near the end of the play. Our full perception of the world-shift that converts Romeo and Juliet from instinctive winners into sacrificial victims thus comes gradually. In this connection the careers of two secondary characters, Friar Laurence and the Nurse, are instructive.

In being and action, these two belong to the comic vision. Friar Laurence is one of the tribe of manipulators, whose job it is to transform or otherwise get round seemingly intractable realities. If his herbs and potions are less spectacular than the paraphernalia of Friar Bacon or John a Kent, he nevertheless belongs to their brotherhood. Such figures abound in romantic comedy, as we have seen, but not in tragedy, where the future is not so manipulable. The Friar's aims are those implicit in the play's comic movement: an inviolable union for Romeo and Juliet and an end to the families' feud.

The Nurse's goal is less lofty but equally appropriate to comedy. She wants Juliet married—to anyone. Her preoccupation with bedding and breeding reminds us of comedy's ancient roots in fertility rites, and it is as indiscriminate as the life force itself. But she conveys no sense of urgency in all this. On the contrary, her garrulity assumes the limitless time of comedy. In this sense her circumlocutions and digressions are analogous to Mercutio's witty games and, for that matter, to Friar Laurence's counsels of patience. "Wisely and slow," the Friar cautions Romeo; "they stumble that run fast" (2.3.94). The Nurse is not very wise, but she is slow. The leisurely time assumptions of both Friar and Nurse contrast with the lovers' impatience, to create first the normal counterpoint of comedy and later a radical split that points us, with the lovers, directly towards tragedy.

Friar Laurence and the Nurse have no place in the new world brought into being by Mercutio's death, the world of limited time, no effective choice, no escape. They

define and sharpen the tragedy by their very failure to find
a part in the dramatic progress, by their growing estrangement from the true springs of the action. "Be patient," is
the Friar's advice to banished Romeo, "for the world is
broad and wide" (3.3.16). But the roominess he perceives
in both time and space simply does not exist for Romeo.
*His* time has been constricted into a chain of days
working out a "black fate," and he sees no world outside
the walls of Verona (17).

Comic adaptability again confronts tragic integrity
when Juliet is forced to marry Paris—and turns to her
Nurse for counsel, as Romeo has turned to Friar Laurence. In the Nurse's response comedy's traditional
wisdom of accommodation is carried to an extreme.
Romeo has been banished, and Paris is after all very pre-
sentable. In short, adjust to the new state of things.

> Then, since the case so stands as now it doth,
> I think it best you married with the County.
> O, he's a lovely gentleman!
> Romeo's a dishclout to him.                         (3.5.218–21)

She still speaks for the life force, against barrenness and
death. Even if Juliet will not accept the dishclout comparison, an inferior husband is better than no husband at
all: "Your first is dead, or 'twere as good he were / As
living here and you no use of him" (226–27).

But her advice is irrelevant, even shocking, in this new
context. There was no sense of jar when Benvolio, a
spokesman for comic accommodation like the Nurse and
the Friar, earlier advised Romeo to substitute a possible
love for an impossible one. True, the Nurse here is urging
Juliet to violate her marriage vows; but Romeo also felt
himself sworn to Rosaline, and for Juliet the marriage
vow is a seal on the integrity of her love for Romeo, not
a separable issue. The parallel points up the move into
tragedy, for while Benvolio's advice sounded sensible in
Act 1 and was in fact unintentionally carried out by
Romeo, the course of action that the Nurse proposes in

Act 3 is unthinkable to the audience as well as to Juliet.
The memory of the lovers' passionate dawn parting that
began this scene is too strong. Juliet and her nurse no
longer speak the same language, and estrangement is
inevitable. "Thou and my bosom henceforth shall be
twain," Juliet vows when the Nurse has left the stage.[10]
Like the slaying of Mercutio, Juliet's rejection of her old
confidante has symbolic overtones. The possibilities of
comedy have again been presented only to be discarded.

Both Romeo and Juliet have now cast off their comic
companions and the alternative modes of being that they
represented. But there is one last hope for comedy. If the
lovers will not adjust to the situation, perhaps the situation can be adjusted to the lovers. This is the usual comic
way with obstinately faithful pairs, and we have at hand
the usual manipulator figure to arrange it.

The Friar's failure to bring off that solution is the final
definition of the tragic world of *Romeo and Juliet*. There is
no villain, only chance and bad timing. In comedy chance
creates that elastic time that allows last-minute rescues. But
here, events at Mantua and at the Capulet tomb will simply
happen—by chance—in the wrong sequence. The Friar
does his best: he makes more than one plan to avert catastrophe. The first, predictably, is patience and a broader field
of action. Romeo must go to Mantua and wait

> till we can find a time
> To blaze your marriage, reconcile your friends,
> Beg pardon of the Prince, and call thee back.
>
> (3.3.150–52)

It is a good enough plan, for life if not for drama, but it
depends on "finding a time." As it turns out, events move
too quickly for the Friar. The hasty preparations for

---

[10] 3.5.241. In the potion scene Juliet's resolve weakens for a moment, but
almost immediately she rejects the idea of companionship. The momentary
wavering only emphasizes her aloneness: "I'll call them back again to comfort me. / Nurse!—What should she do here? / My dismal scene I needs must
act alone" (4.3.17–19).

Juliet's marriage to Paris leave no time for cooling tempers and reconciliations.

His second plan is an attempt to *gain* time: he will create the necessary freedom by faking Juliet's death. This is, of course, a familiar comic formula. Shakespeare's later uses of it are all in comedies.[11] Indeed, the contrived "deaths" of Hero in *Much Ado*, Helena in *All's Well*, Claudio in *Measure for Measure*, and Hermione in *The Winter's Tale* are more ambitiously intended than Juliet's, aimed at bringing about a change of heart in other characters.[12] Time may be important, as it is in *Winter's Tale*, but only as it promotes repentance. Friar Laurence, more desperate than his fellow manipulators, does not hope that Juliet's death will dissolve the Montague-Capulet feud, but only that it will give Romeo a chance to come and carry her off. Time and chance, which in the other plays cooperate benevolently with the forces of regeneration and renewal, work against Friar Laurence. Romeo's man is quicker with the bad news of Juliet's death than poor Friar John with the good news that the death is only a pretense. Romeo himself beats Friar Laurence to the tomb of the Capulets. The onrushing tragic action quite literally outstrips the slower steps of accommodation before our eyes. The Friar arrives too late to prevent one half of the tragic conclusion, and his essential estrangement from the play's world is only emphasized when he seeks to avert the other half by sending Juliet to a nunnery. This last alternative means little to the audience or to Juliet, who spares only a line to reject the possibility of adjustment and continuing life: "Go, get thee hence, for I will not away" (5.3.160).

The Nurse and the Friar show that one way comedy can operate in a tragedy is by its irrelevance. Tragedy is tuned to the extraordinary. *Romeo and Juliet* locates this extraordinariness not so much in the two youthful lovers as in

[11]Or in the comic part of a history, in the case of Falstaff's pretended death on the battlefield at Shrewsbury.

[12]The same effect, if not intention, is apparent in the reported death of Imogen in *Cymbeline*.

the love itself, its intensity and integrity. As the play moves forward, our sense of this intensity and integrity is strengthened by the cumulative effect of the lovers' lyric encounters and the increasing urgency of events, but also by the growing irrelevance of the comic characters.

De Quincey saw in the knocking at the gate in *Macbeth* the resumption of normality after nightmare, "the reestablishment of the goings-on of the world in which we live, [which] first makes us profoundly sensible of the awful parenthesis that had suspended them."[13] I would say, rather, that the normal atmosphere of *Macbeth* has been and goes on being nightmarish, and that it is the knocking episode that turns out to be the contrasting parenthesis, but the notion of sharpened sensibility is important. As the presence of other paths makes us more conscious of the road we are in fact traveling, so the Nurse and the Friar make us more "profoundly sensible" of the love of Romeo and Juliet and its tragic direction.

The play offers another sort of experiment in mingled genres that is less successful, I think. It starts well, in 4.4, with a striking juxtaposition of Capulet preparations for the wedding with Juliet's potion scene. On the one hand is the household group in a bustle over clothes, food, logs for the fire—the everyday necessaries and small change of life. On the other is Juliet's tense monologue of fear, madness, and death. It is fine dramatic counterpoint, and its effect is stronger in stage production, as Granville-Barker observed, when the curtained bed of Juliet is visible upstage during the cheerful domestic goings-on.[14] The counterpoint, of course, depends on the Capulets' ignorance of what is behind those curtains. It comes to an end when in scene 5 Nurse and the others find Juliet's body. But Shakespeare keeps the comic strain alive through the rest of the scene. The high-pitched, repetitive mourning of the Nurse, Paris, and the Capulets sounds more like Pyramus over the body of Thisbe than a serious tragic

---

[13]"On the Knocking at the Gate in *Macbeth*," in *Shakespeare Criticism: A Selection*, ed. D. Nichol Smith (Oxford, 1916), p. 378.

[14]*Prefaces to Shakespeare* (London, 1963), iv, 62–63.

scene. Finally Peter has his comic turn with the musicians. What Shakespeare is attempting here is not counterpoint but the *fusion* of tragic and comic. It doesn't quite work. S. L. Bethell suggests that the mourners' rhetorical excesses direct the audience to remain detached and thus to reserve their tears for the real death scene that will shortly follow.[15] This makes good theatrical sense. It is also possible that the musicians' dialogue, modulating as it does from shock to professional shop to dinner, was meant to set off the tragic action by projecting a sense of the ongoing, normal life that is denied to Romeo and Juliet. Still, the scene tends to leave spectators uneasy—if, in fact, they get to see it at all: often the mourning passages are cut and the musicians' business dropped altogether.[16] Shakespeare's hand is uncertain in this early essay at fusing tragic and comic. Mastery was yet to come, first in the gravediggers' scene in *Hamlet* and then more fully in *King Lear*.

The structural use of comic conventions does work. The result, however, is a particular kind of tragedy. Critics have often remarked, neutrally or with disapproval, that external fate rather than character is the principal determiner of the tragic ends of the young lovers. For the mature Shakespeare, tragedy involves both character and circumstances, a fatal interaction between man and moment. But in *Romeo and Juliet*, although the central characters have their weaknesses, their destruction does not really stem from those weaknesses. We may agree

[15]*Shakespeare and the Popular Dramatic Tradition* (London and New York, 1944), p. 111. Charles B. Lower agrees and argues as well for the more doubtful proposition that the audience needs to be reassured that Juliet is really still alive. Lower convincingly defends the authenticity of a Q1 stage direction, *"All at once cry out and wring their hand[s],"* which, by requiring the laments of Lady Capulet, the Nurse, Paris, and Capulet (4.5.43–64) to be spoken simultaneously like an opera quartet, would increase the scene's burlesque quality. *"Romeo and Juliet*, 4.5: A Stage Direction and Purposeful Comedy," *Shakespeare Studies* 8 (1975): 177–194.

[16]Granville-Barker wrote in 1930 that modern producers usually lowered the curtain after the climactic potion scene and raised it next on Romeo in Mantua, skipping the mourning and the musicians entirely. *Prefaces*, IV, 63–64. The most notable production of more recent years, by Franco Zeffirelli, omitted the musicians. J. Russell Brown, *Shakespeare's Plays in Performance* (London, 1966), p. 177.

with Friar Laurence that Romeo is rash, but it is not rashness that propels him into the tragic chain of events. Just the opposite, it would seem. In the crucial duel between Mercutio and Tybalt, Romeo is trying to keep the combatants apart, to make peace. Ironically, this very intervention leads to Mercutio's death.

> *Mercutio.* Why the devil came you between us? I was hurt
> under your arm.
> *Romeo.* I thought all for the best.                    (3.1.99–101)

If Shakespeare had wanted to implicate Romeo's rash, overemotional nature in his fate, he handled this scene with an ineptness difficult to credit. Judging from the resultant effect, what he wanted was something quite different: an ironic dissociation of character from the direction of events.

Perhaps this same purpose lies behind the elaborate development of comic elements in the early acts before the characters are pushed into the opposed conditions of tragedy. To stress milieu in this way is necessarily to downgrade the importance of individual temperament and motivation. At the crucial moment Romeo displays untypical prudence with the most upright of intentions—and brings disaster on himself and Juliet. In this unusual Shakespearean tragedy, it is not what you are that counts, but the world you live in.

MARIANNE NOVY

# Violence, Love, and Gender
## in *Romeo and Juliet*

In three of Shakespeare's plays, female and male characters share the title. These plays all deviate from the
male-actor-female-audience pattern that dominates in
*Hamlet, Lear, Macbeth,* and *Othello* and resemble the
comedies in other ways as well. In *Romeo and Juliet* and
*Troilus and Cressida,* as in *Antony and Cleopatra,* the
lovers begin as admiring audiences to each other. Juliet
learns to pretend to protect her love of Romeo, and while
her pretense fails, Romeo never distrusts her as the other
heroes distrust women. Cressida pretends from the very
beginning, and in the climactic scene Troilus is an audience to her infidelity with Diomedes. One hero lacks distrust of women, the other seems to learn it by painful
experience (though we can find imagery suggestive of
such distrust in his language earlier); unlike Lady Macbeth, Ophelia, or Desdemona, but more like the women of
comedy, the women maintain or increase their ability to
act throughout the play.

In these plays, then, suspicion of women's acting
cannot be the cause of the disaster. But issues of gender
politics are still important.

Unlike the romantic comedies, these plays all include
war or blood and that calls on men to define their masculinity by violence. In their private world, the lovers may
achieve a mutuality in which both are active and genders
are not polarized. But in the external world, masculinity is

From Marianne Novy, *Love's Argument: Gender Relations in Shakespeare*
(University of North Carolina Press, 1984), pp. 99–109. Used by permission
of the publisher and the author.

identified with violence and femininity with weakness.
Romeo and Juliet establish a role-transcending private
world of mutuality in love. But this world is destroyed,
partly by Romeo's entanglement in the feud, partly by
Juliet's continued life in her parents' house concealing
her marriage.

The minor characters in *Romeo and Juliet* establish a
background of common beliefs current in both plays:
"women, being the weaker vessels, are ever thrust to the
wall" (1.1.17–18) while men glory in their "naked weapon"
(35). In the Nurse's view, there are compensations—
"women grow by men" (1.3.95)—but she assents to her
husband's equation of female sexuality with falling backward.

Two different conventional images of this society link
sex and violence. First, sexual intercourse is seen as
the success of male attacks. For example, Benvolio con-
soles Romeo in his lovesickness for Rosaline by saying,
"A right fair mark, fair coz, is soonest hit" (1.1.210).
Romeo describes the futility of his courtship of her thus,
"She will not stay the siege of loving terms / Nor bide
th'encounter of assailing eyes" (215–16). Romeo has
assayed this siege because he has already been
hit with a different kind of violence—from "Cupid's
arrow" (212). As Mercutio will later put it, he is
"stabbed with a white wench's black eye: run through
the ear with a love song; the very pin of his heart
cleft with the blind bow-boy's butt-shaft" (2.4.14–16).
Rosaline does not feel the same way, and thus "from
Love's weak childish bow she lives unharmed" (1.1.209).
Romeo's imagery conflates his sexual desire for Rosaline
and his consequent desire that she fall in love with
him—imagery of his attacking her and of love's attacking her.

When Romeo meets Juliet, he gives up using such
violent imagery about sexual intercourse: when he uses
it about falling in love, summing up to Friar Laurence
in riddles, his emphasis is on the reciprocity of their
feelings:

I have been feasting with mine enemy,
Where on a sudden one hath wounded me
That's by me wounded.                    (2.3.49–51)

Alternatively, he follows the image with a conceit that
makes Juliet, if accepting, his protection:

Alack, there lies more peril in thine eye
Than twenty of their swords! Look thou but sweet,
And I am proof against their enmity.      (2.2.71–73)

In general, with Juliet he gives up images of himself as
violent aggressor. He speaks more of wanting to touch her
than to conquer her, even if this means wishing away his
own identity. "O that I were a glove upon that hand, /
That I might touch that cheek . . . I would I were thy bird"
(24–25, 182). Romeo is the only Shakespearean tragic
hero who could offer to give up his name, who could say,
"Had I it written, I would tear the word" (57). The strange
nineteenth-century stage tradition of casting women as
Romeo as well as Juliet may have been in part a response
to his lack of violent imagery—except toward his own
name—in their love scenes.

Nevertheless, lack of violence in the imagery does not
mean a lack of sexual energy and attraction, and Shakespeare's dialogue sensitively suggests the power of their
developing relationship. The openness and directness of
Romeo and Juliet stand out against the background of the
romantic comedies, which celebrate the gradual triumph
of love over the inhibitions and defenses of the lovers.
Only in *The Merchant of Venice* do two lovers (Portia and
Bassanio) talk readily and without disguise at their first
meeting. While the lovers in the comedies echo each
other's language and imagery as their affinity grows
behind their disguises, Romeo and Juliet at once match
their shared imagery with more emotional openness.

Throughout this first meeting, Romeo takes the initiative; but at the same time, his language puts aggression at
a distance. He speaks humbly about his "unworthiest

hand" (1.5.95); if his touch is sin, it is "gentle" (96); if it is too rough, he would prefer "a tender kiss" (98). Thus his initiative is that of a pilgrim to a saint and claims to imply the dominance of the woman, not the man. But his saint does not simply stand motionless on her pedestal; she talks back, picking up his imagery and quatrain form, and accepts his hand as showing "mannerly devotion" (100). Even when she claims that "Saints do not move" (107), she is still showing her willingness for the kiss that climaxes the sonnet their interchange has become:

> *Juliet.* Saints do not move, though grant for prayers' sake.
> *Romeo.* Then move not while my prayer's effect I take.
>
> (107–8)

After the kiss, Juliet gives up the imagery of sainthood: "Then have my lips the sin that they have took" (110). She insists on her sharing of his humanity.

The next time they meet, they share the initiative as well. In the balcony scene, Shakespeare uses the soliloquy convention to show each of them in fantasy speaking to the other first, but breaks that convention by showing Romeo as the audience who responds to become actor along with Juliet. Each speech sets the beloved outside the social framework: Romeo compares Juliet to the sun, her eyes to the stars; Juliet more consciously imagines removing him from society: "Deny thy father and refuse thy name" (2.2.34). It is when she makes a direct offer to her fantasy Romeo that the real one breaks in, and proposes a love that will create a private world between the two of them:

> *Juliet.* . . . Romeo, doff thy name;
>    And for thy name, which is no part of thee,
>    Take all myself.
> *Romeo.*        I take thee at thy word.
>    Call me but love, and I'll be new baptized;
>    Henceforth I never will be Romeo.     (47–51)

Like a dreamer startled to find a dream materialize, Juliet is taken aback at Romeo's response. She breaks the fantasy of renaming—"What man art thou . . . ? . . . Art thou not Romeo?" (52, 60)—and momentarily appears to withdraw in fear. Thus the emphasis shifts from shared feeling to male persuasion, as Romeo speaks of the power and value of love, until Juliet responds and acknowledges to the real Romeo what she has said to the fantasy one— "Farewell compliment!" (89). When the interplay of caution and persuasion begins again, Juliet's anxiety oddly focuses on Romeo's oaths, as if his faith could be guaranteed by his *not* swearing. The unreality of her expressions of distrust adds to the charm of this exchange: there are no hints that she finds men untrustworthy, or that Romeo finds women untrustworthy, or even that the family feud leads either of them to doubts about the other (as distinguished from awareness of the practical difficulties). It is as if the only force working against their trust at this point is the feeling that their love is too good to be true. Romeo suggests this as he momentarily, in Juliet's absence, takes over the verbal caution:

> I am afeard,
> Being in night, all this is but a dream,
> Too flattering-sweet to be substantial.        (139–41)

By this time Juliet has given up her hesitation; her avowal evokes the self-renewing power of their mutuality but at the same time grounds it in her own autonomy:

> My bounty is as boundless as the sea,
> My love as deep; the more I give to thee,
> The more I have, for both are infinite.        (133–35)

And as she has been more concerned with the external world in pointing out dangers, she takes the initiative in turning their love from shared fantasy and passion to social institution: "If that thy bent of love be honorable, / Thy purpose marriage, send me word tomorrow" (143–44).

As the movement of their scenes combines mutuality and male persuasion, the words they use about their love can imply both mutuality and patriarchy. "It is my lady" (10), says Romeo of Juliet at the beginning of the balcony scene, and near the end she promises that if they marry "all my fortunes at thy foot I'll lay / And follow thee my lord throughout the world" (147–48). This could reflect either reciprocity of service or a conventional shift from female power in courtship to male power in marriage.

Similarly, when Juliet anticipates her secret wedding night with Romeo, the imagery of female subordination is balanced by imagery of sharing. She speaks of losing her virginity as losing a game, but then it becomes a victory, and her virginity parallel to Romeo's, as she prays to Night, "learn me how to lose a winning match, / Played for a pair of stainless maidenhoods" (3.2.12–13). Here and elsewhere, financial imagery turns Juliet into property more directly than it does Romeo: when she speaks of herself as possessing, the object is less Romeo than love.

> O, I have bought the mansion of a love,
> But not possessed it; and though I am sold,
> Not yet enjoyed.                    (26–28)

Similarly, Romeo calls her "merchandise" for which he would adventure "as far / As that vast shore washed with the farthest sea" (2.2.82–83), while Juliet says "my true love is grown to such excess / I cannot sum up sum of half my wealth" (2.6.33–34).

Romeo and Juliet use the image of woman as property in a way that transcends its source in female social subordination; both of them are far from the financial interest that Lady Capulet suggests in her praise of Paris and the Nurse in her observation that Juliet's husband "shall have the chinks" (1.5.119). Nevertheless, the asymmetry in their use of financial imagery coheres with the asymmetrical demands that the male code of violence will make on Romeo and the female code of docility on Juliet.

Their use of other images is more symmetrical. Both

lovers speak in words at once sensuously descriptive of
beauty and celestially idealizing. Juliet, says Romeo,

> hangs upon the cheek of night
> As a rich jewel in an Ethiop's ear. . . .
> So shows a snowy dove trooping with crows.
>
> (47–48, 50)

Romeo, according to Juliet, "will lie upon the wings of
night / Whiter than new snow upon a raven's back"
(3.2.18–19). Romeo has imagined Juliet as the sun and
her eyes as stars. Juliet overgoes Romeo's praise in
saying that, transformed into stars,

> he will make the face of heaven so fine
> That all the world will be in love with night
> And pay no worship to the garish sun.          (23–25)

Unlike some of Shakespeare's more solipsistic early
lovers, such as Berowne and Proteus, Romeo understands
the value of reciprocity in love. He wants its ritual—
"Th'exchange of thy love's faithful vow for mine"
(2.2.127)—and explains to Friar Laurence, "Her I love
now / Doth grace for grace and love for love allow"
(2.3.85–86); he speaks of "the imagined happiness that
both / Receive in either by this dear encounter"
(2.6.28–29). All this is far from the identification of sex
and violence that the imagery of the servants and Mercutio suggests is more usual in Verona.

Why do Romeo and Juliet keep their love secret not
only from their parents but also from their peers? Romeo
never tells Benvolio or Mercutio of his love for Juliet,
though neither one is so committed to the Montagues that
they would necessarily be hostile. (Benvolio had no
objection to Rosaline as a Capulet; Mercutio belongs to
neither house.) This secrecy helps make Mercutio's fight
with Tybalt inevitable. Romeo's exclusion of Mercutio
from his confidence suggests that his love of Juliet is
not only a challenge to the feud but also a challenge to

associations of masculinity and sexuality with violence. How can Romeo talk of Juliet to someone whose advice is "If love be rough with you, be rough with love, / Prick love for pricking, and you beat love down" (1.4.27-28)?

It is in part because of the difference between their experience of love and Verona's expected distortion of it that Romeo and Juliet try to keep their relationship private. Yet this secrecy is avoidance of a problem that they cannot ultimately escape. When Romeo tries to act according to his secret love of Juliet instead of according to the feud, Tybalt and Mercutio insist on fighting. And when Romeo's intervention—to stop the fight—results in Mercutio's death, it is clear that Verona's definition of masculinity by violence is partly Romeo's definition as well. "O sweet Juliet," he says, "Thy beauty hath made me effeminate" (3.1.115-16), as he prepares for the fight to the death that causes his banishment.

Just before their crucial fight, Tybalt and Mercutio, speaking of Romeo, quibble on the point that "man," a word so important as an ideal, has from the opening scene the less honorific meaning of "manservant."

> *Tybalt.* Well, peace be with you, sir. Here comes my man.
> *Mercutio.* But I'll be hanged, sir, if he wear your livery.
>
> (57-58)

This pun is an analogue of the irony that is precisely in his "manly" vengeance for Mercutio's death that Romeo most decisively loses control of his own fate and becomes, as he says, "fortune's fool" (138). In a sense, as Mercutio's elaboration of his pun suggests without his awareness, a commitment to proving manhood by violence makes one easily manipulated by whoever offers a challenge. "Marry, go before to field, he'll be your follower! / Your worship in that sense may call him man" (59-60). In the larger sense, the code of violence that promises to make Romeo a man actually makes him its man—its pawn.

If Romeo shares Mercutio's belief in the manhood of

violence, he also shares the Friar's wish for reconciliation. But the Friar has his own version of gender polarization that also contributes to the disaster. He repeatedly
uses "womanish" as a synonym for "weak" when
speaking to both Juliet (4.1.119) and Romeo (3.3.110),
and, more crucially for the plot, encourages Juliet to pretend obedience and death through his potion rather than
helping her escape to Romeo (though she has expressed
willingness to leap "From off the battlements of any
tower, / Or walk in thievish ways"—4.1.78–79). His
image of manhood (desirable as an ideal for both sexes) is
emotional control: he chides Romeo for his fury and grief
at banishment by calling him "Unseemly woman in a
seeming man! / And ill-beseeming beast in seeming
both!" (3.3.112–13). The Friar distrusts passionate love,
and, like much of the conventional imagery of the play,
identifies passionate love with violence: "These violent
delights have violent ends" (2.6.9). It is consistent that he
should not encourage Juliet to elopement but rather hopes
to stage their reunion in a context of family reconciliation.

Juliet's confidante, the Nurse, has a more positive attitude toward sexuality, but she too underestimates the
lovers' intense commitment to each other. Like the Friar,
too, she keeps the love secret and encourages Juliet to
appear docile to her parents, and finally to marry Paris,
since Romeo, she says, "is dead—or 'twere as good
he were / As living here and you no use of him" (3.5.
226–27). Thus she is counseling Juliet to a conventional
acceptance of the husband chosen by her parents. While
Juliet refuses this advice, she follows the counsel of pretense that she receives from nurse and friar. The controlled stichomythia of her dialogue with Paris is a sad
contrast to her spontaneous participation in Romeo's
sonnet. Juliet's acceptance of their advice of pretense and
mock death is the point analogous to Romeo's duel with
Tybalt where failure to transcend the gender polarization
of their society makes disaster inevitable.

Yet before their deaths, Romeo and Juliet can transcend
the aggressions and stereotypes of the outside in their

secret world. Fulfilling the promise of the balcony scene, they rename each other "Love" in their aubade scene, and their imagery suggests the creation of a private world with a technique oddly similar to that of the crucial scene in *The Taming of the Shrew*. To keep Romeo with her longer, Juliet transforms the lark into the nightingale and then transforms the sun into "some meteor that the sun exhales / To be to thee this night a torchbearer" (3.5.13–14). Romeo, after initially contradicting her, showing the caution that was primarily hers in the balcony scene, goes along with the game and accepts her transformation, with awareness of the likely cost:

> Let me be ta'en, let me be put to death.
> I am content, so thou wilt have it so.
> I'll say yon gray is not the morning's eye.
> 'Tis but the pale reflex of Cynthia's brow.
>
> (17–20)

The scene in which Kate joins in Petruchio's transformation of the sun into the moon and old Vincentio into a young girl is of course quite different in tone. Kate and Petruchio have been engaged in a farcical combat of wills; they are now returning to Kate's father's house, accompanied by Petruchio's friend Hortensio, rather than in a romantic solitude, and they are under no sentence of death or banishment. But both scenes use a verbal transformation of the world—a creation of a private world through words—as a metaphor for a relationship. Such a private world is crucial to *Shrew*'s mediation between ideologies of patriarchy and companionship in marriage, as well as to the attempt that Romeo and Juliet make love to each other tenderly in a world of violence. The secrecy of their love heightens at once its purity and intensity and its vulnerability. When the private world is established it is already threatened. As soon as Romeo accepts the pretense "it is not day" (25), Juliet resumes her caution and returns them to the real world, where Romeo must flee. Nevertheless, they have an absolute trust in each other; on their departure there is no questioning of each other's truths. . . . Presciently, they imagine death as the only possible obstacle to their reunion.

Shakespeare changed his source to reduce the age of the lovers, and historical evidence suggests that he also made them much younger than the typical age of marriage for Elizabethan aristocrats (twenty for women, twenty-one for men), who married still younger than other classes (median age twenty-four for women, twenty-six for men). However young the members of Shakespeare's original audiences were—probably a high proportion were in their late teens or early twenties—Romeo and Juliet were still younger than almost all of them. The extreme youth of the lovers emphasizes their innocence and inexperience. Anyone who has lived longer than Romeo and Juliet—anyone who has given up a first love—has made more compromises than they have. It is their extreme purity that gives their love its special tragedy. The play expresses both the appeal and the danger of a love in which two people become the whole world to each other. This little world precariously remedies the defects of the larger one—its coldness, its hierarchies, its violence—but the lovers cannot negotiate recognition by the outer world except by their deaths because of their residual commitment to the outer world and its gender ideals.

SYLVAN BARNET

# *Romeo and Juliet*
# on Stage and Screen

In "To the Memorie of the deceased Author, Master W. Shakespeare," a commendatory poem published in the first collection of Shakespeare's works (1623), Leonard Digges wrote,

> Nor shall I e're beleeue, or thinke thee dead
> (Though mist) untill our bankrout Stage be sped
> (Impossible) with some new strain t' out-do
> Passions of *Juliet,* and her *Romeo.*

When Digges published these lines, *Romeo and Juliet* had been on the stage for some twenty-five years. The first printed text of the play, issued in 1597, claims (probably truly) that it "hath been often (with great applause) plaid publiquely"; the second printed text, issued in 1599, says that *Romeo and Juliet* "hath been sundry times publiquely acted." And yet, despite allusions to the play, such as Digges's poem, we have no report of a specific production in England (there are some early references to German productions) until 1662, when William Davenant revived *Romeo and Juliet.*

Despite the absence of early references to productions, we know at least a little about the Elizabethan staging of the play. Because the earliest text, a so-called Bad Quarto (see page 122), probably is based on the memories of actors who had performed in the play, it gives us some idea of what *Romeo and Juliet* was like when it was put on the stage. For instance, certain stage directions in Q1 surely report what the spectators saw. Here are a few of these directions, keyed to the lineation of the present text:

"Enter Juliet somewhat fast, and embraceth Romeo" (2.6.15);

"He offers to stab himselfe, and Nurse snatches the dagger away" (3.3.107);

"Nurse offers to goe in and turnes again" (3.3.161);

"She goeth down from the window" (3.5.68);

"She fals upon her bed within the Curtaines" (4.3.58);

"All at once cry out and wring their hands" (4.1.50);

"She stabs herselfe and falles" (5.3.170).

It is possible, too, that some of the omissions in the Bad Quarto (evident when it is compared to the Good Quarto, which was published two years later) may reflect an Elizabethan cut production of the play. True, most of the cuts in the 1597 text must be due to lapses of memory, but some may faithfully represent an abridged performance. For instance, Benvolio's account (1.1) of the first brawl—ten lines in a later, better text—consists of only two lines in the 1597 version, perhaps because two lines were thought to be enough in production. Similarly, the servants who open 1.5 with talk abut preparing for the banquet are deleted—perhaps because the actors preparing the text did not recall the speech, but possibly because the material was not given in a stage performance. In any case, many later directors have similarly cut these speeches.

One other point should be made about *Romeo and Juliet* on the Elizabethan stage: female parts were played by boys, which mean that Juliet, who is said to be almost fourteen, was in fact played by a performer of approximately that age. Elizabethan child actors were carefully trained, and judging from surviving comments about them, they were remarkably skillful performers. Later centuries have been less successful in their child actors, and attempts to use adolescents in the title roles of the play have usually been unimpressive. Even John Gielgud, when he first played Romeo at nineteen in 1924, was judged inadequate.

Between 1642 and 1660 the London theaters were closed, but with the restoration of Charles II to the throne the theaters reopened. Of Davenant's revival of *Romeo and Juliet* in 1662, the self-assured theater-enthusiast and diarist Samuel Pepys wrote, "To the Opera, and there saw *Romeo and Juliet,* the first time it was ever acted, but it is a play of itself the worst that ever I heard, and the worst acted that ever I saw these people do, and I am resolved to go no more to see the first time of acting." As Pepys's comments on other productions of Shakespeare's plays show, his taste did not run to Elizabethan drama (except when it was heavily adapted to Restoration taste); his comments on the ineptitude of the performers are more surprising, since Thomas Betterton (a leading actor of the period) played Mercutio, and the much-acclaimed Mary Saunderson, later to be Betterton's wife, played Juliet.

A little later—the exact date is not known—James Howard transformed the tragedy of *Romeo and Juliet* into a tragicomedy, keeping the lovers alive at the end. One report says that versions were alternated, "tragical one day and tragicomical another." Howard's adaptation, however, as well as Shakespeare's original, was driven from the stage by an even freer adaptation, Thomas Otway's *Caius Marius* (1679). In this work, set in Republican Rome, Romeo is changed to Caius Marius and Juliet to Lavinia. Otway restored Shakespeare's tragic ending, but Juliet revives briefly before Romeo's death, and in an effort to increase the pathos the lovers exchange dying speeches. *Caius Marius,* virtually an original play, was staged regularly until 1727, utterly displacing Shakespeare's play during these years.

In 1744 *Romeo and Juliet*—somewhat cut, and still with some added passages from Otway, and still with Juliet awakening before Romeo dies—first reappeared on the stage, in a version by Theophilus Cibber, with Cibber playing Romeo, and his daughter Jenny playing Juliet. This version, however, was halted after only nine performances because it was given in an unlicensed theater. In 1748 David Garrick, manager of the theater in Drury Lane, put on his own adaptation of *Romeo and Juliet,* and this adaptation held the stage for the rest of the eighteenth century. During this period, in fact, it was the most frequently performed Shakespeare play on the stage. Its life continued well into the first half of the nineteenth century, for John Philip Kemble's modified version (1803) of Garrick's version was performed until 1845, thus in effect giving Garrick's *Romeo* a run of ninety-seven years. Although Garrick's version marked a significant step in the direction of restoring Shakespeare's texts to the stage, by modern standards Garrick treated the text very badly. Although at first he restored Romeo's early love for Rosaline, when he published his text in 1753 he bowed to critical opinion and, following Otway and Cibber, omitted all reference to Romeo's love for Rosaline. Moreover, again taking a cue from Otway, he restored Juliet to life before Romeo died so that the lovers could exchange words Garrick invented for them. Further, he cut almost half of the play, including the bawdry, and he touched up a good many lines—for instance simplifying some lines for his hearers. In deference to the eighteenth-century opinion that puns do not belong in tragedy, most of the puns are cut—even Mercutio's line that he is "a grave man." After 1750 Garrick added to the beginning of the fifth act a funeral dirge for Juliet. And of course there is added dialogue (about sixty-five lines) between the lovers at the end of the play. Here is a sample from the addition:

> *Romeo.* I thought thee dead! distracted at the sight (Fatal
> speed) drank poison, kiss'd thy cold lips And found within
> thy arms a precious grave—But in that moment—O—
> *Juliet.* And did I wake for this!
> *Romeo.* My powers are blasted, Twixt death and love I'm
> torn—I am distracted! But death's strongest, and I must
> leave thee, Juliet! O cruel, cursed fate!—in sight of
> heav'n—
> *Juliet.* Thou rav'st—lean on my breast—

*Romeo.* Fathers have flinty hearts, no tears can melt 'em
    Nature pleads in vain—children must be wretched.
*Juliet.* O my breaking heart—
*Romeo.* She is my wife—our hearts are twined together;
    Capulet forbear; Paris, loose your hold— Pull not our
    heartstrings thus—they crack—they break—O Juliet! Juliet!
*Juliet.* Stay, stay for me, Romeo; a moment stay; Fate mar
    ries us in death, and we are one. No pow'r shall part us.
    [*Faints on Romeo's body.*]

Garrick went on, after Juliet kills herself, to reduce Friar
Lawrence's long summary (5.3.229–69) by half, and to
reduce lines 270–94 (by the Prince, Balthasar, and the
Boy) to three lines spoken by the Prince. Capulet's and
Montague's speeches of reconciliation are retained, and
the play ends with a speech Garrick composed (drawing
on Shakespeare) for the Prince:

> A gloomy peace this morning with it brings,
> Let Romeo's man and let the boy attend us.
> We'll hence and farther scan these sad disasters.
> Well may you mourn, my lords, now wise too late,
> These tragic issues of your mutual hate.
> From private feuds what dire misfortunes flow;
> Whate'er the cause, the sure effect is woe.

It is easy to laugh at Garrick's verse, and to become
indignant with his cuts and revisions, but acted by
Spranger Barry and Mrs. Cibber (Cibber's estranged
second wife), this version was the talk of the age. When
Barry and Mrs. Cibber abandoned Garrick and Drury
Lane, and went over to the rival theater, Covent Garden,
they continued to perform something close to this version
of *Romeo and Juliet*. The ensuing War of the Theaters
aroused both interest and irritation, for if it allowed theater buffs to compare performers (Garrick and Miss
George Anne Bellamy now took the title roles at Drury
Lane), it also narrowed the choice of plays that one could
see. A theatergoer expressed what must have been a widespread feeling:

"Well, what's tonight?" says angry Ned,
        As up from bed he rouses;
"*Romeo* again!" and shakes his head;
        "Ah, pox on both your houses."

But there was also a good deal of excited commentary about the relative merits of the performers. Perhaps the most engaging judgment was that of the actress Hannah Pritchard, who said that if she were playing Juliet to Garrick's Romeo, his words were so hot and passionate in the garden scene that she would have expected him at any moment to climb up to the window—but if she were playing to Barry's Romeo, his words were so sweet and seductive that she would have gone down to him. One other point should be made about the eighteenth-century productions of *Romeo and Juliet*: they were done in fashionable contemporary dress, not in the Italian Renaissance costumes used in most nineteenth- and twentieth-century productions. Details about Juliet's costume are not known, but Romeo wore a knee-length coat, knee breeches, and a wig with the hair gathered together behind and tied with a knot of ribbon.

Although Garrick's text, in Kemble's adaptation, held the stage during the first four decades of the nineteenth century—even the great William Charles Macready in 1838 used the Garrick version—in 1845 Charlotte Cushman, an American actress in London, returning to Shakespeare's ending, abandoned the added dialogue of the dying lovers in the fifth act. Cushman played Romeo, and her sister, Susan, played Juliet. Since Ellen Tree had played Romeo as early as 1829, and Priscilla Horton had played him in 1834, the novelty was not that a woman played Romeo, but that Shakespeare's text was restored to the stage. On the whole the reviews of Cushman's production were favorable, and the play had a substantial run—substantial enough for Samuel Phelps in 1846 to use Shakespeare's text in his revival of the play.

To say that Shakespeare's text displaced Garrick's is not to say, of course, that Shakespeare's text was faithfully followed down to the last word. Few productions added speeches, but almost all made substantial cuts. Take, for example, Henry Irving's production of 1882, with Irving as Romeo and Ellen Terry as Juliet. Irving, in his usual manner, employed illusionistic sets, for example an elaborate marketplace (fountain, donkeys, and all) for the opening scene, a great hall for the masked ball, and an impressive marble balcony for Juliet. He therefore had to delete or rearrange some scenes, so that the cumbersome sets would not have to be struck, set up again, struck again, and set up again. Moreover Irving, in the tradition of the Victorian actor-managers, cut much in order to emphasize the roles of the star actors. Thus the final scene in the tomb, after the death of the lovers, was completely cut except for the Prince's final four lines, ending the play with a tableau that Ellen Terry described as "magnificent." Henry James, however, wryly commented that the play was not "acted" but was "obstructed, interrupted." Irving, by the way, was forty-three when he played Romeo, and Ellen Terry was thirty-five—ages that are not especially remarkable when one recalls that Garrick played Romeo until he was forty-four, and within living memory Olivia de Havilland was thirty-five, and Katharine Cornell was thirty-six, when they played Juliet.

Under the influence of William Poel, who argued that Shakespeare's plays are best staged in comparatively simple conditions approximating those of Shakespeare's own stage, and of Poel's more imaginative successor, Harley Granville-Barker, most productions of Shakespeare in the first half of the twentieth century were relatively simple and fast-moving when compared with Irving's, but somehow *Romeo and Juliet* remained an exception until fairly recently; reluctant to lose the chance of dazzling with showy spectacle, directors of the twentieth century continued the Victorian tradition of using splendid sets that supposedly evoked the Italian Renaissance. What may well be the most successful production of the twentieth century (1935), however, achieved its greatness not through spectacle but through the acting of

Peggy Ashcroft (Juliet), Edith Evans (the nurse), and John Gielgud and Laurence Olivier (alternating as Romeo and as Mercutio). Gielgud himself, however, in an autobiography entitled *Early Stages*, has expressed reservations about his own performance:

> I know *Romeo and Juliet* by heart, and I have played Romeo three times, yet I cannot say that I have ever pleased myself in it completely. I have always felt I knew exactly how the part should be played, but I have neither the looks, the dash, nor the virility to make a real success of it, however well I may speak the verse and feel the emotion. My Romeo has always been "careful," and I love the language, and revel in it too obviously.

If the staging of the play, at least until the 1960s, continued to smack of the Victorian period, so did the text, which usually was presented with much of the bawdry deleted. But this fault has been amended in our day. Thus, in Terry Hands's 1973 production at Stratford, Mercutio (who was portrayed as a homosexual) obscenely dallied with a life-size female doll during his conjuration of Romeo:

> I conjure thee by Rosaline's bright eyes,
> By her high forehead and her scarlet lip,
> By her fine foot, straight leg, and quivering thigh,
> And the demesnes that there adjacent lie. . . .

> (2.1.17–20)

This production was notable, too, for the set (a severe metallic affair), the costumes (somber), and the manner in which Romeo killed Tybalt (a thrust in the groin with a short dagger).

Probably Hands's choice of a set was dictated by our age's tendency to avoid prettiness and to see the plays through the eyes of Samuel Beckett, but he may also have felt that the one kind of set that surely must be avoided, if unfavorable comparisons were to be avoided, is the showy Renaissance set (very much in Henry Irving's tradition) that Franco Zeffirelli used in his production for the Old Vic in 1960, with John Stride (twenty-four years old) and Judi Dench (twenty-six) in the title parts. One reviewer thought that Stride seemed to be a chubby Marlon Brando, and Dench "a younger Kim Stanley." In an interview in *Shakespeare Survey* 27 Dench forthrightly says that in this heavily cut production Zeffirelli offered youth in place of poetry. Chiefly, however, he offered spectacle, at the expense of actors and of the text. No later director could hope to compete with Zeffirelli in this department; or if a director had any such hopes, they must have been dashed by Zeffirelli's film version—to be discussed in a moment—made in 1968, with its spectacular Renaissance interiors.

In 1968, the Washington, D.C., Summer Shakespeare Festival staged *Romeo and Juliet* at the outdoor Sylvan Theatre, on the slope of the Washington Monument grounds. The play (perhaps taking a cue from the popularity of *West Side Story* by Leonard Bernstein, Arthur Laurents, and Stephen Sondheim) was converted into a play about race: Juliet's family was black. Romeo's white; the setting was New Verona, in Louisiana in the early nineteenth century, and the ball scene was part of the Mardi Gras. A decade later, in 1978, Los Angeles saw a racial version, again with the Capulets black (though Juliet's nurse was white) and the Montagues white. The production seems to have been well received, even though it ran for four hours. (In the Prologue to the play, the Chorus speaks of "the two hours' traffic of our stage," and though most productions of *Romeo and Juliet* run to more than two hours, four hours seems excessively long for what is one of Shakespeare's shorter plays.) Another modern production in Washington—this one at the Folger Shakespeare Theatre in 1986—turned *Romeo and Juliet* into a play about teenage suicide. At least the program note says that the play "addresses a tragic crisis facing our nation—teen suicide," and the production was co-sponsored by the Folger and the Youth Suicide National Center.

One other revival must be mentioned before we look at screen and television versions, Michael Bogdanov's production at Stratford-upon-Avon, in 1986, with Niamh Cusack as Juliet and Sean Bean as Romeo. Eschewing Zeffirelli's untoppable Renaissance Italy, the play was set in Verona at the present time: the Prince was a Mafia don; Romeo and Juliet first met at the Capulets' poolside party; Tybalt (in black leather) drove an Alfa Romeo; Mercutio, Tybalt, and Juliet died to rock music; Romeo injected the poison into his arm (he got a packet, not a potion), and Juliet killed herself with a switchblade knife. Inevitably some of Shakespeare's lines were at odds with the text. For instance, Juliet, awakening to find the dead Romeo, says,

> O churl! Drunk all, and left no friendly drop
> To help me after? I will kiss thy lips.
> Haply some poison yet doth hang on them
> To make me die with a restorative.          (5.3.163–66)

The play ended with the Prince at a press conference, standing in front of two gold statues, reading the first eight lines of the Chorus's opening sonnet, with the tenses changed from present to past. Photographers then snapped pictures of the bereaved parents shaking hands (Lady Montague did not die, as stated in the text at 5.3.210), and finally Benvolio, alone, moved offstage. The implication was that the reconciliation was a media event, and that the tragic loss produced nothing.

Predictably, most academic viewers were unhappy, but the production attracted considerable favorable comment in the press, which saw in it a play that spoke to the materialism and brutality of the late twentieth century. That may not be how most people think of *Romeo and Juliet*, but in fact the play does include materialism and brutality; Bogdanov, making Shakespeare our contemporary, touched on something that in fact is there. But there is no such thing as a free lunch; his emphasis on this aspect had to be paid for, and some people thought the cost too high.

Film versions of *Romeo and Juliet* have been around

for a long time. Apart from at least two silent films of *Romeo and Juliet*, there were two sound films, a 1936 version with Leslie Howard (then forty-two) and Norma Shearer (thirty-one) in the title parts, and a 1954 version, with Laurence Harvey (twenty-seven) and Susan Shentall (young, but her exact age is a well-kept secret). Both of these films cut the text fairly heavily; the 1954 version even omitted such famous passages as Romeo's line about the light in "yonder orchard," and Juliet's speech, "Gallop apace, you fiery-footed steeds."

Neither of these two film versions, however, had anything like the popular success of Franco Zeffirelli's film of 1968. Although he had made extensive cuts in his stage version of 1960, he made even more extensive cuts in the film. Probably half of the text has been dropped in order to "open up" the film, that is, to allow time for the camera to convey a sense of what is supposed to be zesty Renaissance life, for instance by roving through crowded streets. There are lots of torches, lots of eating, lots of swishing of costumes, lots of attention to codpieces, and lots of quick cutting to heighten the activity. Many bits of business are added. For instance, in the middle of Friar John's first speech the Angelus sounds, allowing the Friar to genuflect. In the balcony scene Romeo climbs a tree and supports himself on a ledge so that he may touch Juliet's fingertips (surely part of the point of Shakespeare's scene is that the two lovers are separated), and later he leaps from the balcony and runs through a forest glade. Not all of the additions, however, are so busy; in the fifth act, much of the text is cut in order to allow for a tableau effect as the bodies are laid to rest in an elaborate funeral.

The popular success of Zefirelli's film was due to visual matters and to Nino Rota's music (the sound track became immensely popular with young people) rather than to anything in the text. Especially popular was Zeffirelli's choice of his two leading performers, Leonard Whiting (age seventeen) and Olivia Hussey (age sixteen), both of whom brought an appropriate (and rare) youth and beauty to the roles. Nor were Whiting and Hussey utterly inexperienced performers; Whiting had played in the London company of *Oliver!* when he was twelve, and Hussey had played for two years in London in *The Prime of Miss Jean Brodie*. Nevertheless, despite the fact that a film, unlike a theater production, can keep shooting a scene until the performers get it right, and despite their engaging looks, Whiting and Hussey were not adequate to the language and the emotions of the play. John Simon cruelly but aptly characterized Zeffirelli's film as "a *Romeo and Juliet* for teenyboppers and pederasts."

Baz Luhrmann's film entitled *William Shakespeare's Romeo and Juliet*, with Claire Danes as Juliet and Leonardo Di Caprio as Romeo, was released in 1996. If Terry Hands's 1986 stage production, with its black leather and its switchblades and its red sports car (an Alfa Romeo, of course) sought to make us see *Romeo and Juliet* in a fresh way, so too did Luhrmann's film. Shot in Mexico, its Verona Beach evoked contemporary Miami Beach. Most of the characters are Latino or black except for Romeo and Juliet, who are white. The prologue is spoken by a TV newscaster, there is a shootout at a gas station, Captain Prince arrives in a police helicopter, Mercutio is a drag queen, Romeo shoots pool with Benvolio, and Friar Lawrence sends his message by Federal Express. Obviously in such a version swords and rapiers cannot be used; handguns are used, but they are named "Swords" and "Rapiers" so the text is not altered in this respect, though elsewhere there are cuts, especially in the parts of Paris, the Nurse, Capulet, and Montague. It all sounds odd, maybe even dreadful, but the two principal actors are effective. What most viewers probably find objectionable is not the modernization but the director's willingness to drown out Shakespeare's words with loud music.

The BBC television version (1978) is tolerable, but only that. Its chief virtue is the inclusion of almost the entire text (the chief cut is in Friar Lawrence's long speech in 5.3, beginning at line 229). The set is clearly a studio set, the acting undistinguished except for Michael

Hordern's Capulet. It is perhaps sad to end by saying that this dutiful, traditional production makes viewers think, despite their high-minded disapproval of gimmicks, that maybe there is something to the vigorous reinterpretations of Bogdanov and Lurhmann.

*Bibliographic Note:* For comments on productions, see below, Suggested References, Section 4 (Shakespeare on Stage and Screen, p. 215). For a short book devoted entirely to the play, see Jill L. Levenson's *Romeo and Juliet* (1987), in a series called "Shakespeare in Performance."

# Suggested References

The number of possible references is vast and grows alarmingly. (The *Shakespeare Quarterly* devotes one issue each year to a list of the previous year's work, and *Shakespeare Survey*—an annual publication—includes a substantial review of biographical, critical, and textual studies, as well as a survey of performances.) The vast bibliography is best approached through James Harner, *The World Shakespeare Bibliography on CD-Rom: 1900–Present*. The first release, in 1996, included more than 12,000 annotated items from 1990–93, plus references to several thousand book reviews, productions, films, and audio recordings. The plan is to update the publication annually, moving forward one year and backward three years. Thus, the second issue (1997), with 24,700 entries, and another 35,000 or so references to reviews, newspaper pieces, and so on, covered 1987–94.

Though no works are indispensable, those listed below have been found especially helpful. The arrangement is as follows:

1. Shakespeare's Times
2. Shakespeare's Life
3. Shakespeare's Theater
4. Shakespeare on Stage and Screen
5. Miscellaneous Reference Works
6. Shakespeare's Plays: General Studies
7. The Comedies
8. The Romances
9. The Tragedies
10. The Histories
11. *Romeo and Juliet*

The titles in the first five sections are accompanied by brief explanatory annotations.

## 1. Shakespeare's Times

Andrews, John F., ed. *William Shakespeare: His World, His Work, His Influence,* 3 vols. (1985). Sixty articles, dealing not only with such subjects as "The State," "The Church," "Law," "Science, Magic, and Folklore," but also with the plays and poems themselves and Shakespeare's influence (e.g., translations, films, reputation)

Byrne, Muriel St. Clare. *Elizabethan Life in Town and Country* (8th ed., 1970). Chapters on manners, beliefs, education, etc., with illustrations.

Dollimore, John, and Alan Sinfield, eds. *Political Shakespeare: New Essays in Cultural Materialism* (1985). Essays on such topics as the subordination of women and colonialism, presented in connection with some of Shakespeare's plays.

Greenblatt, Stephen. *Representing the English Renaissance* (1988). New Historicist essays, especially on connections between political and aesthetic matters, statecraft and stagecraft.

Joseph, B. L. *Shakespeare's Eden: the Commonwealth of England 1558-1629* (1971). An account of the social, political, economic, and cultural life of England.

Kernan, Alvin. *Shakespeare, the King's Playwright: Theater in the Stuart Court 1603-1613* (1995). The social setting and the politics of the court of James I, in relation to *Hamlet, Measure for Measure, Macbeth, King Lear, Antony and Cleopatra, Coriolanus,* and *The Tempest.*

Montrose, Louis. *The Purpose of Playing: Shakespeare and the Cultural Politics of the Elizabethan Theatre* (1996). A poststructuralist view, discussing the professional theater "within the ideological and material frameworks of Elizabethan culture and society," with an extended analysis of *A Midsummer Night's Dream.*

Mullaney, Steven. *The Place of the Stage: License, Play, and Power in Renaissance England* (1988). New Historicist analysis, arguing that popular drama became a cultural institution "only by . . . taking up a place on the margins of society."

Schoenbaum, S. *Shakespeare: The Globe and the World*

(1979). A readable, abundantly illustrated introductory book on the world of the Elizabethans.

*Shakespeare's England*, 2 vols. (1916). A large collection of scholarly essays on a wide variety of topics, e.g., astrology, costume, gardening, horsemanship, with special attention to Shakespeare's references to these topics.

## 2. Shakespeare's Life

Andrews, John F., ed. *William Shakespeare: His World, His Work, His Influence*, 3 vols. (1985). See the description above.

Bentley, Gerald E. *Shakespeare: A Biographical Handbook* (1961). The facts about Shakespeare, with virtually no conjecture intermingled.

Chambers, E. K. *William Shakespeare: A Study of Facts and Problems*, 2 vols. (1930). The fullest collection of data.

Fraser, Russell. *Young Shakespeare* (1988). A highly readable account that simultaneously considers Shakespeare's life and Shakespeare's art.

———. *Shakespeare: The Later Years* (1992).

Schoenbaum, S. *Shakespeare's Lives* (1970). A review of the evidence and an examination of many biographies, including those of Baconians and other heretics.

———. *William Shakespeare: A Compact Documentary Life* (1977). An abbreviated version, in a smaller format, of the next title. The compact version reproduces some fifty documents in reduced form. A readable presentation of all that the documents tell us about Shakespeare.

———. *William Shakespeare: A Documentary Life* (1975). A large-format book setting forth the biography with facsimiles of more than two hundred documents, and with transcriptions and commentaries.

## 3. Shakespeare's Theater

Astington, John H., ed. *The Development of Shakespeare's Theater* (1992). Eight specialized essays on theatrical companies, playing spaces, and performance.

Beckerman, Bernard. *Shakespeare at the Globe, 1599–1609* (1962). On the playhouse and on Elizabethan dramaturgy, acting, and staging.

Bentley, Gerald E. *The Profession of Dramatist in Shakespeare's Time* (1971). An account of the dramatist's status in the Elizabethan period.

———. *The Profession of Player in Shakespeare's Time, 1590–1642* (1984). An account of the status of members of London companies (sharers, hired men, apprentices, managers) and a discussion of conditions when they toured.

Berry, Herbert. *Shakespeare's Playhouses* (1987). Usefully emphasizes how little we know about the construction of Elizabethan theaters.

Brown, John Russell. *Shakespeare's Plays in Performance* (1966). A speculative and practical analysis relevant to all of the plays, but with emphasis on *The Merchant of Venice*, *Richard II*, *Hamlet*, *Romeo and Juliet*, and *Twelfth Night*.

———. *William Shakespeare: Writing for Performance* (1996). A discussion aimed at helping readers to develop theatrically conscious habits of reading.

Chambers, E. K. *The Elizabethan Stage*, 4 vols. (1945). A major reference work on theaters, theatrical companies, and staging at court.

Cook, Ann Jennalie. *The Privileged Playgoers of Shakespeare's London, 1576–1642* (1981). Sees Shakespeare's audience as wealthier, more middle-class, and more intellectual than Harbage (below) does.

Dessen, Alan C. *Elizabethan Drama and the Viewer's Eye* (1977). On how certain scenes may have looked to spectators in an Elizabethan theater.

Gurr, Andrew. *Playgoing in Shakespeare's London* (1987). Something of a middle ground between Cook (above) and Harbage (below).

———. *The Shakespearean Stage, 1579–1642* (2nd ed., 1980). On the acting companies, the actors, the playhouses, the stages, and the audiences.

Harbage, Alfred. *Shakespeare's Audience* (1941). A study of the size and nature of the theatrical public, emphasizing the representativeness of its working class and middle-class audience.

Hodges, C. Walter. *The Globe Restored* (1968). A conjectural restoration, with lucid drawings.

Hosley, Richard. "The Playhouses," in *The Revels History of Drama in English*, vol. 3, general editors Clifford Leech and T. W. Craik (1975). An essay of a hundred pages on the physical aspects of the playhouses.

Howard, Jane E. "Crossdressing, the Theatre, and Gender Struggle in Early Modern England," *Shakespeare Quarterly* 39 (1988): 418–40. Judicious comments on the effects of boys playing female roles.

Orrell, John. *The Human Stage: English Theatre Design, 1567–1640* (1988). Argues that the public, private, and court playhouses are less indebted to popular structures (e.g., innyards and bear-baiting pits) than to banqueting halls and to Renaissance conceptions of Roman amphitheaters.

Slater, Ann Pasternak. *Shakespeare the Director* (1982). An analysis of theatrical effects (e.g., kissing, kneeling) in stage directions and dialogue.

Styan, J. L. *Shakespeare's Stagecraft* (1967). An introduction to Shakespeare's visual and aural stagecraft, with chapters on such topics as acting conventions, stage groupings, and speech.

Thompson, Peter. *Shakespeare's Professional Career* (1992). An examination of patronage and related theatrical conditions.

———. *Shakespeare's Theatre* (1983). A discussion of how plays were staged in Shakespeare's time.

## 4. Shakespeare on Stage and Screen

Bate, Jonathan, and Russell Jackson, eds. *Shakespeare: An Illustrated Stage History* (1996). Highly readable essays on stage productions from the Renaissance to the present.

Berry, Ralph. *Changing Styles in Shakespeare* (1981). Discusses productions of six plays (*Coriolanus, Hamlet, Henry V, Measure for Measure, The Tempest,* and *Twelfth Night*) on the English stage, chiefly 1950–1980.

————. *On Directing Shakespeare: Interviews with Contemporary Directors* (1989). An enlarged edition of a book first published in 1977, this version includes the seven interviews from the early 1970s and adds five interviews conducted in 1988.

Brockbank, Philip, ed. *Players of Shakespeare: Essays in Shakespearean Performance* (1985). Comments by twelve actors, reporting their experiences with roles. See also the entry for Russell Jackson (below).

Bulman, J. C., and H. R. Coursen, eds. *Shakespeare on Television* (1988). An anthology of general and theoretical essays, essays on individual productions, and shorter reviews, with a bibliography and a videography listing cassettes that may be rented.

Coursen, H. P. *Watching Shakespeare on Television* (1993). Analyses not only of TV versions but also of films and videotapes of stage presentations that are shown on television.

Davies, Anthony, and Stanley Wells, eds. *Shakespeare and the Moving Image: The Plays on Film and Television* (1994). General essays (e.g., on the comedies) as well as essays devoted entirely to *Hamlet, King Lear,* and *Macbeth.*

Dawson, Anthony B. *Watching Shakespeare: A Playgoer's Guide* (1988). About half of the plays are discussed, chiefly in terms of decisions that actors and directors make in putting the works onto the stage.

Dessen, Alan. *Elizabethan Stage Conventions and Modern Interpretations* (1984). On interpreting conventions such as the representation of light and darkness and stage violence (duels, battles).

Donaldson, Peter. *Shakespearean Films/Shakespearean Directors* (1990). Postmodernist analyses, drawing on Freudianism, Feminism, Deconstruction, and Queer Theory.

Jackson, Russell, and Robert Smallwood, eds. *Players of Shakespeare 2: Further Essays in Shakespearean Performance by Players with the Royal Shakespeare Company* (1988). Fourteen actors discuss their roles in productions between 1982 and 1987.

————. *Players of Shakespeare 3: Further Essays in Shake-*

*spearean Performance by Players with the Royal Shakespeare Company* (1993). Comments by thirteen performers.

Jorgens, Jack. *Shakespeare on Film* (1977). Fairly detailed studies of eighteen films, preceded by an introductory chapter addressing such issues as music, and whether to "open" the play by including scenes of landscape.

Kennedy, Dennis. *Looking at Shakespeare: A Visual History of Twentieth-Century Performance* (1993). Lucid descriptions (with 170 photographs) of European, British, and American performances.

Leiter, Samuel L. *Shakespeare Around the Globe: A Guide to Notable Postwar Revivals* (1986). For each play there are about two pages of introductory comments, then discussions (about five hundred words per production) of ten or so productions, and finally bibliographic references.

McMurty, Jo. *Shakespeare Films in the Classroom* (1994). Useful evaluations of the chief films most likely to be shown in undergraduate courses.

Rothwell, Kenneth, and Annabelle Henkin Melzer. *Shakespeare on Screen: An International Filmography and Videography* (1990). A reference guide to several hundred films and videos produced between 1899 and 1989, including spinoffs such as musicals and dance versions.

Sprague, Arthur Colby. *Shakespeare and the Actors* (1944). Detailed discussions of stage business (gestures, etc.) over the years.

Willis, Susan. *The BBC Shakespeare Plays: Making the Televised Canon* (1991). A history of the series, with interviews and production diaries for some plays.

## 5. Miscellaneous Reference Works

Abbott, E. A. *A Shakespearean Grammar* (new edition, 1877). An examination of differences between Elizabethan and modern grammar.

Allen, Michael J. B., and Kenneth Muir, eds. *Shakespeare's Plays in Quarto* (1981). One volume containing facsimiles of the plays issued in small format before they were collected in the First Folio of 1623.

Bevington, David. *Shakespeare* (1978). A short guide to hundreds of important writings on the subject.

Blake, Norman. *Shakespeare's Language: An Introduction* (1983). On vocabulary, parts of speech, and word order.

Bullough, Geoffrey. *Narrative and Dramatic Sources of Shakespeare*, 8 vols. (1957–75). A collection of many of the books Shakespeare drew on, with judicious comments.

Campbell, Oscar James, and Edward G. Quinn, eds. *The Reader's Encyclopedia of Shakespeare* (1966). Old, but still the most useful single reference work on Shakespeare.

Cercignani, Fausto. *Shakespeare's Works and Elizabethan Pronunciation* (1981). Considered the best work on the topic, but remains controversial.

Dent, R. W. *Shakespeare's Proverbial Language: An Index* (1981). An index of proverbs, with an introduction concerning a form Shakespeare frequently drew on.

Greg, W. W. *The Shakespeare First Folio* (1955). A detailed yet readable history of the first collection (1623) of Shakespeare's plays.

Harner, James. *The World Shakespeare Bibliography*. See headnote to Suggested References.

Hosley, Richard. *Shakespeare's Holinshed* (1968). Valuable presentation of one of Shakespeare's major sources.

Kökeritz, Helge. *Shakespeare's Names* (1959). A guide to pronouncing some 1,800 names appearing in Shakespeare.

———. *Shakespeare's Pronunciation* (1953). Contains much information about puns and rhymes, but see Cercignani (above).

Muir, Kenneth. *The Sources of Shakespeare's Plays* (1978). An account of Shakespeare's use of his reading. It covers all the plays, in chronological order.

Miriam Joseph, Sister. *Shakespeare's Use of the Arts of Language* (1947). A study of Shakespeare's use of rhetorical devices, reprinted in part as *Rhetoric in Shakespeare's Time* (1962).

*The Norton Facsimile: The First Folio of Shakespeare's Plays* (1968). A handsome and accurate facsimile of the first collection (1623) of Shakespeare's plays, with a valuable introduction by Charlton Hinman.

Onions, C. T. *A Shakespeare Glossary*, rev. and enlarged by

R. D. Eagleson (1986). Definitions of words (or senses of words) now obsolete.

Partridge, Eric. *Shakespeare's Bawdy*, rev. ed. (1955). Relatively brief dictionary of bawdy words; useful, but see Williams, below.

*Shakespeare Quarterly*. See headnote to Suggested References.

*Shakespeare Survey*. See headnote to Suggested References.

Spevack, Marvin. *The Harvard Concordance to Shakespeare* (1973). An index to Shakespeare's words.

Vickers, Brian. *Appropriating Shakespeare: Contemporary Critical Quarrels* (1993). A survey—chiefly hostile—of recent schools of criticism.

Wells, Stanley, ed. *Shakespeare: A Bibliographical Guide* (new edition, 1990). Nineteen chapters (some devoted to single plays, others devoted to groups of related plays) on recent scholarship on the life and all of the works.

Williams, Gordon. *A Dictionary of Sexual Language and Imagery in Shakespearean and Stuart Literature*, 3 vols. (1994). Extended discussions of words and passages; much fuller than Partridge, cited above.

# 6. Shakespeare's Plays: General Studies

Bamber, Linda. *Comic Women, Tragic Men: A Study of Gender and Genre in Shakespeare* (1982).

Barnet, Sylvan. *A Short Guide to Shakespeare* (1974).

Callaghan, Dympna, Lorraine Helms, and Jyotsna Singh. *The Weyward Sisters: Shakespeare and Feminist Politics* (1994).

Clemen, Wolfgang H. *The Development of Shakespeare's Imagery* (1951).

Cook, Ann Jennalie. *Making a Match: Courtship in Shakespeare and His Society* (1991).

Dollimore, Jonathan, and Alan Sinfield. *Political Shakespeare: New Essays in Cultural Materialism* (1985).

Dusinberre, Juliet. *Shakespeare and the Nature of Women* (1975).

Granville-Barker, Harley. *Prefaces to Shakespeare*, 2 vols. (1946–47; volume 1 contains essays on *Hamlet, King*

*Lear, Merchant of Venice, Antony and Cleopatra*, and *Cymbeline*; volume 2 contains essays on *Othello, Coriolanus, Julius Caesar, Romeo and Juliet, Love's Labor's Lost*).

————. *More Prefaces to Shakespeare* (1974; essays on *Twelfth Night, A Midsummer Night's Dream, The Winter's Tale, Macbeth*).

Harbage, Alfred. *William Shakespeare: A Reader's Guide* (1963).

Howard, Jean E. *Shakespeare's Art of Orchestration: Stage Technique and Audience Response* (1984).

Jones, Emrys. *Scenic Form in Shakespeare* (1971).

Lenz, Carolyn Ruth Swift, Gayle Greene, and Carol Thomas Neely, eds. *The Woman's Part: Feminist Criticism of Shakespeare* (1980).

Novy, Marianne. *Love's Argument: Gender Relations in Shakespeare* (1984).

Rose, Mark. *Shakespearean Design* (1972).

Scragg, Leah. *Discovering Shakespeare's Meaning* (1994).

————. *Shakespeare's "Mouldy Tales": Recurrent Plot Motifs in Shakespearean Drama* (1992).

Traub, Valerie. *Desire and Anxiety: Circulations of Sexuality in Shakespearean Drama* (1992).

Traversi, D. A. *An Approach to Shakespeare,* 2 vols. (3rd rev. ed, 1968–69).

Vickers, Brian. *The Artistry of Shakespeare's Prose* (1968).

Wells, Stanley. *Shakespeare: A Dramatic Life* (1994).

Wright, George T. *Shakespeare's Metrical Art* (1988).

# 7. The Comedies

Barber, C. L. *Shakespeare's Festive Comedy* (1959; discusses *Love's Labor's Lost, A Midsummer Night's Dream, The Merchant of Venice, As You Like It, Twelfth Night*).

Barton, Anne. *The Names of Comedy* (1990).

Berry, Ralph. *Shakespeare's Comedy: Explorations in Form* (1972).

Bradbury, Malcolm, and David Palmer, eds. *Shakespearean Comedy* (1972).

Bryant, J. A., Jr. *Shakespeare and the Uses of Comedy* (1986).

Carroll, William. *The Metamorphoses of Shakespearean Comedy* (1985).

Champion, Larry S. *The Evolution of Shakespeare's Comedy* (1970).

Evans, Bertrand. *Shakespeare's Comedies* (1960).

Frye, Northrop. *Shakespearean Comedy and Romance* (1965).

Leggatt, Alexander. *Shakespeare's Comedy of Love* (1974).

Miola, Robert S. *Shakespeare and Classical Comedy: The Influence of Plautus and Terence* (1994).

Nevo, Ruth. *Comic Transformations in Shakespeare* (1980).

Ornstein, Robert. *Shakespeare's Comedies: From Roman Farce to Romantic Mystery* (1986).

Richman, David. *Laughter, Pain, and Wonder: Shakespeare's Comedies and the Audience in the Theater* (1990).

Salingar, Leo. *Shakespeare and the Traditions of Comedy* (1974).

Slights, Camille Wells. *Shakespeare's Comic Commonwealths* (1993).

Waller, Gary, ed. *Shakespeare's Comedies* (1991).

Westlund, Joseph. *Shakespeare's Reparative Comedies: A Psychoanalytic View of the Middle Plays* (1984).

Williamson, Marilyn. *The Patriarchy of Shakespeare's Comedies* (1986).

## 8. The Romances (*Pericles, Cymbeline, The Winter's Tale, The Tempest, The Two Noble Kinsmen*)

Adams, Robert M. *Shakespeare: The Four Romances* (1989).

Felperin, Howard. *Shakespearean Romance* (1972).

Frye, Northrop. *A Natural Perspective: The Development of Shakespearean Comedy and Romance* (1965).

Mowat, Barbara. *The Dramaturgy of Shakespeare's Romances* (1976).

Warren, Roger. *Staging Shakespeare's Late Plays* (1990).

Young, David. *The Heart's Forest: A Study of Shakespeare's Pastoral Plays* (1972).

## 9. The Tragedies

Bradley, A. C. *Shakespearean Tragedy* (1904).

Brooke, Nicholas. *Shakespeare's Early Tragedies* (1968).

Champion, Larry. *Shakespeare's Tragic Perspective* (1976).

Drakakis, John, ed. *Shakespearean Tragedy* (1992).

Evans, Bertrand. *Shakespeare's Tragic Practice* (1979).

Everett, Barbara. *Young Hamlet: Essays on Shakespeare's Tragedies* (1989).

Foakes, R. A. *Hamlet versus Lear: Cultural Politics and Shakespeare's Art* (1993).

Frye, Northrop. *Fools of Time: Studies in Shakespearean Tragedy* (1967).

Harbage, Alfred, ed. *Shakespeare: The Tragedies* (1964).

Mack, Maynard. *Everybody's Shakespeare: Reflections Chiefly on the Tragedies* (1993).

McAlindon, T. *Shakespeare's Tragic Cosmos* (1991).

Miola, Robert S. *Shakespeare and Classical Tragedy: The Influence of Seneca* (1992).

———. *Shakespeare's Rome* (1983).

Nevo, Ruth. *Tragic Form in Shakespeare* (1972).

Rackin, Phyllis. *Shakespeare's Tragedies* (1978).

Rose, Mark, ed. *Shakespeare's Early Tragedies: A Collection of Critical Essays* (1995).

Rosen, William. *Shakespeare and the Craft of Tragedy* (1960).

Snyder, Susan. *The Comic Matrix of Shakespeare's Tragedies* (1979).

Wofford, Susanne. *Shakespeare's Late Tragedies: A Collection of Critical Essays* (1996).

Young, David. *The Action to the Word: Structure and Style in Shakespearean Tragedy* (1990).

———. *Shakespeare's Middle Tragedies: A Collection of Critical Essays* (1993).

## 10. The Histories

Blanpied, John W. *Time and the Artist in Shakespeare's English Histories* (1983).

Campbell, Lily B. *Shakespeare's "Histories": Mirrors of Elizabethan Policy* (1947).

Champion, Larry S. *Perspective in Shakespeare's English Histories* (1980).

Hodgdon, Barbara. *The End Crowns All: Closure and Contradiction in Shakespeare's History* (1991).

Holderness, Graham. *Shakespeare Recycled: The Making of Historical Drama* (1992).

————, ed. *Shakespeare's History Plays: "Richard II" to "Henry V"* (1992).

Leggatt, Alexander. *Shakespeare's Political Drama: The History Plays and the Roman Plays* (1988).

Ornstein, Robert. *A Kingdom for a Stage: The Achievement of Shakespeare's History Plays* (1972).

Rackin, Phyllis. *Stages of History: Shakespeare's English Chronicles* (1990).

Saccio, Peter. *Shakespeare's English Kings: History, Chronicle, and Drama* (1977).

Tillyard, E. M. W. *Shakespeare's History Plays* (1944).

Velz, John W., ed. *Shakespeare's English Histories: A Quest for Form and Genre* (1996).

## 11. *Romeo and Juliet*

In addition to the titles listed above in Section 9, The Tragedies, see the following:

Andrews, John F., ed. *Romeo and Juliet: Critical Essays* (1993; contains essays by Mark Van Doren, Derek Traversi, M. M. Mahood, J. L. Calderwood, Marjorie Garber, Coppelia Kahn, Barbara Hodgdon, and others.)

Bevington, David. *Action Is Eloquence: Shakespeare's Language of Gesture* (1984; see esp. pages 111–13).

Charlton, H. B. *Shakespearian Tragedy* (1948).

Clemen, Wolfgang. *Shakespeare's Soliloquies*. Trans. Charity Scott Stokes (1987).

Fergusson, Francis. *Trope and Allegory: Themes Common to Dante and Shakespeare* (1977).

Halio, Jay L., ed. *Shakespeare's "Romeo and Juliet": Texts, Contexts, and Interpretation* (1995).

Hoppe, Harry R. *The Bad Quarto of "Romeo and Juliet": A Bibliographical and Textual Study* (1948).

Knight, G. Wilson. *Principles of Shakespearean Production with Especial Reference to the Tragedies* (1936).

Levenson, Jill L. *Romeo and Juliet* (1987; stage history).

Moore, Olin H. *The Legend of Romeo and Juliet* (1950).

Myers, Henry Alonzo. *Tragedy: A View of Life* (1956; the relevant chapter comparing *Romeo and Juliet* with *A Midsummer Night's Dream* is reprinted in the Signet edition of *A Midsummer Night's Dream2.*

Porter, Joseph A. *Shakespeare's Mercutio: His History and Drama* (1988).

Rabkin, Norman. *Shakespeare and the Common Understanding* (1967).

Traci, Philip J. "Suggestions About the Bawdry in *Romeo and Juliet.*" *South Atlantic Quarterly* 71 (1974): 341–59.